REVELS STUDENT EDITIONS

VOLPONE
Ben Jonson

MANCHESTER
1824

Manchester University Press

REVELS STUDENT EDITIONS

Based on the highly respected Revels Plays, which provide a wide range of scholarly critical editions of plays by Shakespeare's contemporaries, the Revels Student Editions offer readable and competitively priced introductions, text and commentary designed to distil the erudition and insights of the Revels Plays, while focusing on matters of clarity and interpretation. These editions are aimed at undergraduates, graduate teachers of Renaissance drama and all those who enjoy the vitality and humour of one of the world's greatest periods of drama.

GENERAL EDITOR David Bevington

REVELS STUDENT EDITIONS

VOLPONE
Ben Jonson

edited by Brian Parker
and David Bevington

based on The Revels Plays edition
edited by Brian Parker
published by Manchester University Press, 1983

MANCHESTER
UNIVERSITY PRESS
Manchester and New York

distributed in the United States exclusively by
Palgrave Macmillan

Introduction, critical apparatus, etc.
© Brian Parker and David Bevington 1999

The right of Brian Parker and David Bevington to be identified as
the editors of this work has been asserted by them in accordance with
the Copyright, Designs and Patents Act 1988.

Published by Manchester University Press
Oxford Road, Manchester M13 9NR, UK
and Room 400, 175 Fifth Avenue, New York, NY 10010, USA
www.manchesteruniversitypress.co.uk

Distributed in the United States exclusively by
Palgrave Macmillan, 175 Fifth Avenue, New York,
NY 10010, USA

Distributed in Canada exclusively by
UBC Press, University of British Columbia, 2029 West Mall,
Vancouver, BC, Canada V6T 1Z2

British Library Cataloguing-in-Publication Data
A catalogue record for this book is available from the British Library

Library of Congress Cataloging-in-Publication Data applied for

ISBN 978 0 7190 5182 1 *paperback*

First published 1999

16 15 14 13 12 11 10 09   12 11 10 9 8 7 6 5

The publisher has no responsibility for the persistence or accuracy of
URLs for external or any third-party internet websites referred to in this
book, and does not guarantee that any content on such websites is, or
will remain, accurate or appropriate.

Printed in Great Britain
by Bell & Bain Ld, Glasgow

Preface

This Student Revels edition is based on the Revels Plays edition prepared by R. B. Parker and published in 1983. In the present edition, Parker is chiefly responsible for the new introduction and guide to further reading. David Bevington is chiefly responsible for the changes that have been introduced into the text, most of which are non-substantive: added or emended stage directions, modernizing of punctuation, some modernizing of spelling, and numerous matters of series style, such as the placing of stage directions, physical arrangement of paired half-lines, use of italic or roman type, and the like. Together, the editors have reviewed all aspects of the text. Bevington is also chiefly responsible for the commentary notes as they now appear, though making generous use of the notes in the Revels Plays edition. Throughout, the two editors have collaborated closely and have checked and re-checked each other's work, so that in the last analysis this edition is the product of a rewardingly collegial effort.

Brian Parker
David Bevington

Introduction

In their own time and well into the eighteenth century, Ben Jonson was more influential as a comic dramatist than his friend and greatest rival William Shakespeare. This was because he proclaimed himself a classicist: that is, a writer concerned to introduce into English the ideals and techniques of classical drama, as formulated by Aristotle and writers influenced by Aristotle.

Actually, Jonson had first attracted public notice in 1598 by experimenting with aggressively non-Aristotelian comedy, the so-called 'comical satires';[1] but by 1603–5 he had already reversed this tactic with his classical tragedy *Sejanus* (1603) and the prologue to his revision of *Every Man in His Humour* (published in 1616 with a prologue probably written for a court performance in 1605). It was not until the success of *Volpone* in 1606, however, that Jonson's new position was officially recognized, as the exultant dedication of its 1607 edition to the 'two universities' (i.e. Oxford and Cambridge) makes clear.

With *Volpone* Jonson entered on a dozen years of almost unalloyed success, in which he composed all his best plays, collaborated on a lucrative series of court masques with the designer Inigo Jones, wrote a lot of splendid poetry (much of it for influential patrons) was the first playwright to publish his collected writing in a large folio volume with the dignified title of *Works* (1616), was granted an annual pension by King James, and became the focus for a coterie of younger writers who called themselves 'the sons of Ben'. And though his personal success went into steady decline after the death of James I in 1625 and he was almost penniless when he died himself in 1637, from this point onwards Jonson's opinions and example dominated the English literary scene for over a century and a half.[2]

In the Prologue and Epistle to the Reader of the 1607 edition of *Volpone*, Jonson reiterates classical arguments made earlier in his prologue for the revised *Every Man in His Humour*: that the aim of comedy should not be to provoke easy laughter by slapstick farce

1

and bawdry nor to mock actual people, but rather to reform behaviour by holding up for public ridicule general weaknesses of human character (which he called 'humours'); and that the method of such comedy should be to obey the so-called Aristotelian 'unities' of person, place, and time (though not, significantly, the unity that Aristotle himself stressed most, the unity of action).³

In addition to these influential theoretical statements, the text of *Volpone* is crammed with echoes and imitations of famous classical writing. Legacy hunting, for example, which provides the play with its basic plot, was not a notable vice in the time of James I (though one unconvincing contemporary parallel was suggested by John Aubrey in *Brief Lives*), but the play combines attacks on the *captators* (grasping people, legacy hunters) of imperial Rome in Horace's *Satires* 2.5, several of Lucian's *Dialogues of the Dead*, and a section of Petronius's *Satyricon*, with smaller touches borrowed from Juvenal. The characterization of the subplot's Lady Politic Would-be as a non-stop talker, though it may have been coloured by Jonson's own estrangement from his wife (whom he described as 'a shrew but honest'), derives directly from Juvenal's mysogynistic *Satire* 6, with elaborations from *Du Mulier Loquaci*, a Latin translation of a Greek declamation by Libanius of Antioch which became the major source for Jonson's next play, *The Silent Woman* (1609). And the first entertainment performed by Volpone's grotesque attendants, Nano, Androgyno, and Castrone (1.2), which parodies Pythagoras's doctrine of reincarnation, combines Lucian's *Somnium* (*The Dream*, also known as *The Cock*) with details imported from the *De Philosophorum Vitis* of Diogenes Laertius. Some quite extended speeches are deliberately based on well-known classical models: for example, at the very beginning of the play Volpone parodies Ovid's description of the Golden Age in Book I of *Metamorphoses* (1.1.14 ff.); his description of loathsome old age (1.4.144 ff.) reworks Juvenal's Satire 10; and his wooing song to Celia (3.7.165 ff.) translates—but also distorts—a famous love poem by Catullus. The text is packed with such classical echoes and reminiscences, transformed by placing them in different contexts—a technique the Renaissance called 'imitatio' but which modern theory now calls 'intertextuality' or, in some interpretations, 'parody'.⁴

Recognition of such borrowings would certainly have constituted part of *Volpone*'s pleasure for its first audiences, but this does little to explain the play's continuing popularity in later periods when the originals are no longer common knowledge; and, as T. S. Eliot has pointed out in a fine essay,[5] to evaluate Jonson solely by his own neoclassical criteria is to do him less than justice as a theatre artist. Jonson's classicism is complicated by other influences and also by a collusion built up between the Fox and his audience during performance, so that strange crosscurrents and eddies of sympathy play against the classical, didactic mainstream of *Volpone*; and it is precisely because of the conflicts these create that the play has stayed so vividly alive.

BEAST SYMBOLISM AND REYNARD THE FOX

A major aspect of this vivacity is *Volpone*'s debt to the pervasive medieval and Renaissance taste for animal symbolism, those bestiaries and fables whose origins antedate even Aesop, of which the legend of Reynard the Fox was by far the most popular and important. For example, the play's central action of a fox feigning death to trap predatory birds (which is actually based on fact) is a recurrent motif of fox lore in both literature and pictorial representation,[6] as is the Fox's association with intriguing villains in general and, by extension, with the Devil himself. Similarly, vultures were associated with avarice, particularly in lawyers (like Voltore), and specifically by Edward Topsell with those 'which wish the death of their friends, that they may possess their goods',[7] and were also thought to have a keener scent for death than other scavengers; hence Voltore's ability always to arrive first among the legacy hunters (5.2.108–9, 5.6.27). The best-known fable about crows was the story of the crow that bedecked itself with peacock's feathers (reflected, perhaps, in the description of Corvino as 'spruce'—vain of his appearance), and their traditional association with marital constancy would give an extra twist of irony to Corvino's jealousy of, yet willingness to prostitute, his wife. Like old Corbaccio, ravens were considered examples of longevity whose hoarse croaking presaged the death of others, and, as with his disinheriting of Bonario, they were also thought to repudiate their young unless they were as black as themselves. Flies—the final link in the chain of predators (and, presumably, one of the many stinging varieties)—were believed to be particularly irritating to foxes; and 'Musca', the Latin word for fly, was a name frequently given to parasite characters in Latin comedy (Jonson had used it himself in the original version of *Every Man in His Humour*), and was also often used by medieval writers to refer to demonic familiar spirits, a detail that fits in nicely with the play's ironic punning on the idea of 'possession'. Finally, as the abbreviation to 'Pol' implies, the Would-be's in the subplot are seen as noisily voluble and imitative parrots, while Peregrine gets his name from a type of hawk, the 'falco peregrinus', which was 'so called because the young were . . . caught on their passage or "pilgrimage" from their breeding-place' (*OED*, peregrine a. and sb. 4 and B, sb. 3). Peregrine's tormenting of Sir Pol when the latter is disguised as a tortoise recalls a very popular emblem in which the combination of hawk and tortoise symbolized the wisdom of 'hastening slowly' by avoiding both extremes—accommodating the fact that Peregrine is not morally admirable either, but acts overhastily and also maliciously on a false presumption, so that at the end we are left with some sympathy for the foolish but harmless, and now penitent, Sir Pol.

Such general bestiary symbolism would have registered immediately with the original audience, but even more important is *Volpone*'s special indebtedness to the 'beast epic' of *Reynard the Fox*, the most popular story in Europe throughout the Middle Ages and Renaissance, which Jonson has a character refer to specifically—and ironically—in his next play, *The Silent Woman*, as 'an excellent book of moral philosophy . . . a very good book as any is, of the moderns' (4.4.83–91). The development of the Reynard epic is very complicated,[8] but the incidents which were most popular with both writers and visual artists are precisely those which seem relevant to *Volpone*: the two trials of the Fox, accused of attempted rape, then of feigning death to catch predators; the Fox as false doctor and preacher; the Fox as seducing musician; the Fox's self-defeating tendency to jeer; and his final escape from punishment by a court that is itself corrupt.

The central incident of the beast epic is Reynard's trial for rape of the she-wolf, Hersent, and it is this rather than his feigning of death which is the most recurrent aspect of the whole tradition. The earliest version—or 'branch'—of the epic (*c.* 1175) tells of Reynard's trial before the lion, King Noble, for the rape of Hersent, of Noble's scepticism about the charge (since the she-wolf had been Reynard's mistress), and Reynard's eventual escape. Five years later a sequel brought Reynard to a second trial for insolence to Noble and feigning death in order to catch the crow's wife (Celia in the play). And the two stories were then conflated to produce a pattern of the Fox's two trials which closely resembles the two trials of Volpone. There is no equivalent to Noble in the play, of course, though the Venetian court might have been dominated by a replica of the Lion of St Mark which was Venice's official emblem (as it was in a 1972 production at Bristol); but the successive charges of rape and feigning death are the same, and there are also many parallels of detail—such as the Fox's defence by pretending sickness and senility, and the venality of the court which tries him—which are too numerous to be accidental.

One parallel of particular importance is the tradition of the Fox's reckless lechery. This not only covers the switch in Jonson's play from interest in money to interest in Celia (which bothered John Dryden and later neoclassical critics), it also helps to explain the court's willingness to suspect Celia's chastity (since in the epic Reynard's accuser had been his mistress), and sheds light, too, on a curious detail of the subplot when Volpone calls the would-be seductive Lady Pol his 'she-wolf' (5.2.66)—a contradiction of her usual parrot image which seems pointless except in relation to the Reynard story.

There is also a clear parallelism between epic and play in the scene where Volpone adopts the disguise of Scoto of Mantua in order to woo Celia at her window. This combines two favourite incidents of the beast epic: Reynard the false physician (a trick that goes back to Aesop and turns up in nearly all the Reynard 'branches'), and the even more widespread image of Reynard as false preacher. The most common of all the Fox illustrations represents Reynard preaching from a platform (like a mountebank) to a congregation of domestic fowl. He often has a dead bird or two tucked into his cowl; usually there is a helper (like Mosca) behind the pulpit; and in at least one example the congregation actually consists of women not birds. 'If the fox preach', goes a famous proverb, 'it is to spy which is the fattest bird.'

Again, Volpone's bursting into song in the seduction scene (which was also criticized by neoclassical critics and has frequently been cut in performance) would seem much more in character to spectators familiar with the long iconographic tradition of the Fox as false musician. This was particularly popular in the Middle Ages and early Renaissance, with Dürer, for instance, representing *Temptation* by a picture of Reynard playing a fiddle before a cock and hens. And the fact that the Fox was also supposed to have an unpleasant voice might have been used to add an extra ironic twist to Volpone's ineffectual burst into song, which merely succeeds in terrifying Celia.

Finally, there is the same ambiguity of tone at the end of the

Reynard epic as Jonson worries about in his 'Epistle' to *Volpone*. Anarchic identification with the Fox's mischief (which, after all, is usually perpetrated against creatures no better than himself) is balanced in the epic by condemnation of the evils that he represents. Volpone's self-defeating determination to continue to jeer at his victims in Act 5 recalls Reynard's fatal jeering in Chaucer's *Nun's Priest's Tale*. And I think a Jacobean audience might be expected to grasp the irony of Volpone's apparent carelessness about the Avocatori's savage condemnation as he speaks the Epilogue inviting the audience to applaud him, if we remember that in none of the Reynard 'branches' is the Fox finally quelled, though he never escapes until the very last moment. As the French poet Rutebeuf puts it: 'Reynard is dead, Reynard lives, and Reynard reigns'.

Thus four or five key episodes of the play can be recognized as very familiar, even 'expected', scenes from the Reynard tradition, increasing our sense of the play's imaginative unity, and also, I would argue, pushing it away from expectations of psychological and social realism towards a more symbolic mode of drama, like a folk tale.

COMMEDIA DELL'ARTE

This Reynard material combines brilliantly with another context for the play. Not only is *Volpone* packed with Venetian dialect words and local colour (see commentary notes), it also has a fascinating relationship to the early sixteenth-century *commedia dell'arte*. This was an Italian form of improvised farce, particularly associated with Venice, in which a static, recurring cast of characters (called 'masks' because they wore stylized halfmasks)—e.g. old lecherous miser, cheeky servant, pedantic doctor, highminded soldierly young lover, etc.—fleshed out the bare bones of their *scenarios* (or plots) with improvised *burle*, which were individual repertoires of jokes and comic set-pieces that the actors fitted into their roles as they saw occasion. Robert Knoll has remarked on how easily bestiary effects coincide with traditional *commedia* costumes, with their beaky halfmasks, plumes, ragged cloaks, and contorted dance-like postures (as recorded, for example, in the engravings of Jacques Callot);[9] and *Volpone's* relation to the Italian form is both detailed and ironic.

Volpone is one of the few English plays of this period which refers to *commedia* 'masks' specifically. When Corvino returns in 2.3 to find Volpone disguised as Scoto the mountebank wooing Celia, he compares himself to the *commedia*'s miserly old cuckold 'Pantalone', Celia to the bawdy serving girl 'Franciscina', and Volpone-as-Scoto to 'Flamineo', one of the *commedia*'s stock young lovers. These identifications are obviously wrong, however. Corvino is using them sarcastically; and Jonson is relying on his audience's knowledge of *commedia* characters to realize this. If they could recognize such misattributions, however, they could also be expected to recognize the more substantial *commedia* resemblances that permeate the play. Five examples can illustrate this.

The whole set-up of 'Scoto's' wooing of Celia recalls innumerable *commedia* scenes in which a suitor aided by comic servants (called *zannis*, a Venetian corruption of the name 'Giovanni') serenades a wife (or ward or serving girl) at her window and is put to flight by the appearance of a jealous husband (or guardian or master). And when the serenader is disguised as a mountebank (as, for instance, in Fortunio Scala's *Flavio's Fortunes*) or as an apothecary or doctor (as in *Pantalone Spezier* or *Eliza Ali Bassa*), the relationship becomes even clearer.

The Scoto disguise resembles, moreover, the very familiar *commedia* mask of Gratiano, a pedantic Bolognese doctor, whose black mask, cloak, and floppy black hat make a perfect concealment for Volpone, and whose peculiarity is long discourses full of Latin tags, jargon, and pseudo-learning, of which the favourite is a long list of eminent patients, diseases, and cures, as in the play. Gratiano too is usually helped by *zannis*, who attract and entertain the crowd for him, just as Nano the dwarf, Androgyno the hermaphrodite, and Castrone the eunuch, under Mosca's direction, help the Fox perform as Scoto.

It is not Corvino who resembles the central Venetian mask of Pantalone, moreover, but Volpone himself in his character of rich, greedy, complaining, and lecherous *magnifico*, as he is described in the *dramatis personae*. *Magnifico* was traditionally the title of Pantalone, whose Venetian grandee's costume of red tunic, tights, and slippers, covered with a black cloak, is readily adaptable to the russet appearance of a Fox—particularly since his halfmask had a long snout-like nose, a pointed beard, and bristling moustachios, which he thrust forward, animal-like, with belligerent inquisitiveness. Pantalone came to have interestingly contradictory attributes as the role was developed over the years. At one extreme, he was a comically ineffectual old miser who abandoned avarice for lust, only to be deceived by the woman he was pursuing. At the other extreme, he was represented as seriously threatening, a man of energetic middle age, astute and sexually aggressive, with (to quote Allardyce Nicoll) an 'almost animal ferocity and agility'.[10] The character of Volpone exploits this contradictory tradition, and also incorporates such stock Pantalone *burle* as his love of eavesdropping, his inept singing to a lute (which overlaps neatly with the Fox-as-musician), and his trick of exchanging costumes with his servant only to end up with a beating (cf. 5.12.78–82).

Besides these resemblances of interrupted serenade, of Scoto to the *dottore* mask, and of Volpone to the dangerous yet self-deceiving Pantalone, comparison to the *commedia* also clarifies the complicating blandness that seems to be presented with lurking mockery in Jonson's characterization of the 'good' characters, Bonario and Celia. Again Corvino's comparison of his wife to the bawdy 'Franciscina' mask is sarcastic. She and Bonario resemble, rather, typical *commedia* lovers, who lacked the grotesque vitality of the other 'masks'. Traditionally, *commedia* lovers went unmasked, were dressed in the height of contemporary fashion instead of the others' bizarrely stylized costumes, and spoke impeccably lofty sentiments in purest Tuscan Italian, instead of using the comic dialects affected by the rest of the *commedia* characters. However, as the French critic Duchartre puts it, in the context of farce such idealizations are always apt to appear 'just a little bit ridiculous',[11] and this element was particularly exploited in the case of the romantic hero, whose hasty oversimplifications were sometimes exploited for humour—as Jonson exploits Bonario.

Finally, there are possible *commedia* analogues to Mosca and Sir Pol. As tricky servant, Mosca combines characteristics from Pantalone's two main *zannis*, Arlecchino and Brighella; and Sir Pol, the imitative British traveller of the subplot, has interesting resemblances to a mask called Pulchinello. This name derives from *pulchino* (little cockerel), and the character was bird-like in appearance, big-bellied (and sometimes hump-backed) with long thin legs, and half masked, with a parrot-like nose that would also serve nicely for Sir Pol's disguise as a tortoise. (One of Pulchinello's derivatives, Trufaldino, specifically represents himself as a parrot.) His purpose, according to K. M. Lea,[12] was to provide 'strong subplots' by representing a blockhead who tries to be clever, a pointlessly energetic chatterbox who cannot keep a secret (in both French and Italian 'a secret of Pulchinello' means an open secret) and incorporates contemporary gossip into his chatter, and unlike the other *zannis* is usually matched with a wife who deceives him—as Lady Pol *tries* to do—and with whom he quarrels. Even Sir Pol's tortoise disguise has its specific analogue in the scenario of *Pulchinello, Brigand-chief*, in which, while trying to escape arrest, 'Pulchinello slips under a winnowing basket and attempts to reach the wood, crawling like a tortoise'.[13]

These parallels do not prove that the *commedia dell'arte* was a direct 'source' for Volpone, of course, merely that the play incorporates too many resemblance to this famous Italian comic form (with which both Jonson and his actors can be proved beyond a shadow of a doubt to have been familiar) for the likenesses not to have struck a contemporary audience as appropriate for a play ostensibly set in Venice.

THE GOLDEN AGE

A fourth imaginative context is the myth of a Golden Age, to which Jonson immediately relates the play by Volpone's reference to 'that age which [poets] would have the best' (1.1.15), his paraphrase in Volpone's opening aubade of Ovid's famous description of an ideal age without industry or toil (1.1.33–40), and his self-indulgent conclusion to scene 1:

> What should I do
> But cocker up my genius and live free
> To all delights my fortune calls me to? (70–2)

The concept of an ideal past when humanity was sexually unrepressed and lived in harmony with beasts and nature, without money, labour, agriculture, trade, or travel, was central to much Renaissance literature (Harry Levin has an excellent study of it),[14] and Jonson uses the golden age trope frequently elsewhere in his works—including his other great comedy, *The Alchemist*. In *Volpone*, on the other hand, he exploits the myth ironically by leaving the traditional golden age implicit and playing off against each other two perversions of the original ideal. In the first place, he presents it as degenerated to an age of *money*; in the second, as a self-indulgent, self-deceiving Saturnalia.

Degeneration of the Golden Age ideal to mere materialism—greed for 'gold' in the form of money—is the most common irony in the tradition, and it is this that Volpone's opening speeches celebrate so audaciously and that subsequent behaviour by the legacy hunters and Avocatori confirms. The metal gold was supposed not to have existed in the true Golden Age (when mining was unknown), but in his first speech Volpone puts it at the centre of his universe, praising it with religious intensity as brighter than the sun, the unmoved mover and creator of the world, lovelier than sexual beauty, and the ground for all human values. Freedom from toil is no longer based on Nature's bounty, as in Ovid, but on exploiting the greed of other men; and, far from uniting humanity in sexual and social harmony, gold in Venice 'unnaturally' (the word is frequently repeated) breaks the bonds of family and friendship.

Suggestions of sexual abnormality permeate the play, and all its family units are distorted by greed. Volpone's household is a parody of a family, with Mosca as its 'mistress' and the three freaks as its 'children'; Corbaccio repudiates his son; and Celia is reified to gold itself, first by Mosca ('Bright as your gold and lovely as your gold! . . . She's kept as warily as is your gold', 1.5.114, 118), then by her husband, who assures her that, like his money, she will be none the worse for 'touching'. The very term 'family' degenerates from its primary meaning of a marital and parental bond to the secondary one of economic household. The Avocatori fail to live up to the social responsibilities implied by their reiterated title of 'fatherhoods'. And Voltore, who has no marriage or blood ties to betray, by using rhetoric dishonestly betrays not only his profession as lawyer but also the wider human community that Jonson believed could be maintained only by integrity of language.

Greed also distorts the Golden Age relationship between human-ity and animals. Whereas one of the chief glories of the Golden Age was man's ability to communicate with beasts and learn happiness from their example—a belief that, in conjunction with the doctrine of reincarnation, led the followers of the Greek philosopher Py-thagoras to ban meat eating, since to eat an animal in the Golden Age was the destruction of another soul—in *Volpone* men imitate the lust and savagery of animals, not their wisdom. The Pythagorean tenets of reincarnation and vegetarianism are specifically mocked by Volpone's freaks, and, as E. B. Partridge has demonstrated,[15] images of cannibalism abound. Wordplay further links this age of money to the Christian concept of demonic 'possession'. Mosa, the 'fly', is seen as Volpone's familiar spirit, to whose level Volpone descends when he teases the legacy hunters in his disguise as commandatore (or police sergeant). Celia too says she thinks Corvino must be 'possessed'; and the image is dramatically embodied in the last scene when Voltore ludicrously pretends to have been taken over by a blue toad with bat's wings. What really 'possesses' all of them is greed for gold, of course, and the judge's final comment makes clear the several levels of irony in that verb:

> These possess wealth as sick men possess fevers,
> Which trulier may be said to possess them.   (5.12.101–2)

The second, rival perversion of the Golden Age takes the form of untrammelled self-gratification, in which wisdom and folly are re-versed and art degenerates to fantasies of sensuality and power. Historically, its roots are in the classical celebrations of Saturnalia and Carnival, the German peasants' *Bauernhimmel* or Land of Cockayne, or the Lubberland that Jonson mentions in 1614 as an analogue to his comedy *Bartholomew Fair*. Psychologically its appeal can be understood in terms of Freud's 'pleasure principle', accord-ing to which the individual's adjustment to reality on which all social and moral standards are based depends on abandoning the self-centred narcissism of infancy, which reduces everything to terms of its own personality and momentary whim. This adjustment is never wholly complete, however, and infantile self-gratification always surfaces to some extent in adult fantasy, whose products, as de-scribed by Freud, sound like an exact description of the mental world of Volpone: 'imaginary gratifications of ambition, grandiose erotic wishes, dilating the more extravagantly the more reality ad-monishes humility and patience'.[16] Art embodying such fantasy appeals at a very basic, nonrational level, therefore—a level 'below the intellect' as T. S. Eliot recognizes in his essay on Jonson—and this often includes an element of mocking cruelty, since the humili-ation of others is an obvious way to enhance one's own sense of omnipotence. For Freud the function of comedy was precisely to act as a catharsis for this aggressive fantasy, and Jonson appears to have anticipated this theory, if his labelling of *The Silent Woman* as a 'comedy of affliction' (2.6.37) is any indication.

It is at this level that Volpone's main imaginative attraction as a character lies, because reckless self-indulgence like his taps the infantile narcissism of everyone; and its method, as Jonson was always uneasily aware, is close to that of genuine art. Volpone's poetry enthrals us, but Jonson extrapolates the phantasmagoric quality of his mental world in the three freaks—Nano, Castrone, and Androgyno—who play no necessary part in the Aristotelian action of the play but provide theatrical emblems of Volpone's spiritual de-

formity. Since they are extensions of the perverse and childish side
of his imagination, it is when he exposes them to the outside world
by freeing them that his fall begins. Moreover, their entertainments
for him are not only bad art but intentional bad art (cf. 1.2.2–4),
always a sign in Jonson of imaginative corruption and cultural decadence. Significantly, their first entertainment mocks motifs of the
Golden Age and the related teachings of Pythagoras, as it tells how
the soul, derived from the god of art, Apollo, ends by choosing to
inhabit a bisexual fool, Androgyno. A similar descent occurs in
Scoto's account of how Apollo's gift of beauty has been progres-
sively adulterated to become merely a cosmetic at the court of
France. And this spiralling effect of a series of repetitions at progres-
sively lower levels of outrageous performance becomes one of the
basic rhythms of the play.

In fact, the freaks' second entertainment directly associates degeneration with corrupt impersonation. Nano wins a struggle for
precedence among them because his function is the 'pleasing imitation / Of greater men's actions in a ridiculous fashion' (3.3.13–14).
Imaginative corruption thus takes the art form of the play itself, and
mimicry becomes the chief means by which Volpone's saturnalian
world both creates and ultimately destroys itself.

One of the ironies of Jonson's career is that this very great dramatist profoundly distrusted man's instinct for mimesis, his wish to
create a 'virtual reality'. Far from sharing the enthusiasm of
neoplatonic humanists such as Pico della Mirandola that man's
power to change will enable him to become divine, Jonson shared St
Augustine's more traditional belief that man attempting to be a god
sinks lower than the beasts. In his *Discoveries* he warns that 'we so
insist on imitating others, as we cannot (when it is necessary) return
to ourselves . . . and make the habit to another Nature',[17] and this, of
course, is the nemesis of Volpone, who for 'feigning lame, gout,
palsy, and such diseases' is doomed by the Avocatori at the end 'to
lie in prison, cramped with irons, / Till thou be'st sick and lame
indeed' (5.12.122–4).

Before this point, however, we see that acting is one of the Fox's
main delights, indeed a defining aspect of his personality, and the
play as a whole is packed with play-within-the-play situations of
characters dissimulating or watching other characters pretend, as
well as recurrent theatrical comparisons like that of Sir Pol's tortoise
to a puppet show (5.4.77–8), the mountebank scene to the *commedia
dell'arte* (2.3.2–8) or a morality play (2.5.21–2), and Volpone's

wooing of Celia to Venice's famous entertainment for 'the great Valois' (3.7.159 ff.)

The ramifications of such self-referential theatricalism are complex, however. Besides carrying the theme of human over-aspiring, it also affects our understanding of Volpone's motives and controls our theatrical empathy with him. Clearly, acting and the power this gives him over other people excites Volpone more than either gold or sexual possession (1.1.30 ff.; 5.2.10–11); and that this is partly because it is a mode of self-display is revealed by his brag to Celia about admiration of his acting as Antinous in his youth (3.7.162–4), and by the flattery he demands from Mosca for his performance as the mountebank. However, there are also more negative reasons for his attraction to dissimulation: it allows Volpone constantly to humiliate other people; and gradually, as the play proceeds, it becomes clear that he also needs to act because his self-creating mode of life is very susceptible to boredom.[18]

The cause of this compulsiveness peeps out when Volpone summons his freaks' second entertainment in order, in his own phrase, to 'make the wretched time more sweet' while Mosca is away (3.3.2). Time and its passing pervade this play, whose central stage image is of a man acting his own death; and this again can be related to the saturnalian nature of Volpone's cast of mind. The basis of the myth of the Golden Age is that it constituted the reign of Saturn, god of time, and it was not until Saturn was deposed that the world became subject to mortality. Thus, all visions of paradise take place out of time in a spring of unending youth, and the aim of Golden Age art has always been 'to recapture the moment of happiness in eternal stasis'.[19] Thus, though Volpone demurs at Mosca's gross flattery that he will live, if not for ever, at least for many generations (1.2.119–22), in the seduction scene later he himself tells Celia that he is still 'as fresh, / As hot, as high, and in as jovial plight' as when he acted young Antinous thirty-two years earlier (3.7.157–8). And the song he then launches into ('Come, my Celia, let us prove . . .') is an imitation of a famous *carpe diem* ('seize the day') poem by Catullus that was well known to Jonson's contemporaries as the chorus of Tasso's *Aminta*, one of the most famous of all Renaissance plays about the Golden Age.

Volpone trivializes the song, however, by adding a quatrain about not getting caught; and this is typical of his method of dealing with the reminders of time, age, disease, and death which so plentifully bestrew the play. Volpone's technique is to try to control the mortal destiny of which these are reminders by burlesquing both disease and cure, but uneasiness keeps surfacing through his mockery. There is a curiously self-destructive element in Volpone's increasingly hectic behaviour, in fact, in his failures of nerve, his heavy drinking, and his obsessive need for further risks. This element bothered neoclassical critics but it is quite plausible psychologically once it is recognized that self-enhancing fantasy, not mere greed for money, is the main key to his character and to the play's denouement.

THE WOULD-BE SUBPLOT

Another non-classical and complicating aspect of *Volpone* is, of course, the Would-be subplot. In his notebook *Discoveries* Jonson interprets 'unity of action' in non-Aristotelian fashion as a plot that 'being composed of many parts . . . begins to be one as those parts grow or are wrought together',[20] and the parallels and contrasts of the Would-be scenes have been designed to emphasize and complicate our responses to the main plot of *Volpone*, both thematically and rhythmically.

Only Lady Pol is linked directly into the main action, as yet another legacy hunter who comically arrives when Volpone is rapturously expecting Celia and who blackens Celia's reputation in the initial trial scene later. But neither of these involvements is strictly necessary to the plot, and Lady Pol's chief functions are essentially the same as those of Peregrine and Sir Pol: to bridge the gap between Italian setting and London audience, and to provide farcical exaggerations of characters and incidents in the main action. On the one hand, her hand-made cap (3.5.14–15) and garbled medical advice (3.4.52–65) parody the gifts and sinister solicitude of the other legacy hunters—particularly Corbaccio's 'dram' (3.9.14)—while at the same time extending Jonson's mockery of spurious cure-alls; and, like Corvino, she is manipulated by Mosca through sexual jealousy and concern for public reputation. On the other hand, she also affords a comic foil to Celia, not only in her fruitless willingness to be seduced but also in her desire to imitate the skills of Venetian courtesans. Whereas Celia laments her beauty and wishes to disfigure it, Lady Pol is a theoretician of cosmetics and second-hand charm—including a farrago of half-digested culture that recalls the deliberate burlesques of Volpone's freaks—and her impervious self-assertion also parodies the ruthless aggression that is central to the main plot, especially in her general noisiness and the way at first she manages to talk down even the court.

Similarly, Sir Pol's belief in his own shrewdness and cunning, his schemes for power and riches, his sense of rank, his appetite for novelty—especially freaks of natures—and the debunking of these pretensions by the actual trivialities recorded in his diary, all underline similar aspects in Volpone; yet at the same time, the meanness of his petty expenditures provides a comic contrast to the *magnifico*'s genuine extravagance. Sir Pol's naive admiration for Volpone's performance as Scoto merely emphasizes its deliberate speciousness; yet again, by contrast, it reminds us of the Fox's real power of imaginative rhetoric elsewhere in the play. In wishing to enlist Peregrine as admiring confidant, Sir Pol creates a false relationship like Volpone's with Mosca, which makes him vulnerable to the same inversion of power. His admiration for Stone the Fool (2.1.53) not only recalls the vulgarizations of art in the freaks' two entertainments, but also reflects an element of inept acting in the knight himself that contrasts with Volpone's real skill as a performer, as is emphasized by Peregrine's meta-theatrical comment:

> Oh, this knight,
> Were he well known, would be a precious thing
> To fit our English stage.   (2.1.56–8)

All his compromising 'notes' turn out to be plagiarized from playbooks, in fact, and this incompetent theatricality comes to a climax in his grotesque and ineffectual assumption of the role of tortoise, which one of his tormentors compares to London's childish puppet-shows (5.4.77–8).

The effect of the subplot parody is rhythmic, moreover, as well as thematic, depending as much upon its placing as its parallels. An obvious example of this comes in 3.4, where Lady Pol anticipates Volpone's attempt to seduce Celia. This is not only a comic reversal of Volpone's expectations, placing him in a situation where we laugh at instead of with him; it also throws an ironic shadow forward to the real seduction, undermining his stature in that scene too. Moreover, Volpone's recognition in the scene that he is now a victim of his own disguise, so that 'Before, I feigned diseases, now I have one' (3.4.62), will return to haunt him again in 5.1 after the first trial and anticipates his final sentencing by the court to become what he has mimicked. Similarly, the way that Sir Pol's boasts of acumen provide the very means for his exposure in 5.4 anticipates the self-

destructive hubris of Volpone, though the differences are also important. Sir Pol's innocence of the plot for which Peregrine
revenges himself (with a disingenuous cruelty only a little less dis-
turbing than that shown later by the Avocatori) makes Sir Pol less
culpable; and, unlike Volpone, he learns his lesson and is
'dishumoured' in the manner of Jonson's earlier comedy. Volpone's
defiance, on the other hand, and impudent request in the Epilogue
for the audience to applaud him provoke a much more complicated
response, and one that has always been controversial. The subplot
'sports with follies', as Jonson had defined the purpose of comedy in
his Prologue to *Every Man in His Humour*, but the main plot goes
further, to confront us ambiguously with 'crimes'.

THE DENOUEMENT

From Dryden on, neoclassic critics have been uneasy about the
denouement of the play: first, with the way that, after the first trial,
the plot seems to be restarted quite arbitrarily, so that Volpone even
calls it his 'jig' (5.2.59)—a term then used for dances performed
after a play's conclusion; and secondly, with the harshness of the
Avocatori's sentences, which threaten to break the play's comic
tone. Jonson knew exactly what he was doing in the first case, but
was himself worried about the second problem, as he reveals in his
Epistle to the Reader.

Restarting the action in Act 5 is a deliberate though non-classical
technique which Jonson probably learned from the need to bring his
early, virtually plotless 'comical satires' to a satisfactory sense of
closure. In the Chorus to Act 4 of his *The Magnetic Lady* (1632) he
tries to identify such a 'fresh cheat' as the plot's *catastasis* (see
Redwine, xxiii–iv), a term introduced by the Renaissance neoclassical critic Julius Caesar Scaliger. However, Scaliger meant merely the
most complicated moment in a plot, not really a fresh start.

How the technique actually works for Jonson is better understood
by comparison to music. As in seventeenth-century serial composition, the 'fresh cheat' functions as a *reprise* (i.e. summarizing repetition) of the play's main themes, with a change of key, accelerated
tempo, and the two main 'parts' (or roles) reversed.[21] Thus, in Act
5 of *Volpone* the tormenting of the legacy hunters is recapitulated in
accelerated and compressed form, first by the will-reading scene,
then by Volpone's rapid sequence of short scenes in which he teases
the dupes in his disguise as commandatore. The characters are then

all brought together for a final ensemble scene in the second trial, where rapid changes of testimony keep the audience, like the Avocatori, off balance till the end. And, very interestingly, the stage roles of Mosca and Volpone are now totally reversed. The formerly active, buzzing Fly plays a dignified, virtually static *magnifico*, pretending deafness during the will scene (like Volpone earlier) and sycophantically provided with a stool in court by a venal Avocatore; while Volpone by contrast dashes manically around in the costume of a servant, jeering at the legacy hunters and buzzing desperate asides in court to change the testimony of Mosca and Voltore. *Accelerando*, repetition, and inversion thus provide a structural effect of 'closure' that reinforces our psychological awareness that Volpone cannot resist this last disastrous gamble in order to revenge his fear during the first trial and regain a sense of mastery. But our recognition that in fact he is no longer in control of events, combined with increasingly self-conscious reminders of the bestiary dimension of the play (the tortoise, the blue toad with bat's wings, the Avocatori's concluding lines),[22] serve to distance us from identifying too closely with him as he rushes so evidently to disaster.

Nonetheless, as Jonson recognizes, the Avocatori's final sentencing seems too harsh for comedy (at least in reading the play). Like Falstaff in *I Henry IV*, Volpone has established too intimate and comic a link with the audience for that audience to slough him off so abruptly; the Avocatori are corrupt as judges, little better than the rogues they censure; and (as Coleridge, for one, regretted) there is no suggestion that Celia and Bonario may marry to offset the severity of the sentences on the malefactors. Moreover, there is the further problem of the Epilogue, in which Volpone concludes by asking the audience to applaud him. How is this to be reconciled with his savage indictment by the Venetian court?

One clue as to how it may have been handled in performance lies in a structural detail to which too little attention has been paid. This is the oddly anticlimactic order of the court's indictments. Mosca and Volpone are sentenced first, with Mosca delivered over to the *saffi* (the Venetian police) and Volpone less specifically 'removed' (5.12.124). Attention then swings to the minor villains, diverting the audience's focus to less serious, more comically appropriate indictments, with Corbaccio farcically still not able to hear the sentence passed upon him. And it is this anticlimactic arrangement that prepares us for the Epilogue and our sense of the Fox's ultimate survival—a survival that is inevitable because, like Reynard, he

represents something permanent in all of us, an egotistic vitality that
is closely linked to our corruption.

Whereas Volpone panicked miserably after Celia's rescue and was
unnerved during the first trial, he recovers from Mosca's treachery
and the collapse of all his plans with magnificent panache. His
doffing of disguise and contemptuous dismissal of the lesser rogues
(5.12.84 ff.) regain for him immediate command of the stage (and
audience), and he seems to treat his punishment with disdain by
punning on the court's sentence: 'This is called mortifying of a fox'
(see 5.12.125). The anticlimactic minor indictments which then take
attention away from him may have been intended to allow him to
slip away unnoticed—perhaps leaving merely his cloak behind, as in
the proverbial 'To have no more of the Fox than his skin'—so as to
reappear unexpectedly to speak the Epilogue. Such a conclusion
(which has been successfully employed in some modern productions) maintains the comedy's sardonic integrity. This is the Fox's
last trick, in the tradition established by the Reynard beast epic; and
in it he exploits the special complicity built up between Volpone and
the audience. The Fox distinguishes between the Venetian court
and the 'jovially' indulgent audience (Epilogue, 6) and appeals
beyond moral judgement to the theatrical empathy of performance.

THE PLAY IN PERFORMANCE

A final disadvantage of the neoclassical approach to *Volpone* favoured by Jonson himself is that it encourages us to appreciate the
play only as literature rather than in terms of theatrical performance,
as a 'poem', that is, independent of the 'loathèd stage'.[23] But this is
unfair to any play, and particularly to *Volpone*, which has been
performed almost continuously since 1606, except for a 136-year gap
after 1786 (during the periods of sentimental comedy and 'Victorian'
morality); and since its revival in 1921 has not only become the most
frequently produced of all Elizabethan and Caroline plays other than
Shakespeare's most popular works, but has also inspired many adap-
tations and new creations. Its stage history is too complicated to
summarize here,[24] but it is worth briefly considering some of the
main choices that any director must face in mounting the play.
These can be grouped under three categories: first, the interpretation of key roles, and timing of certain actions; secondly, decor, the
kinds of sets and costumes chosen; and thirdly, attempts to maintain
a comic tone despite the Avocatori's cruel sentencing.[25]

Characterization

Two main ways to play Volpone himself have emerged in modern productions, each of which can easily be pushed too far. Sir Donald Wolfit's many productions of the play between 1938 and 1959, in which he took the leading role,[26] represented the Fox as a man in the prime of life whose overbearing energy manifested itself in a savage greed for possession, both material and sexual, combined with a comic 'gusto' that delighted in the performance of roles which, by deceiving other characters, forged a strong link of collusion between Wolfit and the audience. This approach tends to underplay the Fox's moments of alienating weakness, however (Wolfit cavalierly cut them); and, if its comic element is pushed too far, it can also sacrifice our sense of Volpone as an aristocrat and poet, and, even worse, can undermine Jonson's condemnation of his actions. Thus, at Minneapolis in 1964 Douglas Campbell was so funny as a seducer that the audience actually applauded his attempt at rape!

In reaction against the Wolfit line (and influenced also perhaps by Stefan Zweig's German adaptation, which, translated into both English and French, has a modern stage history to rival that of Jonson's original), the other major interpretation of Volpone has been to stress his sense of aristocratic superiority and to explain his mischief-making as motivated solely by boredom. Paul Scofield was so 'magnificent' a Volpone at the National Theatre in 1977 that his downfall had a touch of Marlovian tragedy, while a more sinister, de-Sade-like variation was provided by William Hutt at Stratford, Ontario, in 1971. Ralph Richardson, however, took ironic aloofness too far in his world-weary aristocrat at Stratford-upon-Avon in 1952, so that in one absurd scene Celia actually bent over his prone body to beg him not to assault her.

The characterization of Volpone largely determines that of Nano, Castrone, and Androgyno and, to a lesser extent, of Celia and Mosca. Volpone's attitude to his retainers has ranged from Wolfit's savagery towards what his prompt books contemptuously call the 'queers' to playfulness in both of Tyrone Guthrie's productions (Minneapolis 1964, National Theatre 1968), where they were affectionately referred to as the 'kids'; and these attitudes have determined how grotesquely the three of them should be presented. In the 'decadent' Stratford, Ontario production of 1971, for instance, the Castrone was strikingly fat and bald, dressed all in white satin, Androgyno had naked female breasts and male genitals of mutant size and coloration, and the dwarf emerged from a huge, Castrone-like egg that the other two wheeled in for Volpone's breakfast.

Similarly, representations of Celia have run the gamut from passive, almost masochistic suffering (in Wolfit's versions) to militant morality, and there are two aspects of the staging that can materially affect this. The sexual nastiness of the chastity belt with which Corvino threatens her at 2.5.57 is too often omitted in modern performances (though Wolfit uncompromisingly exploited it); and it is crucial to decide when Celia shall appear at her window to listen to Scoto's spiel. If she appears too soon, enjoys his entertainment, and then throws down her handkerchief, she may seem (as Harold Hobson accused Siobhan Mckenna in the Ralph Richardson production of being) 'like the sort of girl who entices strangers to her bedroom and then screams for help'.[27] It is probably wise to have her appear only at 2.2.198 ff. to throw down her handkerchief in response to Scoto's plea for some token from the crowd in general 'to show I am not contemned of you' (220–7).

Timing is even more crucial for the characterization of Mosca, because it gives quite a different impression of him if we realize that he is treacherous from the start than if he seems merely to get the idea of cheating opportunistically when Volpone decides to nominate him as heir—as Wolfit always insisted, cutting Mosca's acerbic asides that give us earlier warning. The most obvious place for realization is, of course, the Fly's soliloquy in 3.1, which Wolfit contrived to mute but other directors have rightly emphasized; but the 1972 Bristol production created an interesting alternative by allowing Mosca's anger to break through earlier at 1.5.48–9 with 'He's the true father of his family / In all save me'.

There is also the question of how much of a fly Mosca should appear. This may seem like a matter for the next section, except that the most fly-like representation to date was Anthony Quayle's in a production that otherwise did not stress the play's bestiary connections (Stratford-upon-Avon, 1952). Quayle combined physical agility with shiny black clothes and an occasional 'phosphorescently' fixed stare of menace, rubbed his hands together in a motion that was part hypocritical flatterer, part fly massaging its legs, stressed his sibilants, and gave a curious buzzing whenever he laughed. When he read out Volpone's will in 5.3, he even seemed to have six legs, since he was seated at a table whose legs were carved into black shoes and stockings to resemble his own.

Decor

There have been roughly four main kinds of decor in modern productions. Although Wolfit included some bestiary touches and was as opulent in costuming as his straitened budgets allowed, his productions, like most other early versions, set the play as simply as possible, with standard seventeenth-century costumes and a minimum of props, on proscenium stages with a front curtain that allowed short scenes to be acted in front of it and could also be drawn across either half of the stage to suggest a change of venue. The chief advantage of such staging (besides economy) is fluidity, but it offers no comment of its own on the themes or action of the play.

A second, obvious tendency has been to exploit the Venetian setting by evoking an ornate richness that sets the play specifically in time and place and comments on the materialism that Jonson is attacking. Perhaps the most elaborate decor of this kind was Malcolm Pride's designs for Stratford-upon-Avon in 1952, which included a detailed reproduction of the Piazza di San Marco, complete with practical gondolas, that Alan Dent compared to Longhi's glowing canvasses in the Academy at Venice.[28] Such elaborate pictorialness had its costs, however. Despite heavy cutting, set changing made the production last three hours; the theatre's rolling stages clanged noisily together, reminding *Punch* of tram cars; and on one occasion an electrical failure paralysed the lift stage in mid descent, marooning Ralph Richardson in the top half of Volpone's bedroom.

A third solution has been to experiment with modern dress or with transposition to a period that is neither modern nor Jacobean. Joan Littlewood's 1955 production in London had among its props an accordion, a telephone, a cocktail shaker, and a bathchair, with Mosca on a bicycle and the tortoise shell replaced by a frogman's suit, in which Sir Pol made his final exit by diving into the orchestra pit (to great applause). At Stratford, Ontario in 1971 the play's sense of blasphemy and sexual decadence was pointed by setting it in the 1890s Venice of Thomas Mann and Henry James, with the Would-be's as loud Texan tourists encountering a very Jamesian Peregrine in a crowded cafe ('L'addizione, s'il vous plaît').

But perhaps most interesting from an interpretative point of view are decors influenced by the bestiary tradition. There is a touch of this in most productions, but only two have made it central. In Tyrone Guthrie's 1968 version at the National Theatre, besides furs for Volpone and a shiny black suit for Mosca pinched in at the waist and tight on arms and legs, the designer gave six-inch beaks to the birds of prey, with feathered capes and gloves with talons—so that whenever Voltore grasped Mosca's arm, the parasite visibly winced. Actors were sent to study bird behaviour at the Regent's Park zoo; Volpone copied his vocal effects from records of real foxes; and it was Guthrie who first took up the scholars' suggestion of costuming the Would-be's elaborately as parrots.

So much inventive detail was ultimately distracting, however, and bestiary costumes and business were more discreetly handled in a quatercentenary production by the Bristol Old Vic in 1972. This production was unique, moreover, in reflecting bestiary influences also in the set, which consisted mainly of three platforms set on tall scaffolding, with the one at stage left towering as high as twenty feet up into the fly galleries. The birds' entrances were made by swooping down from this on steep diagonal ramps, which not only established the image of circling predators but also allowed some interesting overlapping of scenes of the kind suggested by Jonson's own use of 'noises off' to indicate new arrivals before a scene has finished. There was a central burrow-like entrance for Volpone and a sewer pipe for Mosca, and the whole was painted in a curious greenish gold with lumpy encrustations, simultaneously suggesting ordure and decayed wealth, and was appropriately dominated by a large replica of Venice's insignia, the Lion of St Mark.

Denouement

The problem of reabsorbing the Avocatori's harsh verdicts into a comic tone has bothered every modern director of *Volpone*. Guthrie invented two theatrical solutions: a communal song and wildly escalating laughter from the Avocatori, neither of which worked. Richard David at the Bristol Old Vic was so undecided about whether Volpone should escape after the Epilogue or be repudiated that he changed his ending three times during the run. The only productions that have succeeded with this problem seem to have done so by exploiting the acting motif within the play, its element of self-conscious, acknowledged performance. Wolfit was pre-eminent at this (and, in fact, was once turned down for cinema work because he always acted straight out to the audience). Volpone's decision to unmask is so self-consciously dramatic a climax that it lends itself to spectacular stage effect, and Wolfit introduced a startling vocal effect to emphasize this. After he had been harshly and impressively sentenced, he held his hands, palms outward, over his eyes and gave a strangled, sobbing, animal howl, rising on a long intake of breath to be expelled hissingly with 'This is called mortifying of a fox', prolonging the last sibilant. (In a letter, J. C. Trewin described it to me as the curling, breaking, and ebbing of an enormous wave.) There was no question, then, that Volpone was punished; but Wolfit managed to pull the tones together by his handling of the Epilogue. He spoke it in his own person: not in character as Volpone, but as a variant of his own familiar hanging-from-the-curtain-in-exhaustion call. With his face relaxed, his make-up could be seen as make-up; the actor was visible through the role; and, as he gracefully begged the audience's applause in his Volpone 'poetry' voice, the defeat of the Fox was absorbed into the success of the actor, and the link between Volpone-as-performer and Wolfit-as-performer, played teasingly with throughout, was finally consolidated.

The only other version to find a comparable solution was David William's 1971 production at Stratford, Ontario, and this too relied on an explicit recognition of the play's theatricality. Jonson's anticlimactic order, in which the minor characters are sentenced after the protagonist, allowed Volpone to leave the stage unnoticed while they were being condemned, to reappear on the balcony for the Epilogue, very much at his ease in an Edwardian smoking jacket to oversee the denouement. Whereas Wolfit had solved the tonal problem by obliterating the gap between role and actor, William's effect was to identify Volpone self-referentially with the director.

Theatricality would therefore seem to be essential to *Volpone*. The play gives considerable scope for directorial interpretation, but the most successful modern productions have all been slightly 'stagey', distancing too much identification by use of the bestiary tradition or by direct collusion between the audience and the actor playing Volpone. Seemingly, only when some such dimension is taken into account can the play come to a satisfactory conclusion. Even more than most plays, then, *Volpone* depends for its full effect finally on performance.

A NOTE ON DATE AND EDITIONS[29]

Date

The title page and colophon for *Volpone* in the 1616 folio of Ben Jonson's *Works* state that it was acted by 'the K. MAIESTIES SERVANTS' in 'the yeere 1605', a dating that in the old-style legal calendar could extend to 25 March 1606; and Peregrine's gossip about porpoises and a whale in the Thames (2.1.40–1, 46–7) is said to have occurred on 19 January 1606 and 'a few days after' in Howe's continuation of John Stowe's *Annals* (1615). As the Prologue (l. 14) tells us that the play was invented and written in less than two months, we can confidently date it late 1605 to early 1606.

1607 Quarto edition (Q)

Although the first mention of *Volpone* in the Stationers' Register is not till 3 October 1610, when the publisher Thomas Thorpe transferred his copyright to Walter Burre, the play was first published by Thorpe as a separate quarto volume in 1607, a date made specific by Jonson's subscription to its Epistle: 'From my house in the Blackfriars, this 11th of February, 1607', which is likely, according to Jonson's usual practice, to be a calendar rather than an old-style legal date. Though no printer is named, type analysis has identified him as George Eld, who had already printed other Jonson texts. The edition was set up from a fair copy prepared by Jonson himself, with no theatrical influences; and, like some previous Jonson quartos, it has been consciously modelled on the format of early humanist editions of the Latin dramatists Plautus and Terence, with massed entries at the beginning of each scene and few indications of when characters are to exit.

1616 Folio (F)

Jonson prepared a second edition of *Volpone* for inclusion in the folio of his collected *Works* printed by William Stansby in 1616, where the play appears on pages 439–524. The model for this folio text of the play was a marked-up copy of *Q*, and most of the three thousand or so small differences between the two editions are merely matters of format which would have been decided by the printer. However, there are also other changes by Jonson himself, which include the dropping of several commendatory verses and the placing of others at the head of the whole folio, the excision from the Epistle of *Q*'s allusion to Jonson's notes on *Ars Poetica*, and twenty-nine extra stage directions added in the margins, as well as a few unimportant changes of wording (e.g. 'goodness' for 'virtue' at 4.5.43).

This edition

The present text is mainly a modernized version of *F*, but also incorporates some aspects of *Q* which show theatrical rather than literary usage (e.g. the dashes punctuating Celia's pleas during Volpone's attacks at 3.7.239 ff.). In two instances (Prologue 1 and 2.3.1), the *Q* reading of oaths mentioning God and the devil have been restored, assuming that the *F* readings are excisions or alterations in response to censorship. In at least three other instances ('suff' rance' in 4.6.40, appre 'nded' in 5.1.6, and 'th' hour' in 5.3.8), *Q*'s contractions of individual words have been preserved because they fit the metre; the *F* reading could be a compositor's sophistication or misreading rather than authorial revision. In addition, the *F* reading at 4.6.6 is emended from 'Avo. 4' to '2 Avocatore'.

FURTHER READING

The major reference for Jonson's life and works is still the eleven-volume, old-spelling edition, *Ben Jonson*, edited by C. H. Herford and Percy and Evelyn Simpson (Oxford, 1925–52); but more convenient (and up-to-date) are the introductions and notes of such separate modernized editions of *Volpone* as those by Philip Brockbank (New Mermaids, 1968), John Creaser (London, Medieval and Renaissance Texts, 1978), and R. B. Parker (Revels Plays, 1983).

Among books considering Jonson's work as a whole, Robert E. Knoll, *Ben Jonson's Plays: An Introduction* (Lincoln, Nebr., 1964), J. B. Bamborough, *Ben Jonson* (London, 1970), George Parfitt, *Ben Jonson: Public Poet and Private Man* (London, 1976), Richard Dutton, *Ben Jonson: To the First Folio* (Cambridge, 1983), and Rosalind Miles, *Ben Jonson: His Craft and Art* (London, 1990) offer sound introductory readings. David Riggs provides an unusual psychoanalytical study in *Ben Jonson: A Life* (Cambridge, Mass., 1989); George E. Rowe, *Distinguishing Jonson* (Lincoln, Nebr., 1988), and W. David Kay, *Ben Jonson: A Literary Life* (New York, 1995), place Jonson in a context of other English dramatists of his time; and J. D. Redwine (ed.), *Ben Jonson's Literary Criticism* (Lincoln, Nebr., 1970), anthologizes and analyses Jonson's own literary theories.

In *Jonson's Moral Comedy* (Evanston, Ill., 1971), Alan Dessen relates Jonsonian comedy to the 'estates' morality play tradition; whereas Charles Wheeler, *Classical Mythology in the Plays, Masques and Poems of Ben Jonson* (Princeton, 1938), Douglas Duncan, *Ben Jonson and the Lucianic Tradition* (Cambridge, 1979), and Katherine E. Maus, *Ben Jonson and the Roman Frame of Mind* (Princeton, 1984) see him indebted rather to classical models. Duncan explains Jonson's use of parodic imitation as a technique for imaginatively entrapping audiences, as does Robert Jones, *Engagement with Knavery* (Durham, N.C., 1986); whereas in *Jonson's Parodic Strategy* (Cambridge, Mass., 1987) Robert N. Watson interprets it rather as a technique in which characters themselves self-consciously imitate literary roles. Humanity's penchant for escape into fancy is the leitmotif of Alexander Leggatt's *Ben Jonson: His Vision and His Art* (London, 1981), and other studies with a central thematic approach are Robert Wiltenberg, *Ben Jonson and Self-Love* (Columbia, Mo., 1990) and W. W. E. Slights, *Ben Jonson and the Art of Secrecy* (Toronto, 1994). The latter is particularly interesting about Jonson's relation to the Gunpowder Plot of 1605.

Alvin Kernan, *The Cankered Muse* (New Haven, Conn., 1959) sets Jonson in a framework of seventeenth-century satire. Franz Fricker, *Ben Jonson's Plays in Performance and the Jacobean Theatre* (Bern, 1972), Anne Barton, *Ben Jonson: Dramatist* (Cambridge, 1984), and J. G. Sweeney, *Jonson and the Psychology of Public Theatre* (Princeton, 1985) relate his plays to conditions in the Jacobean theatre. Consideration of *Volpone* in relation to 'City comedy' can be found in Brian Gibbons, *Jacobean City Comedy* (London, rev. edn 1980), and Gail Kern Paster, *The Idea of the City in the Age of Shakespeare* (Athens, Ga., 1985); and this is specifically related to Venice in David McPherson, *Shakespeare, Jonson, and the Myth of Venice* (Newark, Del., 1990). Jonson's critical attitude to emergent capitalism, raised in L. C. Knights's pioneering study, *Drama and Society in the Age of Jonson* (London, 1937), is reformulated in terms of cultural materialism in Jonathan Haynes, *The Social Relations of Jonson's Theatre* (Cambridge, 1992), and interpreted via the theories of Mikhail Bakhtin in Peter Womack's *Ben Jonson* (Oxford, 1986).

In *The Myth of the Golden Age in the Renaissance* (Bloomington, Ind., 1969), Harry Levin contextualizes *Volpone*'s many references to gold. Two studies concentrating more widely on Jonson's imagery and language are Edward B. Partridge, *The Broken Compass: A Study of the Major Comedies of Ben Jonson* (London, 1958), and L. A. Beaurline, *Jonson and Elizabethan Comedy: Essays in Dramatic Rhetoric* (San Marino, Cal., 1978). Stage history is covered by R. G. Noyes, *Ben Jonson on the English Stage, 1660–1776* (Cambridge, Mass., 1935), and Ejner J. Jensen, *Ben Jonson's Comedies on the Modern Stage* (Ann Arbor, Mich., 1985).

Useful single essays include Jonas Barish, 'The Double Plot in *Volpone*', *Modern Philology*, 51 (1953), 83–92; David M. Bergeron, ' "Lend Me Your Dwarf": Romance in *Volpone*', *Medieval and Renaissance Drama in England*, 3 (1986), 99–113; John Creaser, '*Volpone*: The Mortifying of the Fox', *Essays in Criticism*, 25 (1975), 329–56, and 'A Vindication of Sir Politic Would-Be', *English Studies*, 57 (1976), 502–14; P. H. Davison, '*Volpone* and Old Comedy', *Modern Language Quarterly*, 24 (1963), 151–7; G. U. de Sousa, 'Boundaries of Genre in *Volpone* and *The Alchemist*', *Essays in Theatre*, 4 (1986), 134–46; Ian Donaldson, 'Volpone: Quick and Dead', *Essays in Criticism*, 21 (1971), 121–34; William Empson, '*Volpone*', *Hudson Review*, 21 (1968), 651–66; C. J. Gianakaris, 'Identifying Ethical Values in *Volpone*', *Huntington Library Quarterly*, 20 (1959), 233–42; Stephen Greenblatt, 'The False Ending in *Volpone*', *Journal of English and German Philology*, 75 (1976), 90–104; Charles Hallett, 'The Satanic Nature of Volpone', *Philological Quarterly*, 49 (1970), 41–55; Harriet Hawkins, 'Folly, Incurable Disease, and *Volpone*', *Studies in English Literature*, 8 (1968), 335–48; Alexander Leggatt, 'The Suicide of Volpone', *University of Toronto Quarterly*, 39 (1969), 19–32; Harry Levin, 'Jonson's Metempsychosis', *Philological Quarterly*, 22 (1943), 231–9; H. Marchitello, 'Desire and Domination in *Volpone*', *Studies in English Literature*, 31 (1991), 287–308; Ralph Nash, 'The Comic Intent of *Volpone*', *Studies in Philology*, 44 (1947), 26–40; R. B. Parker, '*Volpone* and *Reynard the Fox*', *Renaissance Drama*, n.s. 7 (1976), 3–42, '*Volpone* in Performance, 1921–1972', in *Renaissance Drama*, n.s. 9 (1979), 147–73, and 'Jonson's Venice', in R. Mulryne and M. Shewring (eds), *Theatre of the English and Italian Renaissance* (New York, 1991), pp. 95–112; Leo Salingar, 'Comic Form in Ben Jonson's *Volpone*', in M. Axton and R. Williams (eds), *English Drama: Forms and Development* (Cambridge, 1977), pp. 48–68.

NOTES

1 See W. David Kay, 'The Shaping of Ben Jonson's Career: A Reexamination of Facts and Problems', *Modern Philology*, 67 (1970–1), 224–37, and his *Ben Jonson: A Literary Life* (New York, 1995), pp. 27–62.

2 For a succinct account of Jonson's career, see F. H. Mares (ed.), *The Alchemist*, Revels Plays (Manchester, 1969), pp. xvii–xxxi.

3 Cf. p. 14. For Jonson's literary theories, see J. D. Redwine (ed.), *Ben Jonson's Literary Criticism* (Lincoln, Nebr., 1970).

4 Classical borrowings are recorded in detail in the notes of R. B. Parker (ed.), *Volpone*, Revels Plays (Manchester, 1983); for modern theories of 'imitation with a difference' that need not necessarily be parodic, see Linda Hutcheon, *A Theory of Parody* (New York, 1983), pp. 30–68.

5 T. S. Eliot, *Selected Essays*, new edn (New York, 1950), p. 127.

6 See Parker, *Volpone*, Revels Plays edn, pp. 15–21 and plates 1, 2, 3, and Kenneth Varty, *Reynard the Fox: A Study of the Fox in Medieval Art* (New York, 1967), *passim*.

7 Edward Topsell, *The History of Foure-footed Beasts* (London, 1607), p. 221.

8 See R. B. Parker, '*Volpone* and *Reynard the Fox*', *Renaissance Drama*, n.s. 7 (1976), 3–42, and Lucien Foulet, *Le Roman de Renard* (Paris, 1914).

9 See Parker, *Volpone*, Revels Plays edn, pp. 24–9 and plates 4, 5, 6, and Robert E. Knoll, *Ben Jonson's Plays: An Introduction* (Lincoln, Nebr., 1964), pp. 79–104, esp. 101.

10 Allardyce Nicoll, *The World of Harlequin* (Cambridge, 1963), p. 50.

11 'un tout petit peu ridicules'; P.-L. Duchartre, *La Comédie Italienne* (Paris, 1924), p. 307.

12 K. M. Lea, *Italian Popular Comedy* (Oxford, 1934), 1, p. 102.

13 The scenario is printed in Maurice Sand, *The History of the Harliquinade* (London, 1915), 1, pp. 117–18. Tortoises, moreover, were then one of the exotic sights of Venice for visiting Englishmen: cf. Thomas Coryat, *Coryat's Crudities*, 1611 (Glasgow, 1905), 1, pp. 396: 'I have seene many torteises [in the Venetian markets], whereof I never saw but one in all England'.

14 Harry Levin, *The Myth of the Golden Age in the Renaissance* (Bloomington, Ind., 1969); cf. also J. W. Massingham, *The Golden Age* (London, 1927) and Roy Walker, *The Golden Feast* (London, 1952).

15 Edward B. Partridge, *The Broken Compass: A Study of the Major Comedies of Ben Jonson* (London, 1958), pp. 105–10.

16 Sigmund Freud, *A General Introduction to Psychoanalysis*, trans. Joan Riviere (New York, 1935), p. 325. For Freud's theory of comedy as the catharsis of aggression, see his *Wit and Its Relation to the Unconscious*, trans. A. A. Brill, *The Basic Writings of Sigmund Freud* (New York, 1938); and for Jonson's relation to this attitude, see: R. B. Parker, 'The Problem of Tone in Jonson's "Comicall Satyrs"', *Humanities Association Review*, 28 (Winter 1977), 43–64.

17 C. H. Herford and Percy and Evelyn Simpson, *Ben Jonson* (Oxford, 1925–52), 8, p. 597.

18 Cf. Alexander Leggatt, 'The Suicide of Volpone', *University of Toronto Quarterly*, 39 (1969), 19–32; Stephen J. Greenblatt, 'The False Ending in

Volpone', *Journal of English and German Philology*, 75 (1976), 90–104; Thomas M. Greene, 'Ben Jonson and the Centered Self', *Studies in English Literature*, 10 (1970), 325–48.

19 Levin, *Myth*, p. 194.

20 Herford and Simpson, *Ben Jonson*, 8, p. 647.

21 For these musical techniques of reprise (i.e. summarizing repetition), acceleration, and inversion, see Pauline Johnson, *Form and Transformation in Music and Poetry of the English Renaissance* (New Haven, Conn., 1972), pp. 50, 66, 81.

22 Cf. also 5.2.64–7, 108–9; 5.5.18; 5.8.11–14, 27; 5.9.1; 5.12.85, 125, 150–1.

23 Jonson persistently talked of his plays as 'poems', and after the failure of *The New Inn* he wrote a notorious 'Ode to Himself' (1631), beginning 'Come, leave the loathèd stage', Herford and Simpson, *Ben Jonson* (6, p. 492).

24 For detailed stage history, see R. G. Noyes, *Ben Jonson on the English Stage, 1660–1776* (Cambridge, Mass., 1935), and Ejner J. Jensen, *Ben Jonson's Comedies on the Modern Stage* (Ann Arbor, Mich., 1985).

25 For a fuller discussion of such cruces, see R. B. Parker, '*Volpone* in Performance: 1921–1972', *Renaissance Drama*, n.s. 9 (1979), 147–73.

26 More than any other single person, Donald Wolfit was responsible for the success of *Volpone* in the modern repertoire. See R. B. Parker, 'Wolfit's Fox: An Interpretation of *Volpone*', *University of Toronto Quarterly*, 45 (Spring 1976), 200–20.

27 *Sunday Times*, 20 July 1952.

28 *News Chronicle*, 16 July 1952. For photographs of set and costumes, see Ivor Brown and Angus McBean, *The Shakespeare Memorial Theatre, 1951–53* (London, 1953.)

29 See Parker, *Volpone*, Revels Plays edn, pp. 1–8, for a more extended analysis.

VOLPONE,
OR
THE FOX

[THE DEDICATION.]

TO

THE MOST

NOBLE AND

MOST EQUAL

SISTERS,   5

THE TWO FAMOUS

UNIVERSITIES,

FOR THEIR LOVE

AND

ACCEPTANCE   10

SHOWN TO HIS POEM IN THE

PRESENTATION,

BEN. JONSON,

THE GRATEFUL ACKNOWLEDGER,

DEDICATES   15

BOTH IT AND HIMSELF.

There follows an Epistle, if you
dare venture on the length.

---

4. *EQUAL*] (1) of equal merit; (2) just.

6–7.] Oxford and Cambridge.

11. *POEM*] i.e. play (Jonson is translating the Greek term for 'play').

11–12. *IN THE PRESENTATION*] i.e. when the play was performed at Oxford and Cambridge, some time between the London performance in early 1606 and the publication of the play in February 1607.

Never, most equal sisters, had any man a wit so presently
excellent as that it could raise itself, but there must come both
matter, occasion, commenders, and favourers to it. If this be
true—and that the fortune of all writers doth daily prove it—
it behooves the careful to provide well toward these accidents,   5
and, having acquired them, to preserve that part of reputation
most tenderly wherein the benefit of a friend is also defended.
Hence is it that I now render myself grateful and am studious
to justify the bounty of your act, to which, though your mere
authority were satisfying, yet, it being an age wherein poetry   10
and the professors of it hear so ill on all sides, there will
a reason be looked for in the subject. It is certain, nor can it
with any forehead be opposed, that the too much licence of
poetasters in this time hath much deformed their mistress,
that every day their manifold and manifest ignorance doth   15
stick unnatural reproaches upon her. But for their petulancy,

---

1–3. *Never . . . to it*] i.e. Anyone hoping to succeed as a writer must de-
pend on fit subject matter, favourable opportunity, patrons, and approving
audience.

1. *wit*] intelligence, ability.

presently] immediately.

4. *and that . . . prove it*] and writers' experiences daily show this to be the
case.

5. *to provide . . . accidents*] i.e. to make sure of having good subject matter,
opportunity, patrons, and audience.

7. *wherein . . . defended*] i.e. which will also redound to the credit and
reputation of the patron for beneficence.

8. *studious*] eager.

9. *the bounty . . . act*] i.e. the generosity of your patronage.

9–10. *though . . . satisfying*] though the authority of your endorsement
should be sufficient all by itself.

11. *professors*] practitioners.

hear so ill] are so ill spoken of.

11–12. *there . . . subject*] i.e. suspicious persons will look for some ulterior
motive lying behind your generosity to me.

13. *forehead*] (1) assurance; (2) mind, intellect.

opposed] contradicted.

13–14. *the too . . . poetasters*] the excessive liberties and abuses practised
by talentless rimesters.

14. *their mistress*] i.e. Poetry.

16. *But . . . petulancy*] setting aside the insolence of such fraudulent poetasters.

it were an act of the greatest injustice either to let the learned
suffer or so divine a skill (which indeed should not be attempted with unclean hands) to fall under the least contempt.
For if men will impartially and not asquint look toward the   20
offices and function of a poet, they will easily conclude to
themselves the impossibility of any man's being the good poet
without first being a good man. He that is said to be able to
inform young men to all good disciplines, inflame grown men
to all great virtues, keep old men in their best and supreme   25
state or, as they decline to childhood, recover them to their
first strength; that comes forth the interpreter and arbiter of
nature, a teacher of things divine no less than human, a master
in manners; and can alone, or with a few, effect the business
of mankind: this, I take him, is no subject for pride and   30
ignorance to exercise their railing rhetoric upon. But it will
here be hastily answered that the writers of these days are
other things; that not only their manners, but their natures,
are inverted, and nothing remaining with them of the dignity
of poet but the abused name, which every scribe usurps; that   35
now, especially in dramatic or, as they term it, stage poetry,
nothing but ribaldry, profanation, blasphemy, all licence of
offence to God and man is practised. I dare not deny a great
part of this—and am sorry I dare not—because in some men's
abortive features (and would they had never boasted the light)   40
it is overtrue; but that all are embarked in this bold adventure
for hell is a most uncharitable thought and, uttered, a more

---

19. *unclean*] morally impure.
24. *inform*] shape, form, mould, instruct.
26. *decline to childhood*] slip into senility.
28. *no less than*] as well as, to an equal degree as.
29. *or with a few*] or in a way that few others can match.
29–30. *effect . . . mankind*] carry out the most vital functions of the human
race, by acting as a kind of moral and ethical guide.
30. *I take him*] i.e. as I understand it.
subject] subordinate person.
35. *scribe*] noncreative copyist.
37. *all licence*] excessive liberty.
40. *abortive features*] deformed creations, i.e. botched plays.
boasted the light] come to light, been created.
41. *overtrue*] all too true.
42. *uttered*] when spoken aloud.

malicious slander. For my particular, I can—and from a most
clear conscience—affirm that I have ever trembled to think
toward the least profaneness, have loathed the use of such foul   45
and unwashed bawdry as is now made the food of the scene.
And, howsoever I cannot escape from some the imputation of
sharpness, but that they will say I have taken a pride, or lust,
to be bitter, and not my youngest infant but hath come into
the world with all his teeth, I would ask of these supercilious   50
politics what nation, society, or general order, or state I have
provoked? What public person? Whether I have not, in all
these, preserved their dignity, as mine own person, safe? My
works are read, allowed (I speak of those that are entirely
mine). Look into them: what broad reproofs have I used?   55
Where have I been particular? Where personal—except to
a mimic, cheater, bawd, or buffoon, creatures for their
insolencies worthy to be taxed? Yet to which of these so
pointingly as he might not either ingenuously have confessed
or wisely dissembled his disease? But it is not rumour can   60
make men guilty, much less entitle me to other men's crimes.

---

43. *For my particular*] for my own part.
44–5. *think toward*] incline my thoughts toward.
46. *made . . . scene*] i.e. served up as an (unwholesome) banquet in a play.
47. *howsoever*] albeit, even though.
48. *sharpness*] severity, satirical censoriousness.
but . . . say] without my enemies at once saying that.
lust] liking, craving, vicious pleasure.
49–50. *and . . . teeth*] i.e. and that even the most innocent (and recent) of
my plays has come into existence ready for the attack.
51. *politics*] worldly-wise schemers and know-it-alls.
54. *allowed*] licensed for performance and publication.
54–5. *entirely mine*] i.e. not written in collaboration.
55. *broad*] emphatic, explicit; outspoken; coarse.
57. *mimic*] mime, burlesque actor.
cheater] swindler, dishonest gamester.
58. *taxed*] censured.
58–60. *Yet . . . disease?*] Yet when have I ever attacked any of these types
so pointedly that the indicted person could not have avoided my censure
either by candidly confessing his guilt or by cleverly dissembling his depraved
condition?
60–1. *But . . . guilty*] i.e. name-calling cannot convict me of something I
didn't do.
61. *entitle me to*] impute to me.

I know that nothing can be so innocently writ or carried but
may be made obnoxious to construction. Marry, whilst I bear
mine innocence about me, I fear it not. Application is now
grown a trade with many, and there are that profess to have a   65
key for the deciphering of everything; but let wise and noble
persons take heed how they be too credulous, or give leave to
these invading interpreters to be overfamiliar with their fames,
who cunningly, and often, utter their own virulent malice
under other men's simplest meanings. As for those that will   70
(by faults which charity hath raked up or common honesty
concealed) make themselves a name with the multitude, or, to
draw their rude and beastly claps, care not whose living faces
they intrench with their petulant styles, may they do it without
a rival, for me. I choose rather to live graved in obscurity than   75
share with them in so preposterous a fame. Nor can I blame
the wishes of those severe and wiser patriots who, providing
the hurts these licentious spirits may do in a state, desire
rather to see fools and devils and those antique relics of

---

62. *carried*] managed, conducted, brought off.

63. *obnoxious to construction*] liable to (mis)interpretation.

Marry] lit., 'by the Virgin Mary'; a mild oath.

64. *Application*] i.e. discovering (or inventing) personal allusions and in-
nuendo in a literary work.

65. *there are that*] there are those that.

67. *how*] lest.

68. *fames*] public repute.

69. *utter*] counterfeitly circulate.

71. *by faults*] by exploiting faults in others.

charity . . . up] benevolent fairness has covered over, as ashes are raked
over live coals.

common honesty] common decency.

73. *claps*] applause.

74. *intrench . . . styles*] disfigure cuttingly with (1) their rude writing instruments (*stylus*) and (2) their insolent writing styles.

74–5. *without . . . for me*] without my attempting to rival them; without a
rival, as far as I'm concerned.

75. *graved*] buried.

76. *preposterous*] monstrous, unnatural; lit., with the last first, ass
backwards.

77. *severe*] serious, grave.

providing] foreseeing, exercising foresight concerning.

79–80. *fools . . . barbarism*] i.e. comic types and practices from medieval
drama and ancient nonclassical cultures, whom Jonson deplores as uncivi-
lised but prefers to the savagery of modern-day libelling.

barbarism retrieved, with all other ridiculous and exploded   80
follies, than behold the wounds of private men, of princes, and
nations. For, as Horace makes Trebatius speak, among these

—*Sibi quisque timet, quanquam est intactus, et odit.*

And men may justly impute such rages, if continued, to the
writer as his sports. The increase of which lust in liberty,   85
together with the present trade of the stage in all their
misc'line interludes, what learned or liberal soul doth not
already abhor, where nothing but the filth of the time is
uttered, and that with such impropriety of phrase, such plenty
of solecisms, such dearth of sense, so bold prolepses, so   90
racked metaphors, with brothelry able to violate the ear of a
pagan and blasphemy to turn the blood of a Christian to
water? I cannot but be serious in a cause of this nature,
wherein my fame and the reputations of divers honest and
learned are the question, when a name so full of authority,   95
antiquity, and all great mark is, through their insolence, become the lowest scorn of the age, and those men subject to the
petulancy of every vernaculous orator that were wont to be the

---

80. *exploded*] (1) mocked at as out of fashion; (2) clapped and hooted off
the stage.

82. *these*] i.e. the 'licentious spirits' of 78.

83.] 'Everyone is afraid for himself, even though untouched, and hates
[the critic]' (Horace, *Satires*, 2.1.23).

84–5. *men . . . sports*] i.e. people will justly suppose that such satiric rage,
if carried to extremes, is motivated by the writer's desire for 'sport' or cruel
jesting merely for the entertainment's sake.

85–8. *The increase . . . abhor*] What well-educated and open-hearted person does not already abhor the increase of such pleasure in unrestrained
licence, along with the present practices of the stage in all its miscellaneous
entertainments and variety shows?

90. *solecisms*] improprieties of speech, diction, or grammar.

prolepses] misattributions of time, such as anachronisms.

91. *racked*] overstretched, tortured.

brothelry] lewdness.

94–5. *honest and learned*] honest and learned persons.

95. *a name*] the name of 'poet'; with particular reference to Horace,
whose name Jonson had adopted in *Satiromastix* (1601).

97. *those men*] i.e. poets; the 'honest and learned' persons of 94–5.

98. *vernaculous*] ill-bred, scurrilous.

98–9. *that . . . monarchs*] i.e. (those poets) who were accustomed to the
patronage of the most fortunate of rulers.

care of kings and happiest monarchs. This it is that hath not
only rapt me to present indignation, but made me studious   100
heretofore, and, by all my actions, to stand off from them;
which may most appear in this my latest work—which you,
most learned arbitresses, have seen, judged and, to my crown,
approved—wherein I have laboured, for their instruction and
amendment, to reduce not only the ancient forms, but man-   105
ners of the scene—the easiness, the propriety, the innocence
and, last, the doctrine, which is the principal end of poesy: to
inform men in the best reason of living. And though my
catastrophe may, in the strict rigour of comic law, meet with
censure, as turning back to my promise, I desire the learned   110
and charitable critic to have so much faith in me to think it
was done of industry; for with what ease I could have varied it
nearer his scale, but that I fear to boast my own faculty, I
could here insert. But my special aim being to put the snaffle
in their mouths that cry out, 'We never punish vice in our   115
interludes', etc., I took the more liberty, though not without
some lines of example drawn even in the ancients themselves,
the goings out of whose comedies are not always joyful, but
ofttimes the bawds, the servants, the rivals, yea, and the
masters are mulcted—and fitly, it being the office of a comic   120

---

100. *rapt me*] carried me away, transported me.

103. *arbitresses*] i.e. Oxford and Cambridge, famous 'sisters' and judges of
good taste.

to my crown] as crowning honour to me (playing on the idea of a poet's
laurels).

105. *reduce*] restore, bring back.

the ancient forms] i.e. the classical unities of time, place, and person (see
Prologue 32n.), the distinction between comic and tragic, etc.

105–6. *manners*] dramatic conventions, listed in the rest of the sentence:
i.e. informal and uncontrived style, action suitable for comedy, entertainment both artistically sound and morally instructive.

106. *easiness . . . innocence*] grace, decorum, lack of malicious intent.

108. *inform*] shape, form, mould, instruct (as at 24).

109. *catastrophe*] denouement, final scene.

110. *turning . . . promise*] turning my back on my promise (to avoid a
mixture of the comic and tragic; see 105n.).

112. *of industry*] intentionally, on purpose.

113. *his scale*] the capacity or standard of the critic.

faculty] ability, artistic skill.

118. *goings out*] endings, conclusions.

120. *mulcted*] punished.

poet to imitate justice and instruct to life, as well as purity of
language or stir up gentle affections. To which I shall take the
occasion elsewhere to speak.

For the present, most reverenced sisters, as I have cared to
be thankful for your affections past, and here made the under-   125
standing acquainted with some ground of your favours, let me
not despair their continuance to the maturing of some wor-
thier fruits, wherein, if my muses be true to me, I shall raise
the despised head of poetry again and, stripping her out of
those rotten and base rags wherewith the times have adulter-   130
ated her form, restore her to her primitive habit, feature, and
majesty, and render her worthy to be embraced and kissed of
all the great and master spirits of our world. As for the vile and
slothful, who never affected an act worthy of celebration or are
so inward with their own vicious natures as they worthily fear   135
her and think it a high point of policy to keep her in contempt
with their declamatory and windy invectives, she shall out of
just rage incite her servants (who are *genus irritabile*) to spout
ink in their faces, that shall eat, farther than their marrow, into
their fames; and not Cinnamus the barber with his art shall be   140

121–2. *to imitate . . . affections*] to represent justice in art, to offer instruction concerning the good in life, to set an example of purity of language, and
to stir up the most exalted of emotions.

123. *elsewhere to speak*] i.e. in a commentary on Horace's *Ars Poetica*
which was burned in 1623 when Jonson's library caught fire.

124. *as*] inasmuch as.

cared] striven.

125–6. *the understanding*] those who understand.

127. *despair their continuance*] despair of the continuation of your
favours towards me.

130–1. *the times . . . form*] these bad times have defiled and corrupted
Poetry's beauty, as though prostituting her.

131. *primitive habit*] original clothing.

134. *affected*] (1) attempted, aspired to; (2) admired.

135. *inward with*] (1) intimately associated with; (2) secretly aware of.

136. *her*] Poetry.

138. *her servants*] i.e. poets.

genus irritabile] class of people easily aroused.

138–9. *spout ink*] i.e. write satirically. Ink was often made of gall, a bitter
and burning substance well suited as an image for satire.

140. *Cinnamus the barber*] Martial, in *Epigram* 6.24, alludes to Cinnamus
as one who, for all his skill in surgery (since barbers were often surgeons as
well), would not be able to efface the branding marks inflicted by Martial's
satiric wrath.

able to take out the brands, but they shall live, and be read, till
the wretches die, as things worst deserving of themselves in
chief, and then of all mankind.

From my house in the Blackfriars,
this 11. of February, 1607.   145

142–3. *in chief*] in the first place.
144. *Blackfriars*] a fashionable residential district in London near the
Thames, where there was also a private theatre.

THE PERSONS OF THE PLAY

VOLPONE, *a magnifico.*
MOSCA, *his parasite.*
NANO, *a dwarf.*
CASTRONE, *an eunuch.*
ANDROGYNO, *a[n] hermaphrodite.*   5
VOLTORE, *an advocate.*
CORBACCIO, *an old gentleman.*
BONARIO, *a young gentleman* [*son to* CORBACCIO].
CORVINO, *a merchant.*
CELIA, *the merchant's wife.*   10
[SIR] POLITIC WOULD-BE, *a[n English] knight.*
FINE MADAME WOULD-BE, *the knight's wife.*
PEREGRINE, *a[n English] gent[leman]-traveller.*
Avocatori, *four magistrates.*
Notario, *the register.*   15
Commandatori, *officers* [*of justice*].
Mercatori, *three merchants.*
Servitor[i], *servant[s].*

---

1. *VOLPONE*] a sly fox.

magnifico] an honorary title bestowed on the magnates of Venice; any person in an exalted position; also an alternative name for the 'Pantalone' or lean and foolish old man of the *commedia dell'arte.*

2. *MOSCA*] any kind of flying insect, especially of the stinging sort, like a gadfly.

parasite] one who eats at the expense of another, a flatterer and hanger-on; a standard type in the 'New' Comedy of Plautus and Terence.

3. *NANO*] a dwarf (Latin, *nanus*). *CASTRONE* and *ANDROGYNO* are similarly explained etymologically by the definitions provided by Jonson: *eunuch* or castrated man, and *hermaphrodite*, a person having both male and female sexual organs.

6. *VOLTORE*] a vulture.

advocate] legal counsel for the defence.

7. *CORBACCIO*] a raven.

8. *BONARIO*] honest, good, uncorrupt, naive.

9. *CORVINO*] a crow.

10. *CELIA*] from Latin *Caelia*, the heavenly one.

13. *PEREGRINE*] (1) a traveller; (2) a pilgrim hawk.

14. *Avocatori*] Venetian public prosecutors, to whom Jonson assigns the function of judges.

15. *Notario*] notary, functioning as clerk of the court.

16. *Commandatori*] uniformed deputies of the court charged with summoning those who were to appear at trial.

Women [*two attendants on* LADY WOULD-BE].   20
[Grege, *or crowd.*]

THE SCENE
VENICE.

---

22. *VENICE*] in Elizabethan times, a rich city-state that was seen as a European hub of political intrigue, artistic sophistication, and moral decadence.

THE ARGUMENT.

V OLPONE, childless, rich, feigns sick, despairs,
O ffers his state to hopes of several heirs,
L ies languishing; his parasite receives
P resents of all, assures, deludes; then weaves
O ther cross plots, which ope themselves, are told.   5
N ew tricks for safety are sought; they thrive, when, bold,
E ach tempts th' other again, and all are sold.

1–7.] The Argument's acrostic form is in imitation of the Roman comedy writer, Plautus.
1. *despairs*] i.e. his life is despaired of.
2. *state*] estate.
5. *told*] exposed.
7. *sold*] (1) betrayed; (2) tricked.

Prologue

Now, luck God send us, and a little wit
    Will serve to make our play hit,
According to the palates of the season;
    Here is rhyme not empty of reason.
This we were bid to credit from our poet,   5
    Whose true scope, if you would know it,
In all his poems still hath been this measure:
    To mix profit with your pleasure;
And not as some, whose throats their envy failing,
    Cry hoarsely, 'All he writes is railing',   10
And, when his plays come forth, think they can flout
    them
    With saying, 'He was a year about them'.
To these there needs no lie but this his creature,
    Which was, two months since, no feature;
And, though he dares give them five lives to mend it,   15
    'Tis known, five weeks fully penned it,

1–36.] The Prologue was probably spoken by Androgyno, Nano, and Castrone.

1–4.] i.e. 'Public taste being what it is, we only need luck and a little cunning to make our play a hit; [be that as it may,] here is rhyme not empty of reason.'

5. *credit . . . poet*] trust in by Ben Jonson.

6. *scope*] objective, purpose.

7. *measure*] prescribed extent, moderate intent, plan of action, poetic design.

8.] Jonson restates Horace, *Ars Poetica*, 343.

9. *as some*] e.g. Thomas Dekker and John Marston, who had reproved Jonson for 'railing' (10) and slowness in composition (12).

whose . . . failing] whose throats are incapable of uttering all the envy that is intended.

13–14.] Nothing is needed to give the lie to such accusations other than the present creation (i.e. the play), which, two months ago, did not even exist.

44

From his own hand, without a coadjutor,
    Novice, journeyman, or tutor.
Yet thus much I can give you as a token
    Of his play's worth: no eggs are broken,   20
Nor quaking custards with fierce teeth affrighted,
    Wherewith your rout are so delighted;
Nor hales he in a gull, old ends reciting,
    To stop gaps in his loose writing;
With such a deal of monstrous and forced action   25
    As might make Bedlam a faction;
Nor made he his play for jests stol'n from each table,
    But makes jests to fit his fable.
And so presents quick comedy refined
    As best critics have designed.   30
The laws of time, place, persons he observeth;
    From no needful rule he swerveth.
All gall and copp'ras from his ink he draineth;

17–18. *without . . . tutor*] without a collaborator, apprentice, occasional helper (literally, someone paid by the day), or supervisor and corrector.

21.] i.e. Jonson's play will use no crude farce like throwing eggs or pretending to quake with fear before a snarling bully. 'Cowardy custard' is still a schoolboy insult in England.

22. *your rout*] the usual playgoing rabble.

23. *hales*] hauls, pulls.

a gull . . . reciting] a simpleton telling stale old jokes.

25. *forced action*] strained and artificial acting.

26.] such as might seem appropriate in London's chief insane asylum, creating faction among the inmates. 'Bedlam' ('Bethlem' and 'Bet'lem' in Q and F) was the lunatic asylum of St Mary of Bethlehem in the London suburbs, where people often visited to laugh at the inmates.

27–8.] He does not piece a plot together out of scavenged jokes, but invents jokes that rise naturally from the situation.

27. *for . . . table*] (1) out of left-overs from others' feasts; (2) out of stolen *bon mots*, witty table talk.

28. *fable*] plot.

29. *quick*] lively.

30. *best critics*] i.e. classical authorities like Aristotle and Horace.

designed] designated, specified.

32. *needful rule*] Jonson omits the classical 'unity of action' because he preferred multiple plots.

33. *gall and copp'ras*] (1) oak-gall and vitriol (iron sulphate), both used in the manufacture of ink; (2) rancour and bitterness. *Gall* also suggests the bilious secretion of the liver, thought to produce asperity. See The Epistle, 138–9 and n.

Only a little salt remaineth,
Wherewith he'll rub your cheeks, till, red with
  laughter, 35
They shall look fresh a week after.

---

34. *salt*] sediment; also, stinging wit.

Volpone, or the Fox
Act 1

[*Enter*] MOSCA [*and discovers*] VOLPONE [*in his bed*].

Volpone. [*Rising*] Good morning to the day; and next, my
  gold!
  Open the shrine that I may see my saint.
    [*Mosca draws a curtain to disclose Volpone's treasure.*]
  Hail, the world's soul, and mine! More glad than is
  The teeming earth to see the longed-for sun
  Peep through the horns of the celestial Ram   5
  Am I to view thy splendour darkening his,
  That, lying here amongst my other hoards,
  Show'st like a flame by night, or like the day
  Struck out of chaos, when all darkness fled

1.1.0.1. discovers] i.e. draws back the bedcurtains. The scene is located
in Volpone's chambers throughout Act 1, and the action is continuous.
Volpone could begin the scene by entering with Mosca, rather than rising
from bed, but the bed is certainly needed later in the act.

2. *shrine . . . saint*] Volpone begins the play with a mock prayer that parodies the traditional Christian matins.

3. *the world's soul*] (1) the sun (Latin *sol*); (2) gold as symbolic of the sun,
here worshipped as a deity. See n. 10.

5. *the celestial Ram*] the sign of Aries in the zodiac, which the sun sup-
posedly enters on 21 March, the vernal equinox, to begin the spring season.
(A centuries-long precession of the calendar means that this is no longer
strictly accurate.)

6. *darkening his*] outshining the sun itself.

7.] which gold, lying here amidst my jewels and other treasures.

8. *flame by night*] Volpone combines a classical image for gold with the
pillar of fire that guided the Israelites to the Promised Land (Exodus, 13.21).

8–9. *or . . . chaos*] Volpone's gold outshines its surroundings much as
the first day of Creation stood out from the surrounding chaos when God
'divided the light from the darkness' (Genesis, 1.2–4). Volpone's speech is
filled with comic blasphemies.

Unto the centre. O thou son of Sol,   10
But brighter than thy father, let me kiss,
With adoration, thee, and every relic
Of sacred treasure in this blessèd room.
Well did wise poets by thy glorious name
Title that age which they would have the best,   15
Thou being the best of things, and far transcending
All style of joy in children, parents, friends,
Or any other waking dream on earth.
Thy looks when they to Venus did ascribe,
They should have giv'n her twenty thousand cupids,   20
Such are thy beauties and our loves. Dear saint,
Riches, the dumb god that giv'st all men tongues,
That canst do nought and yet mak'st men do all things,
The price of souls, even hell, with thee to boot,
Is made worth heaven. Thou art virtue, fame,   25
Honour, and all things else. Who can get thee,
He shall be noble, valiant, honest, wise—

---

10. *centre*] centre of the earth.

Sol] the sun personified, as in Latin *Sol*; punning on 'soul' in 3, just as *son* puns on 'sun'.

12. *relic*] (1) remnant, small bit; (2) venerated object.

13. *blessèd*] (1) fortunate, pleasurable, blissful; (2) consecrated; (3) wealthy (as in Latin *beatus*).

15. *that . . . best*] i.e. the mythical Golden Age, when humans gathered food without labour and lived in harmony without laws, trade, industry, or war (see Ovid, *Metamorphoses*, 1.89–112). See also 33–61 for Volpone's ironic expansion of this kind of prosperity, and Introduction, pp. 9–14.

16. *the best of things*] Gold is alchemically the most perfect of all metals, but this materialism foreshadows all the characters' downfalls at the play's end.

17. *style*] kind; fashion, mode; title.

19.] i.e. when poets (such as Ovid and Virgil) called Venus *aurea*, 'golden', thus ascribing to her the look of gold.

20. *twenty thousand cupids*] i.e. an inordinate 'cupidity' for wealth, not just one Cupid representing sexual love.

21. *our loves*] our adoration of gold.

22.] Proverbially, silence is golden, yet gold prompts everyone to be voluble in its praise.

24–5. *The price . . . heaven*] i.e. the price of everlasting damnation would not be too much to pay for the 'heaven' of wealth when you are added into the bargain. (Wealth thus replaces Christ's sacrifice, 'the price of souls'.)

25–6. *Thou . . . else*] i.e. with wealth one can buy a reputation for virtue and honour.

26. *Who*] any person who.

27. *shall be*] will be accounted.

Mosca. And what he will, sir. Riches are in fortune
    A greater good than wisdom is in nature.
Volpone. True my belovèd Mosca. Yet I glory   30
    More in the cunning purchase of my wealth
    Than in the glad possession, since I gain
    No common way: I use no trade, no venture;
    I wound no earth with ploughshares; fat no beasts
    To feed the shambles; have no mills for iron,   35
    Oil, corn, or men, to grind 'em into powder;
    I blow no subtle glass; expose no ships
    To threat'nings of the furrow-facèd sea;
    I turn no monies in the public bank
    Nor usure private—
Mosca.   No, sir, nor devour   40
    Soft prodigals. You shall ha' some will swallow
    A melting heir as glibly as your Dutch
    Will pills of butter, and ne'er purge for 't;
    Tear forth the fathers of poor families
    Out of their beds, and coffin them, alive,   45
    In some kind, clasping prison, where their bones
    May be forthcoming when the flesh is rotten.
    But your sweet nature doth abhor these courses;
    You loathe the widow's or the orphan's tears

28–9. *Riches . . . nature*] i.e. To achieve riches through good luck is better than to be naturally wise.

31. *cunning purchase*] skillful acquisition; crafty getting.

33. *venture*] speculation, risky enterprise.

35. *shambles*] slaughterhouse.

36. *'em*] (1) iron, olive oil, grain; (2) men.

37. *subtle glass*] intricate, delicate glassware, for which Venice is still famous.

39. *turn*] exchange, speculate with.

40. *usure private*] private moneylending.

41. *Soft*] (1) easily imposed on; (2) easy to bite.

41–2. *You . . . heir*] there are some unscrupulous operators who will gulp down a money-squandering inheritor of his family fortune.

42–3. *as glibly . . . butter*] The Dutch were frequently mocked for eating lots of butter.

43. *pills*] gobs, mouthfuls.

purge] vomit, or take a laxative.

46. *clasping*] (1) embracing (as though in kindness); (2) manacling.

47. *forthcoming*] (1) carted out of the prison; (2) sticking out of the skin.

49. *loathe*] feel intense aversion for the very possibility that.

Should wash your pavements, or their piteous cries   50
Ring in your roofs and beat the air for vengeance—
Volpone. Right, Mosca, I do loathe it.
Mosca.   And besides, sir,
You are not like the thresher that doth stand
With a huge flail, watching a heap of corn,
And, hungry, dares not taste the smallest grain,   55
But feeds on mallows and such bitter herbs;
Nor like the merchant who hath filled his vaults
With Romagnia and rich Candian wines,
Yet drinks the lees of Lombard's vinegar.
You will not lie in straw whilst moths and worms   60
Feed on your sumptuous hangings and soft beds.
You know the use of riches, and dare give, now,
From that bright heap, to me, your poor observer,
Or to your dwarf, or your hermaphrodite,
Your eunuch, or what other household trifle   65
Your pleasure allows maint'nance.
Volpone.   Hold thee, Mosca,
Take of my hand. [*He gives him money.*] Thou strik'st
   on truth in all,
And they are envious term thee parasite.
Call forth my dwarf, my eunuch, and my fool,
And let 'em make me sport.   [*Exit* MOSCA.]
                              What should I do   70
But cocker up my genius and live free

---

50. *pavements*] paved areas.
56. *mallows*] wild herbs that could be cooked and eaten, but were proverbially poor fare.
58. *Romagnia*] a sweet wine from Greece (Romanie).
Candian] from Crete.
59. *Lombard's vinegar*] i.e. Lombardy's notoriously poor wine.
61. *hangings*] bedcurtains.
63. *poor observer*] humble attendant.
65–6. *trifle . . . maint'nance*] unworthy menial whom you are pleased to
employ.
66. *Hold thee*] (1) Here, accept this coin; (2) Stop, that's enough praise.
67. *strik'st on truth*] speak the pure truth, hit the nail on the head.
68. *term*] who call.
69–70. *dwarf . . . sport*] Renaissance noblemen frequently supported persons with physical impairments as entertainers.
71. *cocker up my genius*] (1) indulge my appetites, especially sexual desire;
(2) humour my aptitude for creativity.

To all delights my fortune calls me to?
I have no wife, no parent, child, ally,
To give my substance to; but whom I make
Must be my heir; and this makes men observe me.　　　75
This draws new clients daily to my house,
Women and men of every sex and age,
That bring me presents, send me plate, coin, jewels,
With hope that when I die (which they expect
Each greedy minute) it shall then return　　　　　　80
Tenfold upon them; whilst some, covetous
Above the rest, seek to engross me whole,
And counterwork the one unto the other,
Contend in gifts, as they would seem in love—
All which I suffer, playing with their hopes,　　　　85
And am content to coin 'em into profit,
And look upon their kindness, and take more,
And look on that, still bearing them in hand,
Letting the cherry knock against their lips,
And draw it by their mouths, and back again.—　　　90
How now!

Act i Scene 2

NANO, ANDROGYNO, [and] CASTRONE [enter, to entertain]
VOLPONE, MOSCA [following them].

Nano.　　　　Now, room for fresh gamesters, who do will you
　　　　　　　　to know

---

74. *make*] designate.
75. *observe*] (1) be obsequious to; (2) take notice of.
76. *clients*] petitioners, dependents on patronage.
78. *plate*] gold or silver plate.
82. *engross me whole*] buy me up wholesale so as to achieve a monopoly.
83.] and undermine each other, as in siege warfare.
84.] outbid each other with gifts, to seem the more loving.
85. *suffer*] allow, permit.
88. *bearing . . . hand*] leading them on, beguiling them.
89–90.] i.e. I tantalize them as in the game of chop-cherry or bob-cherry, in which the players try to bite a suspended cherry without using their hands.

1. *room*] the traditional cry of entertainers asking for access to the playing space as they enter.
gamesters] merry-makers, entertainers.

> They do bring you neither play nor university
>   show,
> And therefore do entreat you that whatsoever
>   they rehearse
>   May not fare a whit the worse for the false
>   pace of the verse.
> If you wonder at this, you will wonder more
>   ere we pass,   5
>   For know, here [*Indicating Androgyno*] is
>   enclosed the soul of Pythagoras,
> That juggler divine, as hereafter shall follow—
>   Which soul, fast and loose, sir, came first from
>   Apollo,
> And was breathed into Aethalides, Mercurius
>   his son,
>   Where it had the gift to remember all that
>   ever was done.   10
> From thence it fled forth, and made quick
>   transmigration
>   To goldilocked Euphorbus, who was killed in
>   good fashion
> At the siege of old Troy by the cuckold of
>   Sparta.

---

2. *neither . . . show*] neither a public theatre play nor a learned entertainment such as the universities favoured.

3. *rehearse*] recite.

4. *the false . . . verse*] i.e. the loose four-stress 'tumbling' metre of much medieval drama, consciously archaic and 'antic'.

6. *Pythagoras*] ancient Greek authority (sixth century B.C.) for the doctrine of the transmigration of souls. Nano's burlesque is based closely on Lucian's parody in his *Dream, or The Cock*, and on Diogenes Laertius's discussion of Pythagoras in Book 8 of his *De Philosophorum Vitis*.

7. *juggler*] trickster.

8. *fast and loose*] i.e. hard to pin down, as in the old cheating game by that name in which a victim is inveigled into betting that he can pin 'fast' an intricately folded belt that the cheater then effortlessly 'looses'.

9. *Aethalides . . . son*] herald of the Argonauts and son of Mercury. He was gifted with an encyclopedic memory; see next n.

10. *all . . . done*] all that ever happened.

12. *Euphorbus*] a Trojan warrior in Homer's *Iliad*, Bks 16–17.

13. *the cuckold of Sparta*] Menelaus, whose wife, Helen, was stolen by Paris. See the *Iliad*, 17.1 ff., for his slaying of Euphorbus.

Hermotimus was next (I find it in my charta)
To whom it did pass, where no sooner it was
    missing   15
    But with one Pyrrhus of Delos it learned to
    go a-fishing;
And thence did it enter the sophist of Greece.
    From Pythagore, she went into a beautiful
    piece
Hight Aspasia, the meretrix; and the next toss of
    her
    Was again of a whore she became a
    philosopher,   20
Crates the cynic—as itself doth relate it.
    Since, kings, knights, and beggars, knaves,
    lords, and fools gat it,
Besides ox and ass, camel, mule, goat, and
    brock,
    In all which it hath spoke as in the cobbler's
    cock.
But I come not here to discourse of that
    matter,   25
    Or his one, two, or three, or his great oath, 'By
    quater!'

---

14. *Hermotimus*] a Greek philosopher, c. 500 B.C.

charta] charter, paper, source.

16. *Pyrrhus*] a Greek philosopher who had been a fisherman of Delos,
according to Diogenes Laertius.

17. *the sophist of Greece*] the wise man of Greece, Pythagoras.

18. *piece*] person; often said contemptuously of a woman.

19–21.] named Aspasia, the 'courtesan' (who was mistress of Pericles,
fifth-century Athenian leader); and the next transmigration changed her
from a whore to a philosopher, Crates of Thebes (364–285 B.C.), pupil of
Diogenes—as the soul tells the story and as the story says. ('Toss of her'
suggests a whore's turning of a trick. 'Again' in 20 belongs logically after
'philosopher'.)

22. *Since*] since then.

gat it] received the soul in transmigration.

23. *brock*] badger.

24. *the cobbler's cock*] i.e. Lucian's parody (see 6 n.), in which a cock
relates his story to a cobbler named Micyllus, who dreams of riches.

26–7.] Pythagoras taught that the universe could be understood as permu-
tations of the 'quater(nion)', the first four whole numbers, 1, 2, 3, 4, which,

His musics, his *trigon*, his golden thigh,
   Or his telling how elements shift; but I
Would ask how of late thou hast suffered
   translation,
   And shifted thy coat in these days of
   reformation?   30

Androgyno. Like one of the reformèd, a fool, as you see,
   Counting all old doctrine heresy.

Nano. But not on thine own forbid meats hast thou
   ventured?

Androgyno. On fish, when first a Carthusian I entered.

Nano. Why, then thy dogmatical silence hath left
   thee?   35

Androgyno. Of that an obstreperous lawyer bereft me.

Nano. O wonderful change! When sir lawyer forsook
   thee,
   For Pythagore's sake, what body then took
   thee?

Androgyno. A good dull mule.

---

added together, total 10, as demonstrated geometrically by the 'trigon' or equilateral triangle of four units per side. His followers swore by this as the symbol of cosmic and moral harmony, the One and the All. Music symbolizes for Pythagoras the mystical relationship of such numbers and heavenly bodies. Pythagoras' *golden thigh*, a token of his godhead, is mentioned by Lucian and Diogenes Laertius, among others.

  28. *how elements shift*] i.e. how the four elements of earth, air, fire, and water contend with one another and recombine to form all corporeal things.

  29. *translation*] change, transmigration.

  30. *shifted thy coat*] changed your (religious) allegiance.

  reformation] presumably the Puritan rather than the Protestant reformation; see next note.

  31. *the reformèd*] the Puritans.

  as you see] Androgyno may be dressed in a fool's coat.

  32. *old doctrine*] Puritans condemned both Roman Catholicism and Anglicanism.

  33.] But haven't you ventured to eat food forbidden by your religious beliefs? (Puritans and Pythagoreans alike observed strict dietary laws, as do many sects and faiths.)

  34. *Carthusian*] a member of an austere Benedictine monastic order, allowed fish but not meat, and under a vow of silence (see next note).

  35. *dogmatical silence*] Both the Carthusians and the Pythagoreans were under a vow of silence.

  36. *obstreperous*] making a loud noise (Latin, *obstrepere*). When the soul entered a lawyer, it inevitably became loquacious.

Nano.	And how, by that means,
	Thou wert brought to allow of the eating of
	beans? 40
Androgyno.	Yes.
Nano.	But from the mule into whom didst thou pass?
Androgyno.	Into a very strange beast, by some writers
	called an ass;
	By others a precise, pure, illuminate brother
	Of those devour flesh, and sometimes one
	another,
	And will drop you forth a libel, or a sanctified
	lie, 45
	Betwixt every spoonful of a Nativity pie.
Nano.	Now quit thee, for heaven, of that profane
	nation,
	And gently report thy next transmigration.
Androgyno.	To the same that I am.
Nano.	A creature of delight,
	And, what is more than a fool, an
	hermaphrodite? 50
	Now, pray thee, sweet soul, in all thy variation,

40.] Beans were forbidden by Pythagoras' dietary laws, but a mule might eat them as fodder.

43. *precise*] adhering strictly to rules—a term often applied satirically, as here, to English Calvinists and Puritans.

illuminate] i.e. seeing the true light.

brother] The Puritans often spoke of themselves as brethren.

44.] i.e. of those who (hypocritically) eat forbidden meat and prey on each other, despite their protestations of brotherly love.

45. *drop you*] drop. (The *you* is colloquial.)

libel] Puritans were often castigated for their scurrilous polemics.

46.] The Puritans are seen here as hypocritically gluttonous and as sanctimoniously pious in their speech, preferring 'Nativity' to 'Christmas' because of the association with the Catholic 'mass'.

47. *nation*] sect, group.

49. *To . . . am*] i.e. I was then transmigrated into my present shape.

50. *more . . . fool*] (1) completely foolish; (2) blessed paradoxically with a special kind of zaniness. Nano asks in mock wonder why Androgyno would wish to cease his transmigrations by remaining a hermaphrodite, but hints at the commonplace notion that hermaphrodites, being of both sexes, could lay claim to unusual insight and pleasure. See 54 and note.

51. *in . . . variation*] of all the various shapes you have assumed.

Which body wouldst thou choose to take up
thy station?
Androgyno.   Troth, this I am in, even here would I tarry.
Nano.   'Cause here the delight of each sex thou
canst vary?
Androgyno.   Alas, those pleasures be stale and forsaken.   55
No, 'tis your fool wherewith I am so taken,
The only one creature that I can call blessèd,
For all other forms I have proved most
distressèd.
Nano.   Spoke true, as thou wert in Pythagoras still.
This learnèd opinion we celebrate will,   60
Fellow eunuch, as behooves us, with all our
wit and art,
To dignify that whereof ourselves are so
great and special a part.
Volpone. Now, very, very pretty! Mosca, this
Was thy invention?
Mosca.   If it please my patron,
Not else.
Volpone. It doth, good Mosca.
Mosca.   Then it was, sir.   65

[NANO *and* CASTRONE *sing.*]

SONG

Fools, they are the only nation
Worth men's envy or admiration;
Free from care or sorrow-taking,

53.] To tell the truth, I would prefer to stay as I am now.

54.] Is that because you can now experience in rich variety the pleasures
that both sexes enjoy?

56. *your fool*] i.e. this fool that people talk about. (Also at 71–2 etc.)
Androgyno insists that he cherishes the paradoxical wisdom and licence of
the allowed fool more than sexual variety.

58. *proved*] found by experience to be. Androgyno has come to the conclusion that most shapes of existence are distressful; only the fool enjoys the
perfect freedom of his licence.

59. *as*] as if.

60. *celebrate will*] will celebrate.

62. *that*] i.e. folly.

66. *nation*] sect, group (as at 47).

Selves and others merry making.
All they speak or do is sterling.   70
Your fool, he is your great man's dearling,
And your lady's sport and pleasure;
Tongue and bauble are his treasure.
E'en his face begetteth laughter,
And he speaks truth free from slaughter;   75
He's the grace of every feast,
And, sometimes, the chiefest guest;
Hath his trencher and his stool
When wit waits upon the fool.
    Oh, who would not be   80
    He, he, he?   *One knocks without.*

Volpone. Who's that? Away!
                [*Exeunt* NANO *and* CASTRONE.]
                Look, Mosca.

Mosca.   Fool, begone!
                  [*Exit* ANDROGYNO.]
'Tis Signor Voltore, the advocate;
I know him by his knock.

Volpone.   Fetch me my gown,
My furs, and night-caps. Say my couch is changing,   85
And let him entertain himself awhile
Without i' th' gallery.   [*Exit* MOSCA.]
                Now, now, my clients

69.] making merry both themselves and others.

70. *sterling*] of standard quality, accepted as excellent.

71. *dearling*] i.e. darling (in obsolete spelling for the rhyme).

73. *bauble*] a fool's baton or stick, with playful suggestion also of 'phallus' and 'babble'. *Tongue* may also hint at sexual meaning, since by his tongue the fool is to provide his lady's 'sport and pleasure' (72).

75. *free from slaughter*] i.e. free from punishment; with impunity. Often rhymed with 'laughter'. Licensed fools were permitted to joke about any subject.

77. *the chiefest guest*] i.e. sitting at the head of the table, nearest the lord.

78. *trencher*] wooden platter.

79.] i.e. when wit serves the fool's purposes, or listens intently to the fool's words, or allows folly to take precedence.

80–1.] Who would not wish to be a fool? (Imitating in 'He, he, he' the sound of laughter and also perhaps pointing at Androgyno.)

85. *furs*] worn by the sick for warmth; also, suitable for a 'fox' to be wearing. Two 'night-caps' might also give the effect of fox's ears.

couch is changing] bed is being changed.

Begin their visitation. Vulture, kite,
Raven, and gorcrow, all my birds of prey,
That think me turning carcass, now they come.   90
I am not for 'em yet.

[*Re-enter* MOSCA, *with the gown, etc.*]

            How now? The news?
Mosca. [*Helping him dress*] A piece of plate, sir.
Volpone.   Of what bigness?
Mosca.   Huge,
Massy, and antique, with your name inscribed
And arms engraven.
Volpone.   Good!—and not a fox
Stretched on the earth, with fine delusive sleights,   95
Mocking a gaping crow? Ha, Mosca?
Mosca. [*Laughing*]   Sharp, sir.
Volpone. Give me my furs. Why dost thou laugh so, man?
Mosca. I cannot choose, sir, when I apprehend
What thoughts he has without now, as he walks:
That this might be the last gift he should give;   100
That this would fetch you; if you died today,
And gave him all, what he should be tomorrow;

---

88. *kite*] a kind of hawk. Voltore, Corbaccio, and Corvino are accounted
for in Volpone's list (88–9) by the vulture, raven, and gorcrow or carrion
crow (see 'The Persons of the Play'), leaving the *kite* unaccounted for or
possibly referring to the rapacious Lady Would-be. In any case, the image of
a raptor that feeds on flesh or carrion is obviously appropriate to the expected
visitors.

89. *gorcrow*] carrion crow, from Old English *gor*, 'mud, filth'.

91. *for 'em*] (1) to receive them; (2) to die and thus serve their purposes.

92. *plate*] silver- or gold-plated tableware.

94. *arms*] coat of arms.

95. *sleights*] crafty stratagems. Volpone is thinking of a fox fable, such as
that in which the fox tricks the crow to sing and thereby drop the cheese held
in its beak, or that in which the fox shams death to catch predators. Volpone
will be metaphorically 'stretched on the earth' when he receives his visitors
lying on his sickbed.

98. *apprehend*] imagine.

99. *without*] outside, in the gallery adjoining (see 87).

100. *should*] would have to.

101. *fetch you*] take you in, bring you around.

102. *be*] be worth.

What large return would come of all his ventures;
How he should worshipped be and reverenced,
Ride with his furs and footcloths, waited on   105
By herds of fools and clients, have clear way
Made for his mule, as lettered as himself;
Be called the great and learnèd advocate;
And then concludes there's nought impossible.

Volpone. [*Climbing into bed*] Yes, to be learnèd, Mosca.
Mosca.   Oh, no: rich   110
Implies it. Hood an ass with reverend purple,
So you can hide his two ambitious ears,
And he shall pass for a cathedral doctor.

Volpone. My caps, my caps, good Mosca. Fetch him in.
Mosca. Stay, sir; your ointment for your eyes.
Volpone.   That's true.   115
Dispatch, dispatch! I long to have possession
Of my new present.

Mosca. [*Anointing Volpone's eyes*] That, and thousands more,
I hope to see you lord of.
Volpone.   Thanks, kind Mosca.
Mosca. And that, when I am lost in blended dust,

---

103. *ventures*] i.e. the money Voltore has invested in wooing Volpone; cf.
1.4.80.

105. *footcloths*] 'large, richly-ornamented cloths laid over the back of a
horse [or mule; cf. 107] and hanging down to the ground on either side'
(*OED*). A sign of rank.

107. *mule*] a mount often used by lawyers riding in ceremonial
processions.

lettered] learned.

110. *Yes . . . learnèd*] i.e. Yes, there is one thing impossible for such a fool
as Voltore: to be truly learned.

111. *reverend purple*] i.e. the crimson hood and robes of a Doctor of
Divinity.

112. *So*] provided that.

113. *doctor*] learned cleric.

115. *ointment*] i.e. to make the eyes appear watery and gummy with ageing
and disease.

116. *Dispatch*] Finish up quickly.

119–20.] Mosca flatters his master by expressing a hope that Volpone will
outlive him and a hundred subsequent attendants.

119. *lost . . . dust*] blended with the dust, dissolved into the elements after
death.

And hundred such as I am in succession—   120
Volpone. Nay, that were too much, Mosca.
Mosca.   You shall live
    Still to delude these harpies.
Volpone.   Loving Mosca!
    'Tis well. My pillow now, and let him enter.
                                        [*Exit* MOSCA.]
    Now, my feigned cough, my phthisic, and my gout,
    My apoplexy, palsy, and catarrhs,   125
    Help, with your forcèd functions, this my posture,
    Wherein this three year I have milked their hopes.
    He comes; I hear him. [*He coughs.*] Uh! uh! uh!
    uh! Oh—

ACT I   SCENE 3

            [*Enter*] MOSCA [*with*] VOLTORE.

Mosca. [*To Voltore*] You still are what you were, sir.
        Only you,
    Of all the rest, are he commands his love;
    And you do wisely to preserve it thus
    With early visitation and kind notes
    Of your good meaning to him, which, I know,   5

---

122. *Still*] (1) till that time; (2) for ever.

harpies] fabulous monsters, part woman, part rapacious bird—an image appropriate to grasping, rapacious persons, and perhaps hinting at costuming of the birds of prey visiting Volpone.

124. *phthisic*] literally 'pulmonary consumption', but used more generally of asthma. The chronic, barking cough of the old and dying was often called 'the fox's cough'.

125. *apoplexy*] stroke.

palsy] a condition marked by uncontrollable tremor of limbs, feebleness, and muscular rigidity.

catarrhs] inflammations and watery discharge of the mucous membranes in the nose and eyes.

126. *forcèd*] (1) produced by effort; (2) artificially produced (?).
posture] imposture.

1.3.2. *he*] he who.
4. *notes*] tokens, i.e. gifts.
5. *meaning to*] intentions towards.

Cannot but come most grateful. [*To Volpone*] Patron!
  Sir!
  Here's Signor Voltore is come—
Volpone. [*Faintly*]   What say you?
Mosca. Sir, Signor Voltore is come this morning
  To visit you.
Volpone.   I thank him.
Mosca.   And hath brought
  A piece of antique plate, bought of St Mark,   10
  With which he here presents you.
Volpone.   He is welcome.
  Pray him to come more often.
Mosca.   Yes.
Voltore. [*To Mosca*]   What says he?
Mosca. He thanks you and desires you see him often.
Volpone. Mosca.
Mosca.   My patron?
Volpone.   Bring him near. Where is he?
  I long to feel his hand.
Mosca. [*Prompting Voltore*] The plate is here, sir.   15
Voltore. How fare you, sir?
Volpone.   I thank you, Signor Voltore.
  Where is the plate? Mine eyes are bad.
Voltore. [*Putting it into his grasp*]   I'm sorry
  To see you still thus weak.
Mosca. [*Aside*]   That he is not weaker.
Volpone. You are too munificent.
Voltore.   No, sir; would to heaven
  I could as well give health to you as that plate.   20
Volpone. You give, sir, what you can. I thank you. Your
    love
  Hath taste in this, and shall not be unanswered.
  I pray you see me often.
Voltore.   Yes, I shall, sir.

---

10. *of St Mark*] i.e. from one of the famous goldsmiths' shops in the Piazza di San Marco of Venice.

18. *That . . . weaker*] i.e. What you really mean is that you're sorry he is not even weaker.

22. *Hath taste*] i.e. makes itself felt, proves itself; shows good judgement.
unanswered] unrewarded.

Volpone. Be not far from me.

Mosca. [*To Voltore*]   Do you observe that, sir?

Volpone. Hearken unto me still; it will concern you.   25

Mosca. [*To Voltore*] You are a happy man, sir; know your
     good.

Volpone. I cannot now last long—

Mosca. [*Whispering, aside*]   You are his heir, sir.

Voltore. Am I?

Volpone.   I feel me going—uh! uh! uh! uh!—
     I am sailing to my port—uh! uh! uh! uh!—
     And I am glad I am so near my haven.   30

Mosca. Alas, kind gentleman! Well, we must all go—

Voltore. But Mosca—

Mosca.   Age will conquer.

Voltore.   Pray thee, hear me.
     Am I inscribed his heir for certain?

Mosca.   Are you?
     I do beseech you, sir, you will vouchsafe
     To write me i' your family. All my hopes   35
     Depend upon your worship. I am lost
     Except the rising sun do shine on me.

Voltore. It shall both shine and warm thee, Mosca.

Mosca.   Sir,
     I am a man that have not done your love
     All the worst offices. Here I wear your keys,   40
     See all your coffers and your caskets locked,
     Keep the poor inventory of your jewels,
     Your plate, and moneys, am your steward, sir,
     Husband your goods here.

Voltore.   But am I sole heir?

Mosca. Without a partner, sir, confirmed this morning;   45

---

30. *haven*] with a pun on 'heaven'.
33. *inscribed*] written down in the will.
35. *write . . . family*] set me down in your household book.
36. *your worship*] an honorific title, like 'Your Honour'.
37. *Except*] unless.
39–40. *I am . . . offices*] I am one who has not served you badly.
40. *your keys*] i.e. the keys of Volpone's household, now in effect yours.
(Actually, Mosca does not get possession of all the keys until 2.4.)
44. *Husband*] manage prudently.

The wax is warm yet, and the ink scarce dry
Upon the parchment.
Voltore.   Happy, happy me!
By what good chance, sweet Mosca?
Mosca.   Your desert, sir;
I know no second cause.
Voltore.   Thy modesty
Is loath to know It. Well, we shall requite it.   50
Mosca. He ever liked your course, sir; that first took him.
I oft have heard him say how he admired
Men of your large profession, that could speak
To every cause, and things mere contraries,
Till they were hoarse again, yet all be law;   55
That, with most quick agility, could turn
And re-turn, make knots and undo them,
Give forkèd counsel; take provoking gold
On either hand, and put it up: these men,
He knew, would thrive with their humility.   60
And, for his part, he thought he should be blessed
To have his heir of such a suffering spirit,
So wise, so grave, of so perplexed a tongue,
And loud withal, that would not wag, nor scarce
Lie still, without a fee; when every word   65
Your worship but lets fall is a *chequin!*   *Another knocks.*

---

46. *wax*] wax of the official seal on the will.
48. *desert*] deserving.
50. *know*] acknowledge.
51. *your course*] your way of doing things (esp. your skill as a lawyer).
took him] (1) attracted him; (2) caught him.
53. *large profession*] (1) liberal vocation; (2) wide-ranging advocacy; (3) great pretensions.
54. *mere contraries*] on wholly opposite sides of the argument.
58. *forkèd*] equivocal, of doubtful or double meaning.
provoking] inciting, stimulating, inciting, bribing.
59. *On either hand*] from either side of a lawsuit.
put it up] pocket it; put up with it.
60. *humility*] an ironical reference to lawyers' feigned modesty in accepting fees.
62. *suffering*] longsuffering (said ironically, as in 60).
63. *perplexed*] complicated and devious.
64. *withal*] in addition.
66. chequin] Venetian gold coin.

Who's that? One knocks. I would not have you seen,
   sir.
And yet—pretend you came and went in haste;
I'll fashion an excuse. And, gentle sir,
When you do come to swim in golden lard,   70
Up to the arms in honey, that your chin
Is borne up stiff with fatness of the flood,
Think on your vassal; but remember me.
I ha' not been your worst of clients.
Voltore.   Mosca—
Mosca. When will you have your inventory brought, sir?   75
Or see a copy of the will? [*Knock repeated.*] Anon!
[*To Voltore*] I'll bring 'em to you, sir. Away, begone;
Put business i' your face.   [*Exit* VOLTORE.]
Volpone. [*Springing up*]   Excellent, Mosca!
Come hither, let me kiss thee.
Mosca.   Keep you still, sir.
Here is Corbaccio.
Volpone.   Set the plate away.   80
The vulture's gone, and the old raven's come.

ACT 1   SCENE 4

Mosca. Betake you to your silence and your sleep.
  [*Volpone gets in bed; Mosca puts the plate away.*] Stand
  there and multiply. Now we shall see

---

73. *vassal*] slave, servant; with perhaps a pun on 'vessel', carrying Voltore
through the *flood* of riches.
  but] only.
74. *clients*] playing on the original meaning of 'a plebeian under the
patronage of a patrician' (*OED* 1), a dependant or hanger-on, and the
narrower legal meaning appropriate to Voltore's profession, 'one whose
cause an advocate pleads' (*OED* 3).
76. *Anon!*] Coming! (Mosca calls out to the person at the door.)
78. *Put . . . face*] look busy, pretend to be in haste (as at 68).
79. *kiss*] Cf. 1.4.137, 1.5.37SD, and 5.3.103–4.

1.4.2. *Stand . . . multiply*] Mosca blasphemously uses the language of God
in the act of creating the world and its creatures (Genesis, 1.28) to express a
wish that the gold plate might breed more such gifts. Breeding gold is a kind
of usury, generally forbidden to Christians (cf. Shylock in *MerVen*, 1.3.94,
speaking of gold and silver: 'I cannot tell, I make it breed as fast').

A wretch who is indeed more impotent
Than this can feign to be, yet hopes to hop
Over his grave.

[*Enter* CORBACCIO.]

        Signor Corbaccio!   5
You're very welcome, sir.
Corbaccio.   How does your patron?
Mosca. Troth, as he did, sir; no amends.
Corbaccio. [*Mishearing*]   What? Mends he?
Mosca. [*Loudly*] No, sir: he is rather worse.
Corbaccio.   That's well. Where is he?
Mosca. Upon his couch, sir, newly fall'n asleep.
Corbaccio. Does he sleep well?
Mosca.   No wink, sir, all this night,   10
Nor yesterday; but slumbers.
Corbaccio.   Good! He should take
Some counsel of physicians. I have brought him
An opiate here from mine own doctor—
Mosca. He will not hear of drugs.
Corbaccio.   Why? I myself
Stood by while 'twas made, saw all th' ingredients,   15
And know it cannot but most gently work.
My life for his, 'tis but to make him sleep.
Volpone. [*Aside*] Ay, his last sleep, if he would take it.
Mosca.   Sir,
He has no faith in physic.
Corbaccio.   Say you? Say you?
Mosca. He has no faith in physic. He does think   20
Most of your doctors are the greater danger,
And worse disease t' escape. I often have

---

4. *this*] i.e. Volpone, who feigns the kind of impotence that Corbaccio
suffers as a real condition.

16. *work*] (1) effect a cure; (2) do Volpone in.

17. *My life for his*] i.e. I'd be willing to wager my life against his (with a
hidden suggestion of Corbaccio's thriving at the expense of Volpone's life).

18. *last sleep*] i.e. death.

19. *physic*] medicine.

21, 23, 25. *your doctors . . . your physician*] doctors in general. Cf. 1.2.56
and n.

Heard him protest that your physician
Should never be his heir.
Corbaccio. Not I his heir?
Mosca. Not your physician, sir.
Corbaccio. Oh, no, no, no, 25
I do not mean it.
Mosca. No, sir, nor their fees
He cannot brook; he says they flay a man
Before they kill him.
Corbaccio. Right, I do conceive you.
Mosca. And then, they do it by experiment,
For which the law not only doth absolve 'em, 30
But gives them great reward; and he is loath
To hire his death so.
Corbaccio. It is true, they kill
With as much licence as a judge.
Mosca. Nay, more;
For he but kills, sir, where the law condemns,
And these can kill him too.
Corbaccio. Ay, or me, 35
Or any man. How does his apoplex?
Is that strong on him still?
Mosca. Most violent.
His speech is broken, and his eyes are set,
His face drawn longer than 'twas wont—
Corbaccio. How? How?
Stronger than he was wont?
Mosca. No, sir; his face 40
Drawn longer than 'twas wont.

23–4. *physician . . . heir*] A doctor who stands to inherit might be tempted
to hasten the death of his patient—a proverbial idea.

27. *brook*] endure.

flay] literally 'strip the skin off'; here 'strip him of money'.

28. *conceive*] understand.

29. *by experiment*] i.e. by trying out remedies on their patients.

34. *he*] a judge.

35. *And these . . . too*] i.e. whereas doctors can kill anybody without legal
sentence having been passed—even the judge himself.

36–54.] As Mosca comments on each symptom, Volpone enacts it—
amusingly doing so after the words have been said.

36. *apoplex*] apoplexy, a stroke.

38. *set*] staring at a fixed point.

Corbaccio.   Oh, good!
Mosca.   His mouth
    Is ever gaping, and his eyelids hang.
Corbaccio.   Good.
Mosca. A freezing numbness stiffens all his joints,
    And makes the colour of his flesh like lead.
Corbaccio.   'Tis good.
Mosca. His pulse beats slow and dull.
Corbaccio.   Good symptoms still.   45
Mosca. And from his brain—
Corbaccio.   Ha? How? Not from his brain?
Mosca. Yes, sir, and from his brain—
Corbaccio.   I conceive you; good.
Mosca. Flows a cold sweat, with a continual rheum
    Forth the resolvèd corners of his eyes.
Corbaccio. Is 't possible? Yet I am better, ha!   50
    How does he with the swimming of his head?
Mosca. Oh, sir, 'tis past the scotomy; he now
    Hath lost his feeling, and hath left to snort;
    You hardly can perceive him that he breathes.
Corbaccio. Excellent, excellent; sure I shall outlast him!   55
    This makes me young again, a score of years.
Mosca I was a-coming for you, sir.
Corbaccio.   Has he made his will?
    What has he giv'n me?
Mosca.   No, sir.
Corbaccio.   Nothing? Ha?
Mosca. He has not made his will, sir.
Corbaccio.   Oh, Oh, Oh.
    What then did Voltore, the lawyer, here?   60

---

48. *rheum*] watery discharge.
49. *Forth . . . corners*] from the watering and spongy corners.
50. *Yet*] (1) again, still; (2) despite the fact that I am old too.
52. *scotomy*] dizziness accompanied by dimness of sight (*OED*).
53. *left*] ceased.
   snort] breathe stertorously—a common symptom in comatose patients.
57. *I was . . . sir*] I was coming to fetch you before it was too late (but with hidden suggestion also: 'I have been setting a trap for you'; sometimes spoken in the theatre as a cunning aside).
58. *No, sir*] Mosca means that Volpone has not yet made his will, as he explains in 59, but Corbaccio takes him to be saying that Volpone has left him nothing.

Mosca. He smelled a carcass, sir, when he but heard
　　My master was about his testament;
　　As I did urge him to it for your good—
Corbaccio. He came unto him, did he? I thought so.
Mosca. Yes, and presented him this piece of plate.　　　　65
Corbaccio. To be his heir?
Mosca.　　　　　　　　I do not know, sir.
Corbaccio.　　　　　　　　　　　　True,
　　I know it too.
Mosca. [*Aside*]　　By your own scale, sir.
Corbaccio.　　　　　　　　　　Well,
　　I shall prevent him yet. See, Mosca, look:
　　Here I have brought a bag of bright *chequins*
　　Will quite weigh down his plate.
Mosca. [*Taking the bag*]　　　　Yea, marry, sir!　　70
　　This is true physic, this your sacred medicine;
　　No talk of opiates to this great elixir.
Corbaccio. 'Tis *aurum palpabile*, if not *potabile*.
Mosca. It shall be ministered to him in his bowl?
Corbaccio. Ay, do, do, do.
Mosca.　　　　　　　　Most blessèd cordial!　　　75
　　This will recover him.
Corbaccio.　　　　　　　Yes, do, do, do.
Mosca. I think it were not best, sir.
Corbaccio.　　　　　　　　What?
Mosca.　　　　　　　　　　　To recover him.
Corbaccio. Oh, no, no, no; by no means.
Mosca.　　　　　　　　　　Why, sir, this
　　Will work some strange effect if he but feel it.

---

62. *about his testament*] making his will.
67. *By . . . scale*] i.e. judging by your own scale of values.
68. *prevent him*] anticipate and thus forestall Voltore.
70. *weigh down*] outweigh; perhaps suggested by Mosca's 'scale' (67).
72.] Opiates cannot compare with money as the great alchemical essence supposed to ensure eternal life and transmute all baser metals into gold (suggesting also that there is no need to talk about using the opiates that Corbaccio has brought at 12–13).
73.] i.e. 'gold that can be felt, if not drunk'. Potable gold was 'a preparation of nitro-muriate of gold deoxidized by some volatile oil' and used as as a stimulant (*OED*). Perhaps Mosca continues the joke by pouring out the *chequins* into Volpone's medicine bowl (74).
75. *cordial*] heart stimulant.
79. *feel*] See n. 73 on *aurum palpabile*, gold that can be felt.

Corbaccio. 'Tis true, therefore forbear; I'll take my venture;   80
    Give me 't again.
Mosca.   At no hand. Pardon me.
    You shall not do yourself that wrong, sir. I
    Will so advise you, you shall have it all.
Corbaccio. How?
Mosca.   All, sir; 'tis your right, your own; no man
    Can claim a part; 'tis yours without a rival,   85
    Decreed by destiny.
Corbaccio.   How? How, good Mosca?
Mosca. I'll tell you, sir. This fit he shall recover—
Corbaccio. I do conceive you.
Mosca.   And, on first advantage
    Of his gained sense, will I re-importune him
    Unto the making of his testament,   90
    And show him this.   [*He points to the money.*]
Corbaccio.   Good, good.
Mosca.   'Tis better yet,
    If you will hear, sir.
Corbaccio.   Yes, with all my heart.
Mosca. Now, would I counsel you, make home with speed;
    There, frame a will whereto you shall inscribe
    My master your sole heir.
Corbaccio.   And disinherit   95
    My son?
Mosca.   Oh, sir, the better; for that colour
    Shall make it much more taking.
Corbaccio.   Oh, but colour?
Mosca. This will, sir, you shall send it unto me.
    Now, when I come to enforce, as I will do,
    Your cares, your watchings, and your many prayers,   100

---

80. *venture*] venture capital, the gold he has brought. Cf. 1.2.103n.

81. *At no hand*] by no means.

84. *How?*] (1) How can that be, naming me as sole heir? (2) How can you do it?

88. *advantage*] opportunity.

89. *gained sense*] regained consciousness and awareness.

94. *frame*] devise.

96. *colour*] pretence, plausible appearance of things.

97. *taking*] (1) successful; (2) acceptable, attractive.

Oh, but colour?] Oh, it's only pretence, is it?

99. *enforce*] urge, emphasize the claims of.

Your more than many gifts, your this day's present,
And, last, produce your will—where, without thought
Or least regard unto your proper issue,
A son so brave and highly meriting,
The stream of your diverted love hath thrown you   105
Upon my master and made him your heir—
He cannot be so stupid, or stone dead
But out of conscience and mere gratitude—
Corbaccio. He must pronounce me his?
Mosca.   'Tis true.
Corbaccio.   This plot
Did I think on before.
Mosca.   I do believe it.   110
Corbaccio. Do you not believe it?
Mosca.   Yes, sir.
Corbaccio.   Mine own project.
Mosca. Which, when he hath done, sir—
Corbaccio.   Published me his heir?
Mosca. And you so certain to survive him—
Corbaccio.   Ay.
Mosca. Being so lusty a man—
Corbaccio.   'Tis true.
Mosca.   Yes, sir—
Corbaccio. I thought on that too. See, how he should be   115
The very organ to express my thoughts!
Mosca. You have not only done yourself a good—
Corbaccio. But multiplied it on my son?
Mosca.   'Tis right, sir.
Corbaccio. Still my invention.
Mosca.   'Las, sir, heaven knows
It hath been all my study, all my care,   120

---

103. *proper issue*] own child, true offspring.

104. *brave*] fine, splendid.

110. *I do believe it*] In performance, Mosca sometimes utters these words ironically, half under his breath, as though to say, 'Does this fool really suppose this was his idea?' Corbaccio has trouble hearing the remark.

114. *lusty*] healthy, vigorous (but with an ironic suggestion of 'lustful', a ridiculous prospect in one as old as Corbaccio).

115. *he*] Mosca.

116. *organ*] mouthpiece, instrument.

119. *Still my invention*] This too was something I thought of.

(I e'en grow grey withal) how to work things—
Corbaccio. I do conceive, sweet Mosca.
Mosca.   You are he
    For whom I labour here.
Corbaccio.   Ay, do, do, do.
    I'll straight about it.   [*Going*]
Mosca. [*Aside*]   Rook go with you, raven!
Corbaccio. I know thee honest.
Mosca. [*Aside*]   You do lie, sir—
Corbaccio.   And—   125
Mosca. [*Aside*] Your knowledge is no better than your ears,
    sir.
Corbaccio. I do not doubt to be a father to thee.
Mosca. [*Aside*] Nor I to gull my brother of his blessing.
Corbaccio. I may ha' my youth restored to me, why not?
Mosca. [*Aside*] Your worship is a precious ass—
Corbaccio.   What sayst thou?   130
Mosca. I do desire your worship to make haste, sir.
Corbaccio. 'Tis done, 'tis done; I go.   [*Exit.*]
Volpone. [*Leaping from his couch*] Oh, I shall burst!
    Let out my sides, let out my sides—
Mosca.   Contain
    Your flux of laughter, sir. You know this hope
    Is such a bait it covers any hook.   135
Volpone. Oh, but thy working and thy placing it!
    I cannot hold; good rascal, let me kiss thee.
                    [*He embraces him.*]
    I never knew thee in so rare a humour.

---

124. *straight*] straightaway, at once.

Rook . . . raven] i.e. 'May you be cheated, you cheat', playing on *Corbaccio* = 'raven' and *rook* = 'to cheat'.

124–9 SD. Aside] Mosca may speak these lines in a normal voice, but not loud enough to be heard by the deaf Corbaccio.

126. *Your . . . ears*] i.e. 'What you think you know (cf. 125) is no more reliable than your (deaf) ears'.

128. *gull my brother*] i.e. cheat Bonario, Corbaccio's real son; with a glance at Jacob's cheating of Esau (Genesis, 27).

133. *Let . . . sides*] i.e. Loosen my clothes (so I can laugh).

134. *flux*] (1) flow, flood; (2) morbid discharge; evacuation of bowels.

this hope] i.e. this prospect of inheriting Volpone's wealth.

137. *hold*] i.e. contain my delight.

138. *rare a humour*] excellent a temperament, ingenious a disposition.

Mosca. Alas, sir, I but do as I am taught:
  Follow your grave instructions, give 'em words, 140
  Pour oil into their ears, and send them hence.
Volpone. 'Tis true, 'tis true. What a rare punishment
  Is avarice to itself!
Mosca.   Ay, with our help, sir.
Volpone. So many cares, so many maladies,
  So many fears attending on old age, 145
  Yea, death so often called on, as no wish
  Can be more frequent with 'em, their limbs faint,
  Their senses dull, their seeing, hearing, going,
  All dead before them, yea, their very teeth,
  Their instruments of eating, failing them— 150
  Yet this is reckoned life! Nay, here was one
  Is now gone home, that wishes to live longer—
  Feels not his gout nor palsy, feigns himself
  Younger by scores of years, flatters his age
  With confident belying it, hopes he may 155
  With charms like Aeson have his youth restored,
  And with these thoughts so battens as if fate
  Would be as easily cheated on as he,
  And all turns air!   *Another knocks.*
    Who's that there, now? A third?
Mosca. Close, to your couch again; I hear his voice. 160
  It is Corvino, our spruce merchant.
Volpone. [*Lying down as before*] Dead.

---

140. *give 'em words*] deceive them with speech.

141. *oil*] i.e. flattery.

146. *called on*] invoked, wished for.

148. *going*] movement.

149. *All . . . them*] i.e. their five senses are deadened even before they have died.

154–5. *flatters . . . belying it*] i.e. flatters himself by lying brazenly about his age.

156. *Aeson*] Jason's father, who was restored to youth by the magical charms of his daughter-in-law Medea.

157. *battens*] grows fat, gloats.

158. *cheated on*] cheated.

159. *all turns air*] (1) makes light of everything; (2) everything becomes insubstantial delusion.

160. *Close*] Conceal yourself; be quiet.

161. *spruce*] trim, dapper.

Dead] i.e. I'm playing dead.

Mosca. Another bout, sir, with your eyes. [*Anointing them*]
　　Who's there?

ACT I   SCENE 5

[*Enter*] CORVINO.

Mosca. Signor Corvino! Come most wished for! Oh,
　　How happy were you, if you knew it, now!
Corvino. Why? What? Wherein?
Mosca.　　　　　　　　The tardy hour is come, sir.
Corvino. He is not dead?
Mosca.　　　　　　Not dead, sir, but as good;
　　He knows no man.
Corvino.　　　　　How shall I do then?
Mosca.　　　　　　　　　　Why, sir?　　　　5
Corvino. I have brought him here a pearl.
Mosca.　　　　　　　　　Perhaps he has
　　So much remembrance left as to know you, sir.
　　He still calls on you; nothing but your name
　　Is in his mouth. Is your pearl orient, sir?
Corvino. Venice was never owner of the like.　　　　10
Volpone. [*Faintly*] Signor Corvino!
Mosca.　　　　　　　　Hark!
Volpone.　　　　　　　　Signor Corvino!
Mosca. He calls you. Step and give it him. [*To Volpone*]
　　He's here, sir,
　　And he has brought you a rich pearl.
Corvino.　　　　　　　　How do you, sir?
　　[*To Mosca*] Tell him it doubles the twelfth carat.
Mosca.　　　　　　　　　　　Sir,
　　He cannot understand, his hearing's gone;　　　　15
　　And yet it comforts him to see you—
Corvino.　　　　　　　　Say
　　I have a diamond for him, too.
Mosca.　　　　　　　　　Best show 't, sir;

1.5.1. *Come*] you come.
8. *still*] continually.
9. *orient*] shining, lustrous, as from the East.
14. *doubles . . . carat*] Twenty-four carets is maximum weight for pearls.

Put it into his hand; 'tis only there
He apprehends. He has his feeling yet.
                    [*Volpone seizes the diamond.*]
    See how he grasps it!
Corvino.   'Las, good gentleman!   20
    How pitiful the sight is!
Mosca.   Tut, forget, sir.
    The weeping of an heir should still be laughter
    Under a visor.
Corvino.   Why, am I his heir?
Mosca. Sir, I am sworn; I may not show the will
    Till he be dead. But here has been Corbaccio,   25
    Here has been Voltore, here were others too,
    I cannot number 'em they were so many,
    All gaping here for legacies; but I,
    Taking the vantage of his naming you,
    'Signor Corvino, Signor Corvino', took   30
    Paper, and pen, and ink, and there I asked him
    Whom he would have his heir? 'Corvino.' Who
    Should be executor? 'Corvino.' And
    To any question he was silent to,
    I still interpreted the nods he made,   35
    Through weakness, for consent; and sent home
        th' others,
    Nothing bequeathed them but to cry and curse.
Corvino. Oh, my dear Mosca!   *They embrace.*
                    Does he not perceive us?
Mosca. No more than a blind harper. He knows no man,
    No face of friend, nor name of any servant,   40
    Who 'twas that fed him last, or gave him drink;

---

20. *grasps it*] The language invites comic action: Corvino is quite surprised to see with what a swift and firm grasp Volpone scoops up the
diamond. A similar comic moment may accompany Voltore's putting his
plate into Volpone's hand at 1.3.15.

22–3. *laughter . . . visor*] joy concealed beneath pretence of sorrow, as if
wearing a mask.

30. *'Signor . . . Corvino'*] Mosca may imitate Volpone's feeble voice.
Donald Wolfit used to have Volpone himself say the name, coincidentally
with Mosca's pauses.

38. *Does . . . us?*] The line may suggest that Volpone can be heard in
muffled laughter.

Not those he hath begotten, or brought up,
Can he remember.
Corvino.   Has he children?
Mosca.   Bastards,
Some dozen or more that he begot on beggars,
Gypsies, and Jews, and blackmoors, when he was
    drunk.   45
Knew you not that, sir? 'Tis the common fable.
The dwarf, the fool, the eunuch are all his;
He's the true father of his family
In all save me; but he has giv'n 'em nothing.
Corvino. That's well, that's well. Art sure he does not hear
    us?   50
Mosca. Sure, sir? Why, look you, credit your own sense.
    [*Shouting in Volpone's ear*] The pox approach and add to
        your diseases,
If it would send you hence the sooner, sir.
For your incontinence, it hath deserved it
Throughly and throughly, and the plague to boot!   55
    [*To Corvino*] You may come near, sir. [*To Volpone*]
        Would you would once close
Those filthy eyes of yours, that flow with slime
Like two frog-pits, and those same hanging cheeks,
Covered with hide instead of skin—[*To Corvino*] Nay,
    help, sir—
That look like frozen dishclouts set on end!   60
Corvino. Or like an old smoked wall, on which the rain
    Ran down in streaks!

---

46. *fable*] story, report (not 'fiction').

48. *father . . . family*] Mosca plays on *paterfamilias*, 'head of a household'.

50. *Art . . . us?*] The line suggests a reaction on Volpone's part to Mosca's jibe. Cf. notes at 30 and 38.

51. *credit . . . sense*] i.e. believe your own eyes and ears.

52 ff.] The humour of these insults operates at three levels: Mosca and Corvino at the expense of the 'invalid'; Mosca and Volpone at Corvino's expense; but also Mosca (and the audience) at Volpone's expense?

52. *The pox*] syphilis.

54–5.] As for your uncontrolled sexual appetites, such debauchery thoroughly deserves the punishment it gets by way of syphilis, and the plague in addition.

58. *frog-pits*] scummy ponds inhabited by frogs.

60.] (Cheeks) that look like frozen dishcloths set up on end.

Mosca.   Excellent, sir, speak out.
   You may be louder yet; a culverin
   Dischargèd in his ear would hardly bore it.
Corvino. His nose is like a common sewer, still running.   65
Mosca. 'Tis good! And what his mouth?
Corvino.   A very draught.
Mosca. [*Snatching up a pillow*] Oh, stop it up—
Corvino.   By no means.
Mosca.   Pray you, let me.
   Faith, I could stifle him rarely with a pillow
   As well as any woman that should keep him.
Corvino. Do as you will, but I'll be gone.
Mosca.   Be so.   70
   It is your presence makes him last so long.
Corvino. I pray you, use no violence.
Mosca.   No, sir? Why?
   Why should you be thus scrupulous, pray you, sir?
Corvino. Nay, at your discretion.
Mosca.   Well, good sir, begone.
Corvino. I will not trouble him now to take my pearl?   75
Mosca. Pooh! Nor your diamond. What a needless care
   Is this afflicts you? [*He takes the pearl.*] Is not all here
      yours?
   Am not I here, whom you have made? Your creature,
   That owe my being to you?
Corvino.   Grateful Mosca!
   Thou art my friend, my fellow, my companion,   80
   My partner, and shalt share in all my fortunes.
Mosca. Excepting one.
Corvino.   What's that?

---

63. *culverin*] an early firearm.
64. *bore*] pierce, penetrate.
66. *draught*] privy, drain, sink.
68. *rarely*] excellently.
69. *keep*] look after, care for.
77 SD.] Other options have been used by actors, such as having Volpone clutch both jewels at this point or even (as Donald Wolfit did) putting the pearl in his mouth to keep it away from Corvino, but at 75 Corvino seems to suggest that he has not yet presented the pearl to Volpone. He did present the diamond at 19–20.

Mosca.   Your gallant wife, sir.
                        [*Exit* CORVINO.]
  [*To Volpone*] Now he is gone; we had no other means
  To shoot him hence but this.
Volpone.   My divine Mosca!
  Thou hast today outgone thyself.   *Another knocks.*
                    Who's there?   85
  I will be troubled with no more. Prepare
  Me music, dances, banquets, all delights;
  The Turk is not more sensual in his pleasures
  Than will Volpone.   [*Exit* MOSCA.]
             Let me see: a pearl!
  A diamond! Plate! *Chequins*! Good morning's
    purchase.   90
  Why, this is better than rob churches yet,
  Or fat by eating, once a month, a man.

               [*Enter* MOSCA.]

  Who is 't?
Mosca.   The beauteous Lady Would-be, sir,
  Wife to the English knight, Sir Politic Would-be—
  This is the style, sir, is directed me—   95
  Hath sent to know how you have slept tonight,
  And if you would be visited?
Volpone.   Not now.
  Some three hours hence—
Mosca.   I told the squire so much.
Volpone. When I am high with mirth and wine, then, then.

---

  82. *gallant*] glamorous.
  82.1.] The full comic surprise of Corvino's precipitous and wordless exit at the mere mention of his 'gallant wife' confirms what Mosca then says in 83–4, that only the mention of her would have prompted the jealous Corvino to leave so suddenly.
  88. *The Turk*] Mahomet III, Sultan of the Ottoman empire, was notorious for his extravagant sensuality.
  90. *purchase*] haul, booty.
  91. *yet*] still, by far (modifying 'better').
  92.] i.e. or grow rich by charging (exorbitant) monthly interest rates.
  95.] this is the manner of address, sir, that I was directed to use.
  98. *squire*] attendant bringing the message.

'Fore heaven, I wonder at the desperate valour   100
Of the bold English, that they dare let loose
Their wives to all encounters!
Mosca.   Sir, this knight
Had not his name for nothing: he is politic,
And knows, howe'er his wife affect strange airs,
She hath not yet the face to be dishonest.   105
But had she Signor Corvino's wife's face—
Volpone. Hath she so rare a face?
Mosca.   Oh, sir, the wonder,
The blazing star of Italy! A wench
O' the first year! A beauty, ripe as harvest!
Whose skin is whiter than a swan, all over,   110
Than silver, snow, or lilies! A soft lip,
Would tempt you to eternity of kissing!
And flesh that melteth in the touch to blood!
Bright as your gold, and lovely as your gold!
Volpone. Why had not I known this before?
Mosca.   Alas, sir,   115
Myself but yesterday discovered it.
Volpone. How might I see her?
Mosca.   Oh, not possible;
She's kept as warily as is your gold,
Never does come abroad, never takes air
But at a window. All her looks are sweet   120
As the first grapes or cherries, and are watched
As near as they are.
Volpone.   I must see her—
Mosca.   Sir,
There is a guard of ten spies thick upon her,

---

100. *desperate*] reckless. (English women at this time had much more social freedom than Mediterranean women.)

103. *he is politic*] i.e. he preens himself on being sagacious and knowledgeable in the ways of men.

105.] (1) she lacks the audacity to be an adulteress; (2) she is too unattractive to succeed as one.

109. *O'. . . year*] (1) of a vintage crop or harvest; (2) in the first season of her womanhood.

113. *to blood*] (1) to blushes; (2) to responsive desire.

119. *abroad*] out of the house.

122. *near*] closely, jealously.

All his whole household, each of which is set
Upon his fellow, and have all their charge,   125
 . When he goes out, when he comes in, examined.
Volpone. I will go see her, though but at her window.
Mosca. In some disguise then.
Volpone.   That is true. I must
Maintain mine own shape still the same. We'll think.

                                   [*Exeunt.*]

124–6.] Whenever Corvino (*he* in 126) leaves or returns to his house, he demands a report from the servants, whose 'charge' or instruction is to spy on Celia and each other.

128–9. *I must . . . same*] i.e. I must continue my pose as a dying man; therefore, I must woo Celia in some other disguise.

Act 2

[*Enter* SIR] POLITIC WOULD-BE [*and*] PEREGRINE.

Sir Politic. Sir, to a wise man all the world's his soil.
It is not Italy, nor France, nor Europe
That must bound me, if my fates call me forth.
Yet, I protest, it is no salt desire
Of seeing countries, shifting a religion,   5
Nor any disaffection to the state
Where I was bred, and unto which I owe
My dearest plots, hath brought me out; much less
That idle, antique, stale, grey-headed project
Of knowing men's minds and manners, with Ulysses;   10
But a peculiar humour of my wife's,
Laid for this height of Venice, to observe,
To quote, to learn the language, and so forth.—
I hope you travel, sir, with licence?
Peregrine.   Yes.

2.1.1. *soil*] country. A proverbial sentiment.
4. *protest*] insist.
salt] inordinate; wanton.
5. *shifting a religion*] converting from one religion to another.
8. *plots*] plans, projects.
out] abroad, out of my own country.
10.] Homer's *Odyssey* begins, line 4: 'Many were the men whose cities he saw and whose minds he learned'.
11. *peculiar*] (1) particular; (2) singular, odd.
humour] whim.
12. *Laid . . . height*] directed towards this latitude. *Height* may also suggest 'high degree of quality', as well as the famous Rialto or merchants' exchange of Venice, whose name was derived from *rivo alto*, high or lofty bank.
13. *quote*] make notes on; see 4.1.133ff.
14. *licence*] travel permit from the Privy Council.

Sir Politic. I dare the safelier converse.—How long, sir,   15
  Since you left England?
Peregrine.   Seven weeks.
Sir Politic.   So lately!
  You ha' not been with my lord ambassador?
Peregrine. Not yet, sir.
Sir Politic.   Pray you, what news, sir, vents our climate?
  I heard, last night, a most strange thing reported
  By some of my lord's followers, and I long   20
  To hear how 'twill be seconded.
Peregrine.   What was 't, sir?
Sir Politic. Marry, sir, of a raven that should build
  In a ship royal of the king's.
Peregrine. [*Aside*]   This fellow,
  Does he gull me, trow? Or is gulled? [*To Sir Politic*] Your
      name, sir?
Sir Politic. My name is Politic Would-be.
Peregrine. [*Aside*]   Oh, that speaks him.   25
  [*To Sir Politic*] A knight, sir?
Sir Politic.   A poor knight, sir.
Peregrine.   Your lady
  Lies here in Venice for intelligence
  Of tires, and fashions, and behaviour

---

15. *I dare . . . converse*] English travellers were forbidden to converse with
unlicensed travellers.

17.] English travellers were enjoined to report to the English ambassador
in any countries they visited. From 1604 to 1612 the English ambassador to
Venice was Jonson's friend Sir Henry Wotton.

18. *vents our climate*] issues forth from our country. Jonson is satirizing a
recent craze for sensational news sheets.

20. *my lord's*] the English ambassador's.

21. *To hear . . . seconded*] to hear confirmation.

22–3.] A raven building in a ship's rigging was regarded as a portent of
disaster.

22. *should build*] is reported to have built.

24. *gull*] trick, fool.

trow?] i.e. 'do you suppose?'

25. *speaks*] defines.

26. *poor*] insignificant; said with self-deprecating (and false) modesty.

27–9.] Venetian courtesans were famed for their elegant dress, cosmetics,
and coiffures, as well as for their skill in music and erudite conversation.

27. *Lies*] stays.

intelligence] news.

28. *tires*] attires, especially head-dresses.

Among the courtesans? The fine Lady Would-be?
Sir Politic. Yes, sir; the spider and the bee oft-times   30
    Suck from one flower.
Peregrine.   Good Sir Politic,
    I cry you mercy! I have heard much of you.
    'Tis true, sir, of your raven.
Sir Politic.   On your knowledge?
Peregrine. Yes, and your lion's whelping in the Tower.
Sir Politic. Another whelp?
Peregrine.   Another, sir.
Sir Politic.   Now heaven!   35
    What prodigies be these? The fires at Berwick!
    And the new star! These things concurring, strange!
    And full of omen! Saw you those meteors?
Peregrine. I did, sir.
Sir Politic.   Fearful! Pray you, sir, confirm me:
    Were there three porpoises seen above the Bridge,   40
    As they give out?
Peregrine.   Six, and a sturgeon, sir.

30–1. *the spider . . . flower*] This proverbial saying suggests that Lady Pol
will not be sullied by acquiring elegance from the courtesans.

32. *cry you mercy*] beg your pardon.

33. *of your raven*] what people say about the raven you mentioned.

34.] Lions had been kept in the Tower of London for many years, but the
birth of cubs there in August of 1604 and February of 1605 was an exciting
new event (according to John Stow's *Annals*). Both lived only a short time.

36.] Strange apparitions of fighting men and shots of ordnance were
reported at Berwick in December of 1604—probably *aurora borealis*.

37. *the new star*] a supernova explosion, suddenly appearing on 30
September 1604 and remaining visible seventeen months; the subject of
much prophesying.

38. *those meteors*] i.e. the Berwick fires and 'the new star', regarded as
belonging to a category of ominous signs of disorder in the heavens that
included meteors and shooting stars.

40–7. *three porpoises . . . Woolwich*] Stow reports in his *Annals* that on 19
January 1606 a great porpoise was taken alive in a small stream feeding the
Thames at West Ham (below London, in point of fact), and a great whale
was seen a few days later within eight miles of the city. Woolwich, again, is
downstream from London. Sir Pol's story is exaggerated, since the encountering of such sea mammals upstream from London Bridge (*the Bridge*, 40)
is considerably less likely.

41. *a sturgeon*] Peregrine is teasing Sir Pol; sturgeons were common in the
Thames, and 'Six' is an even more gross exaggeration of the event recorded
by Stow than is Sir Pol's 'three'.

Sir Politic. I am astonished!

Peregrine.   Nay, sir, be not so;
I'll tell you a greater prodigy than these—

Sir Politic. What should these things portend!

Peregrine.   The very day
(Let me be sure) that I put forth from London,   45
There was a whale discovered in the river
As high as Woolwich, that had waited there,
Few know how many months, for the subversion
Of the Stode fleet.

Sir Politic.   Is 't possible? Believe it,
'Twas either sent from Spain, or the Archdukes—   50
Spinola's whale, upon my life, my credit!
Will they not leave these projects? Worthy sir,
Some other news.

Peregrine.   Faith, Stone the fool is dead,
And they do lack a tavern fool extremely.

Sir Politic. Is Mas' Stone dead?

Peregrine.   He's dead, sir; why? I hope   55
You thought him not immortal? [*Aside*] Oh, this knight,
Were he well known, would be a precious thing
To fit our English stage. He that should write
But such a fellow should be thought to feign
Extremely, if not maliciously.

---

48. *subversion*] scuttling.

49. *the Stode fleet*] the ships of the English Merchant Adventurers, who had settled at Stade on the Elbe estuary in northern Germany after being forced out of nearby Hamburg in 1597. The idea of a whale attempting to subvert a fleet is more satirical hyperbole intended for Sir Pol to swallow, and may be based on encounters of British ships with large numbers of whales off Holland in 1602.

50. *the Archdukes*] the title given to the Infanta Isabella and her husband Albert when the Spanish Netherlands were ceded to them before the death of Philip II of Spain. James I's peace with the Archdukes and Philip III, signed in 1604, was not popular with some English.

51. *Spinola's whale*] Ambrosio Spinola, general of the Spanish army in the Netherlands, was popularly credited with inventing ingenious weapons, including a whale trained to drown London by 'snuffing up the Thames and spouting it upon the city'.

my credit] upon my honour.

53. *Stone the fool*] a cheeky jester at James's court who was whipped in 1605 for mocking an important embassy to Spain.

54. *Mas'*] Master.

Sir Politic.   Stone dead!   60
Peregrine. Dead. Lord! How deeply, sir, you apprehend it!
     He was no kinsman to you?
Sir Politic.   That I know of.
     Well, that same fellow was an unknown fool.
Peregrine. And yet you knew him, it seems?
Sir Politic.   I did so. Sir,
     I knew him one of the most dangerous heads   65
     Living within the state, and so I held him.
Peregrine. Indeed, sir?
Sir Politic.   While he lived, in action.
     He has received weekly intelligence,
     Upon my knowledge, out of the Low Countries,
     For all parts of the world, in cabbages,   70
     And those dispensed again to ambassadors
     In oranges, muskmelons, apricots,
     Lemons, pome-citrons, and suchlike—sometimes
     In Colchester oysters, and your Selsey cockles.
Peregrine. You make me wonder!
Sir Politic.   Sir, upon my knowledge.   75
     Nay, I've observed him at your public ordinary

---

60. *Stone dead*] with an absurd play on the expression 'stone dead' (e.g.
1.4.107). Sir Pol's prolonged shock at the death of a court fool betrays his
foolishness.

61. *apprehend*] feel.

62.] Peregrine jocosely hints that Sir Pol and Stone are two of a kind.
That] not that.

63. *unknown*] not known for what he really was—i.e. a spy. Sir Pol sees
spies everywhere.

66. *held*] regarded (with a suggestion also that Sir Pol thinks he has held
this danger to the state in check).

67. *in action*] i.e. involved in subversive activities.

70. *in cabbages*] a major export from the Low Countries to England. Sir
Pol, in his ridiculous paranoia, presumes that they were used to conceal
secret dispatches, which were then sent on to English ambassadors hidden in
other, more glamorous foodstuffs.

73. *pome-citrons*] citrons or limes.

74. *Colchester oysters*] oysters from Colchester, Essex, a seaport east of
London long famous for its seafood.

your Selsey cockles] shellfish from Selsea, in Sussex, to the south of
London. *Your* suggests 'you know the kind I mean', and is a habit of speech
of Sir Pol betraying his wish to sound knowledgeable about intimate secrets.

76. *him*] Stone the fool.

your public ordinary] an eating house providing meals at a fixed price—you
know the kind I mean.

Take his advertisement from a traveller
(A concealed statesman) in a trencher of meat,
And instantly, before the meal was done,
Convey an answer in a toothpick.
Peregrine.   Strange!   80
How could this be, sir?
Sir Politic.   Why, the meat was cut
So like his character, and so laid, as he
Must easily read the cypher.
Peregrine.   I have heard
He could not read, sir.
Sir Politic.   So 'twas given out,
In polity, by those that did employ him;   85
But he could read, and had your languages,
And to 't as sound a noddle—
Peregrine.   I have heard, sir,
That your baboons were spies, and that they were
A kind of subtle nation near to China.
Sir Politic. Ay, ay, your *Mamaluchi*. Faith, they had   90
Their hand in a French plot or two; but they
Were so extremely given to women as

---

77. *advertisement*] instructions, information.

78. *concealed statesman*] secret agent serving the state.

trencher] wooden plate.

80. *toothpick*] Toothpicks were all the fashion at this time (see 4.1.139)—and here an absurdly small object for espionage, though a carved ivory box containing toothpicks might be used to conceal a message.

82. *character*] cypher, code. The fashionable practice of cutting meat into letter shapes is here laughed at as another absurd method of espionage.

84. *given out*] reported, alleged.

85. *In polity*] in craftiness, as a blind.

86. *had your languages*] could speak any language you care to mention.

87. *And to 't . . . noddle*] and besides he had as good a head.

88–9.] Baboons were imported and put on show as great curiosities. Peregrine lampoons the notion that they have been imported as spies, and are really a kind of *subtle* or cunning people from some exotic nation in the Far East.

90. Mamaluchi] Sir Pol absurdly confuses the Mamluks or Mamelukes, former Circassian slaves who seized power in Egypt in 1254 and who served after 1517 as local governors there under Turkish domination, with baboons and Chinese. The word 'Mamelukes' was also applied to fighting slaves serving the Pope.

92. *given to women*] Baboons were popularly thought to be lecherous; many of the most powerful Mamelukes, on the other hand, were eunuchs.

They made discovery of all; yet I
Had my advices here, on Wednesday last,
From one of their own coat, they were returned,   95
Made their relations, as the fashion is,
And now stand fair for fresh employment.
Peregrine. [*Aside*]   Heart!
This Sir Pol will be ignorant of nothing.
[*To Sir Politic*] It seems, sir, you know all.
Sir Politic.   Not all, sir. But
I have some general notions. I do love   100
To note and to observe; though I live out,
Free from the active torrent, yet I'd mark
The currents and the passages of things
For mine own private use, and know the ebbs
And flows of state.
Peregrine.   Believe it, sir, I hold   105
Myself in no small tie unto my fortunes
For casting me thus luckily upon you,
Whose knowledge, if your bounty equal it,
May do me great assistance in instruction
For my behaviour and my bearing, which   110
Is yet so rude and raw—
Sir Politic.   Why, came you forth
Empty of rules for travel?
Peregrine.   Faith, I had

---

93. *made discovery of*] disclosed, revealed.
94. *advices*] dispatches.
95. *one . . . coat*] one of their livery, i.e. serving on their side; with a playful reference to the custom of clothing monkeys and baboons in order to put them on display.
   they were returned] that the supposed spies had come back from their involvement in a 'French plot' (91).
96. *relations*] reports.
97. *fair*] ready.
   Heart!] by God's heart! (an oath).
98.] This Sir Pol insists on presenting himself as in the know about everything that is going on.
101. *out*] abroad.
102. *Free . . . torrent*] not actively involved in politics.
106. *tie*] obligation.
108. *bounty*] generosity (in sharing knowledge).

Some common ones from out that vulgar grammar
Which he that cried Italian to me taught me.
Sir Politic. Why, this it is that spoils all our brave bloods,   115
Trusting our hopeful gentry unto pedants,
Fellows of outside and mere bark. You seem
To be a gentleman of ingenuous race—
I not profess it, but my fate hath been
To be where I have been consulted with,   120
In this high kind, touching some great men's sons,
Persons of blood and honour—
Peregrine.   Who be these, sir?

Act 2 Scene 2

> [*Enter*] MOSCA [*and*] NANO [*disguised as zanies and
> followed by*] Grege [*the crowd*].

Mosca. [*To Nano*] Under that window, there 't must be. The
    same.   [MOSCA *and* NANO *set up a rostrum.*]
Sir Politic. Fellows to mount a bank! Did your instructor

---

113. *vulgar*] (1) in the vernacular; (2) low-bred, ordinary.

grammar] guide book, set of rules. Peregrine could have a particular one in mind, perhaps *Second Fruits* (1591) by John Florio, one of Jonson's Italian friends in London.

114. *cried*] i.e. taught by pronouncing.

115. *brave bloods*] dashing young gallants.

116. *gentry*] (1) gentlemen; (2) refined manners.

117. *outside . . . bark*] mere external show; concern for the appearance merely, not the substance of learning. With a possible play in *bark* on a loud animal noise, picking up on 'cried' in 114.

118. *ingenuous race*] noble lineage and disposition. (The sense of 'guileless' comes at a later date.) Sir Pol pauses as he considers Peregrine's potential.

119. *I . . . it*] i.e. I do not tutor young men as a profession.

121. *In . . . kind*] about important matters of this sort. Sir Pol is fatuously offering himself as a kind of avuncular gentlemanly advisor to the young man.

122. *blood*] noble birth.

2.2.0.1. zanies] clowns assisting the mountebank; see next note.

2. *Fellows . . . bank*] The word 'mountebank' derives from Italian *monta in banco*, 'mount on a bench'. A mountebank is an itinerant quack, often assisted by a professional clown.

In the dear tongues never discourse to you
Of the Italian mountebanks?
Peregrine.   Yes, sir.
Sir Politic.   Why,
    Here shall you see one.
Peregrine.   They are quacksalvers,   5
    Fellows that live by venting oils and drugs.
Sir Politic. Was that the character he gave you of them?
Peregrine. As I remember.
Sir Politic.   Pity his ignorance.
    They are the only knowing men of Europe,
    Great general scholars, excellent physicians,   10
    Most admired statesmen, professed favourites
    And cabinet counsellors to the greatest princes—
    The only languaged men of all the world.
Peregrine. And I have heard they are most lewd impostors,
    Made all of terms and shreds, no less beliers   15
    Of great men's favours than their own vile med'cines,
    Which they will utter upon monstrous oaths,
    Selling that drug for twopence ere they part
    Which they have valued at twelve crowns before.
Sir Politic. Sir, calumnies are answered best with silence.   20
    Yourself shall judge. [*To Mosca and Nano*] Who is it
        mounts, my friends?
Mosca. Scoto of Mantua, sir.
Sir Politic.   Is 't he? Nay, then
    I'll proudly promise, sir, you shall behold
    Another man than has been phant'sied to you.
    I wonder yet that he should mount his bank   25

---

3. *dear tongues*] modern languages. *Dear* = of high estimation and worth.
5. *quacksalvers*] ignorant pretenders to medical skill; quacks.
6. *venting*] vending.
12. *cabinet*] private.
13. *only languaged men*] most skilled speakers.
14. *lewd*] ignorant.
15. *terms and shreds*] jargon and snippets of quotation, etc.
beliers] false allegers, misrepresenters.
17. *utter*] sell fraudulently.
19. *crowns*] silver coins stamped with a crown.
22. *Scoto of Mantua*] an Italian actor who visited England between 1576 and 1583, impressing audiences with his juggling and sleight-of-hand.
24. *phant'sied to you*] i.e. suggested to your fancy or imagination.

Here, in this nook, that has been wont t' appear
In face of the Piazza! Here he comes.

[*Enter* VOLPONE, *disguised as a mountebank.*]

Volpone. [*To Nano*] Mount, zany.
Grege. [*Gathering excitedly*] Follow, follow, follow, follow,
    follow!
Sir Politic. See how the people follow him! He's a man
May write ten thousand crowns in bank here. Note;   30

> [*Volpone mounts the rostrum. Throughout his appearance*
> *in this scene, Peregrine and Sir Pol continue to*
> *speak confidentially to each other.*]

Mark but his gesture. I do use to observe
The state he keeps in getting up.
Peregrine.   'Tis worth it, sir.
Volpone. Most noble gentlemen and my worthy patrons, it
    may seem strange that I, your Scoto Mantuano, who was
    ever wont to fix my bank in face of the public Piazza, near   35
    the shelter of the portico to the Procuratia, should now,
    after eight months' absence from this illustrious city of
    Venice, humbly retire myself into an obscure nook of the
    Piazza.
Sir Politic. Did not I now object the same?
Peregrine.   Peace, sir.   40
Volpone. Let me tell you: I am not, as your Lombard proverb
    saith, cold on my feet, or content to part with my com-
    modities at a cheaper rate than I accustomed. Look not

---

27. *In face of*] facing.

28. Grege] the crowd (Latin).

30. *May . . . bank*] who can write a cheque for 10,000 crowns. Sir Pol
gullibly imagines 'Scoto' to be wealthy.

31. *use*] make it my practice.

32. *state*] stateliness, ceremoniousness.

'*Tis . . . sir*] Peregrine offers praise with a hidden mock: the fatuous attention you pay Scoto is fully deserved by the man you mistakenly adulate.

36. *the portico . . . Procuratia*] the arcade fronting the residence of Venice's
governing hierarchy, the procurators of St Mark's, on the north side of the
Piazza di San Marco.

40. *object the same*] ask the same question (at 25–7).

42. *cold . . . feet*] i.e. obliged, through poverty and need, to sell cheap (as
he goes on to explain).

for it. Nor that the calumnious reports of that impudent
detractor and shame to our profession (Alessandro   45
Buttone, I mean), who gave out in public I was condemned *a sforzato* to the galleys for poisoning the
Cardinal Bembo's—cook, hath at all attached, much less
dejected me. No, no, worthy gentlemen! To tell you true,
I cannot endure to see the rabble of these ground   50
ciarlitani that spread their cloaks on the pavement as if
they meant to do feats of activity and then come in lamely
with their mouldy tales out of Boccaccio, like stale
Tabarin, the fabulist, some of them discoursing their
travels and of their tedious captivity in the Turks' galleys,   55
when indeed, were the truth known, they were the
Christians' galleys, where very temperately they ate bread
and drunk water as a wholesome penance enjoined them
by their confessors for base pilferies.

Sir Politic. Note but his bearing and contempt of these.   60

Volpone. These turdy-facey-nasty-patey-lousy-fartical rogues,
with one poor groatsworth of unprepared antimony finely
wrapped up in several *scartoccios*, are able very well to kill

---

45–6. *Alessandro Buttone*] a rival mountebank.

47. a sforzato] against my will, like a galley-slave.

48. *Cardinal Bembo's—cook*] Pietro Bembo (1470–1547) was a Venetian
scholar who appears in Castiglione's *The Courtier* as one who spiritualizes
erotic love. The dash or pause here may hint that the cook was something
more to the Cardinal than just cook.

attached] seized, laid hold of (much as any misfortune or sickness might
seize a person).

50–1. *ground* ciarlitani] lowly charlatans working on the ground, without
a 'bank' or bench.

52. *feats of activity*] acrobatics.

53. *Boccaccio*] author of the *Decameron*, a collection of salacious stories.

54. *Tabarin, the fabulist*] a famous Venetian *zanni*, adept at drawing
crowds by his storytelling.

57–9. *where . . . pilferies*] 'Scoto' jests that the Christian galley-owners
imposed hard labour and a minimal diet on their slaves as though out of
concern for their spiritual welfare, teaching them 'wholesome penance',
when the more probable truth is that the slaves were simply being punished
and exploited. Sir Pol is taken in by all this.

62. *groatsworth*] fourpence worth.

unprepared antimony] native trisulphide (or 'grey antimony'), used in alchemical experiments and as an ingredient for medicines and cosmetics.

63. *several* scartoccios] several paper containers for spice, used by
apothecaries.

their twenty a week, and play; yet these meagre, starved
spirits, who have half stopped the organs of their minds   65
with earthy oppilations, want not their favourers among
your shrivelled, salad-eating artisans, who are overjoyed
that they may have their ha'p'orth of physic; though it
purge 'em into another world, 't makes no matter.

Sir Politic. Excellent! Ha' you heard better language, sir?   70

Volpone. Well, let 'em go. And, gentlemen, honourable gentlemen, know that for this time our bank, being thus
removed from the clamours of the *canaglia*, shall be the
scene of pleasure and delight; for I have nothing to sell,
little or nothing to sell.   75

Sir Politic. I told you, sir, his end.

Peregrine.   You did so, sir.

Volpone. I protest, I and my six servants are not able to make
of this precious liquor so fast as it is fetched away from
my lodging by gentlemen of your city, strangers of the
terra firma, worshipful merchants, ay, and senators too,   80
who, ever since my arrival, have detained me to their uses
by their splendidous liberalities—and worthily. For what
avails your rich man to have his magazines stuffed with
moscadelli or of the purest grape when his physicians

---

64. *and play*] i.e. and yet continue on in their frivolous entertainments (?).

66. *earthly oppilations*] mundane, gross obstructions resulting in mental stagnation.

want] lack.

67. *salad-eating*] a dig at Italians for a less than manly diet.

68. *ha'p'orth of physic*] half-pennyworth of medicinal purge. Salad was sometimes prescribed as a laxative.

71. *let 'em go*] let's say no more about them.

72. *bank*] benchlike platform.

73. *the* canaglia] the mob; 'rascally people only fit for dog's company' (Florio).

76. *end*] goal, purpose; also at 92. Peregrine sardonically appears to agree with Sir Pol while taking quite a different view of 'Scoto's' *end*, which as he sees it is to make a quick profit, not, as Sir Pol insists, to better the condition of mankind.

79–80. *strangers . . . firma*] foreigners dwelling in Venetian-controlled territories on the mainland.

80. *worshipful*] distinguished, honourable.

82. *splendidous*] splendid, munificent.

83. *magazines*] storehouses.

84. moscadelli] Muscatel wine.

or of] or wine of.

prescribe him, on pain of death, to drink nothing but   85
water cocted with aniseeds? Oh, health, health! The
blessing of the rich, the riches of the poor! Who can buy
thee at too dear a rate, since there is no enjoying this
world without thee? Be not then so sparing of your
purses, honourable gentlemen, as to abridge the natural   90
course of life—

Peregrine. You see his end?

Sir Politic.   Ay, is 't not good?

Volpone. For when a humid flux, or catarrh, by the mutability
of air, falls from your head into an arm or shoulder or any
other part, take you a ducat, or your *chequin* of gold, and   95
apply to the place affected; see what good effect it can
work. No, no, 'tis this blessed *unguento*, this rare extrac-
tion, that hath only power to disperse all malignant humours that proceed either of hot, cold, moist, or windy
causes—   100

Peregrine. I would he had put in 'dry' too.

Sir Politic.   Pray you, observe.

Volpone. To fortify the most indigest and crude stomach, ay,
were it of one that through extreme weakness vomited
blood, applying only a warm napkin to the place, after the
unction and fricace; for the *vertiginè* in the head, putting   105
but a drop into your nostrils, likewise behind the ears—a
most sovereign and approved remedy; the *mal caduco*,

---

86. *cocted*] boiled.

92.] See 76 and note.

96–7. *see . . . work*] i.e. gold cannot cure rheumatism or similar ills.

97. unguento] unguent, ointment.

98. *only*] unique.

99–101. *hot . . . 'dry'*] As Peregrine drily observes, the opposite of 'moist'
in the Galenic scheme of humours theory should be 'dry'. The basic characteristics of air (hot and moist), fire (hot and dry), water (cold and moist),
and earth (cold and dry) were thought to produce in the body the four humours
of sanguine (hot and moist), choleric (hot and dry), phlegmatic (cold and
moist), and melancholic (cold and dry), which had to be correctly balanced
for good health.

102. *indigest and crude*] (1) not digesting; (2) sour.

105. *unction*] application of ointment.

fricace] massage.

vertiginè] vertigo, dizziness.

107. *sovereign*] superlative, potent, unrivalled.

107–8. mal caduco] epilepsy.

cramps, convulsions, paralyses, epilepsies, *tremor cordia*,
retired nerves, ill vapours of the spleen, stoppings of the
liver, the stone, the strangury, *hernia ventosa, iliaca passio*;   110
stops a *dysenteria* immediately; easeth the torsion of the
small guts; and cures *melancholia hypocondriaca*, being
taken and applied according to my printed receipt.
(*Pointing to his bill and his glass*.) For this is the physician,
this the medicine; this counsels, this cures; this gives   115
the direction, this works the effect; and, in sum, both
together may be termed an abstract of the theoric and
practic in the Aesculapian art. 'Twill cost you eight
crowns. [*To Nano*] And, Zan Fritada, pray thee sing a
verse extempore in honour of it.   120
Sir Politic. How do you like him, sir?
Peregrine.   Most strangely, I!
Sir Politic. Is not his language rare?
Peregrine.   But alchemy
    I never heard the like, or Broughton's books.

                                        [*Nano sings.*]

                        SONG
Nano. Had old Hippocrates, or Galen,

108–11. tremor cordia . . . passio] palpitation of the heart, shrunken sin-
ews, hysteria or depression, obstructions in the liver, kidney stone, impeded
urination, hernia that is full of wind and swollen (?), obstruction in the small
intestine.

111. dysenteria] severe diarrhoea.

torsion] cramps, spasmodic pain; colic.

112. melancholia hypocondriaca] melancholy originating in the *hypo-
condria* or abdomen under the ribs on each side of the stomach.

113. *receipt*] recipe.

114 SD. bill . . . glass] the recipe and a flagon.

118. *Aesculapian*] medical, named after Aesculapius, Greek god of
medicine.

119. *Zan Fritada*] literally, 'Jack Pancake', a famous Venetian zany.

121. *strangely*] (1) exceptionally; (2) unfavourably. Sir Pol is expected to
understand only the first.

122. *But*] except for.

123. *Broughton's books*] Hugh Broughton (1549–1612) was a puritan
divine and rabbinical scholar whose obscure pedantry Jonson also satirizes in
The Alchemist, 4.5.1–32.

124. *Hippocrates*] the Greek physician, c. 460 B.C., whose ideas on medicine Galen systematized into the theory of humours (c. 130 A.D.); see 99–101
n. above.

That to their books put med'cines all in,   125
But known this secret, they had never
(Of which they will be guilty ever)
Been murderers of so much paper,
Or wasted many a hurtless taper;
No Indian drug had e'er been famed,   130
Tobacco, sassafras not named;
Ne yet of guacum one small stick, sir,
Nor Raymond Lully's great elixir;
Ne had been known the Danish Gonswart,
Or Paracelsus with his longsword.   135

Peregrine. All this, yet, will not do. Eight crowns is high.

Volpone. No more.—Gentlemen, if I had but time to discourse to you the miraculous effects of this my oil, sur-
named *Oglio del Scoto*, with the countless catalogue of
those I have cured of th' aforesaid and many more dis-   140
eases, the patents and privileges of all the princes and
commonwealths of Christendom, or but the depositions
of those that appeared on my part before the Signiory of

---

125. *med'cines all*] all medicines.

126. *this secret*] i.e. Scoto's formula.

128.] Galen was said to have written almost five hundred treatises on medicine.

129.] or burned many a harmless candle, working at night.

131. *Tobacco, sassafras*] newly introduced from America for medicinal use, especially as mild sedatives and in the treatment of syphilis.

132. *Ne*] nor. (Also in 134.)

guacum] products of the guaiacum tree from the West Indies used medicinally.

133.] Raymond Lully (1235–1315) was a Spanish scholar, astrologer, and missionary, wrongly reputed to be an alchemist and discoverer of the philosopher's stone—the 'great elixir' able to bestow eternal life.

134.] nor would the Danish Gonswart have been known. (Gonswart may be Johan Gansfort, or Wessel, a fifteenth-century scholar; or perhaps an invented name combining the herbs 'Danewort', i.e. Dwarf Elder, and 'Goutwart', used to cure gout.)

135. *Paracelsus*] a pioneer of chemical medicine (1493–1541) who is supposed to have kept a familiar spirit or secret medicines in the hollow pommel of his longsword.

136.] Peregrine's wry reflection indicates not his own unwillingness to buy at the stated price of eight crowns but his sure sense that the pitchman is about to start coming down in what he asks—as indeed he does at 180 ff.

143–4. *Signiory . . . Sanità*] a ministry of health set up in 1485 to license physicians and mountebanks.

the Sanità and most learned College of Physicians, where
I was authorised, upon notice taken of the admirable   145
virtues of my medicaments and mine own excellency in
matter of rare and unknown secrets, not only to disperse
them publicly in this famous city, but in all the territories
that happily joy under the government of the most pious
and magnificent states of Italy! But may some other gal-   150
lant fellow say, 'Oh, there be divers that make profession
to have as good and as experimented receipts as yours!'
Indeed, very many have assayed, like apes, in imitation of
that which is really and essentially in me, to make of this
oil, bestowed great cost in furnaces, stills, alembics, con- 155
tinual fires, and preparation of the ingredients (as indeed
there goes to it six hundred several simples, besides some
quantity of human fat, for the conglutination, which we
buy of anatomists), but, when these practitioners come to
the last decoction, blow, blow, puff, puff—and all flies *in*   160
fumo. Ha, ha, ha! Poor wretches! I rather pity their folly
and indiscretion than their loss of time and money, for
those may be recovered by industry, but to be a fool born
is a disease incurable. For myself, I always from my youth
have endeavoured to get the rarest secrets, and book   165
them, either in exchange or for money; I spared nor cost
nor labour where anything was worthy to be learned. And
gentlemen, honourable gentlemen, I will undertake, by
virtue of chemical art, out of the honourable hat that
covers your head to extract the four elements, that is to   170

150–1. *But . . . say*] but some other young man of fashion might say.
151. *divers*] some persons.
152. *experimented*] i.e. tested by experiment.
154–5. *of this oil*] some of this oil.
155. *stills, alembics*] distilling equipment.
157. *several simples*] separate medicinal herbs; separate ingredients.
158. *conglutination*] gluing together.
159. *anatomists*] dissectors of the human body.
160. *decoction*] boiling down.
blow . . . puff] the efforts made by the alchemist's assistant operating the
bellows to intensify the fire.
160–1. in fumo] up in smoke.
162. *indiscretion*] failure of discernment or discrimination.
165. *book*] record.
166. *in exchange*] i.e. in exchange for secrets of my own.

say, the fire, air, water, and earth, and return you your felt
without burn or stain. For, whilst others have been at the
balloo, I have been at my book, and am now past the
craggy paths of study, and come to the flowery plains of
honour and reputation.   175
Sir Politic. I do assure, you sir, that is his aim.
Volpone. But to our price.
Peregrine.   And that withal, Sir Pol.
Volpone. You all know, honourable gentlemen, I never valued
this *ampulla*, or vial, at less than eight crowns; but for this
time I am content to be deprived of it for six: six crowns   180
is the price, and less, in courtesy, I know you cannot offer
me. Take it or leave it, howsoever, both it and I am at
your service. I ask you not as the value of the thing, for
then I should demand of you a thousand crowns: so the
Cardinals Montalto, Fernese, the great Duke of Tuscany,   185
my gossip, with divers other princes, have given me; but
I despise money. Only to show my affection to you,
honourable gentlemen, and your illustrous state here, I
have neglected the messages of these princes, mine own
offices, framed my journey hither, only to present you   190
with the fruits of my travels. [*To Nano and Mosca*] Tune
your voices once more to the touch of your instruments,
and give the honourable assembly some delightful
recreation.
Peregrine. What monstrous and most painful circumstance   195
Is here, to get some three or four *gazets*,

---

171. *felt*] felt hat.
173. balloo] i.e. balloon, a ball game played by six or seven young men,
each wearing spiked wooden bracelets on one of his arms.
177. *withal*] as well. Peregrine deflates Sir Pol's insistence that Scoto is a
man of honour by adding that he is also interested in the bottom line.
179. ampulla] a thin vial made of glass.
182. *Take . . . howsoever*] whether you purchase it or not.
183. *as*] as corresponding to.
184. *demand*] ask.
186. *gossip*] i.e. godparent of one's children and hence a friend. 'Scoto' is
dropping names.
190. *offices*] affairs, duties.
framed] devised, planned.
195. *circumstance*] irrelevantly detailed and circuitous account.
196. gazets] Venetian coins, worth less than an English penny.

Some threepence i' th' whole—for that 'twill come to!

[*During the*] SONG [CELIA *appears at a window above*].

Nano. [*Sings*] You that would last long, list to my song;
Make no more coil, but buy of this oil.
Would you be ever fair and young,   200
Stout of teeth and strong of tongue,
Tart of palate, quick of ear,
Sharp of sight, of nostril clear,
Moist of hand and light of foot?
Or I will come nearer to 't,   205
Would you live free from all diseases?
Do the act your mistress pleases,
Yet fright all aches from your bones?
Here's a med'cine for the nones.

Volpone. Well, I am in a humour, at this time, to make a   210
present of the small quantity my coffer contains, to the
rich in courtesy, and to the poor for God's sake. Wherefore, now mark: I asked you six crowns, and six crowns at
other times you have paid me. You shall not give me six
crowns, nor five, nor four, nor three, nor two, nor one;   215
nor half a ducat; no, nor a *moccenigo*. Six—pence it will
cost you, or six hundred pound; expect no lower price,

---

197. *i' th' whole*] as the entire receipts.

197.1.] Celia may appear at this point, or earlier, or shortly before she
drops her handkerchief at 227.1. The longer she is visible, the more opportunity and risk there is in suggesting, through her reactions to the scene
below, credulity, or flirtatiousness, or frivolity.

198. *list*] listen.

199. *coil*] fuss.

202. *Tart*] keen.

204. *Moist of hand*] a sign of youth and libidinousness.

207. *the act*] the sexual act.

208. *aches*] a disyllable 'aitches', referring to syphilis.

209. *nones*] nonce, occasion.

212. *for God's sake*] i.e. for charity. A conventional phrase.

216. *ducat*] The Venetian gold ducat was worth about nine shillings, the
silver ducat (presumably meant here) about three shillings and sixpence.

moccenigo] a small coin worth about nine (old) pence.

216-17. *Six . . . pound*] This sudden introduction of English money may
indicate that these lines are spoken directly to Sir Pol and Peregrine. The
dash after 'six' marks the point where 'Scoto' notices the Englishmen.

217. *or six . . . pound*] i.e. or else I am not going any lower.

for, by the banner of my front, I will not bate a *bagatine*:
that I will have, only, a pledge of your loves, to carry
something from amongst you to show I am not con-   220
temned by you. Therefore, now toss your handkerchiefs
cheerfully, cheerfully; and be advertised that the first
heroic spirit that deigns to grace me with a handkerchief,
I will give it a little remembrance of something beside,
shall please it better than if I had presented it with a   225
double *pistolet*.

Peregrine. Will you be that heroic spark, Sir Pol?

      Celia at the window throws down her handkerchief.
Oh, see! The window has prevented you.

Volpone. Lady, I kiss your bounty; and for this timely grace
you have done your poor Scoto of Mantua, I will return   230
you, over and above my oil, a secret of that high and
inestimable nature shall make you for ever enamoured on
that minute wherein your eye first descended on so mean
(yet not altogether to be despised) an object. Here is a
powder concealed in this paper, of which, if I should   235
speak to the worth, nine thousand volumes were but as
one page, that page as a line, that line as a word, so short
is this pilgrimage of man (which some call life) to the
expressing of it. Would I reflect on the price, why, the
whole world were but as an empire, that empire as a   240
province, that province as a bank, that bank as a private
purse, to the purchase of it. I will only tell you: it is the
powder that made Venus a goddess, given her by Apollo,
that kept her perpetually young, cleared her wrinkles,

---

218. *the banner . . . front*] i.e. the banner displayed before my mountebank's stall advertising my wares.

    bate] abate.

    a bagatine] a small Italian coin worth about one twelfth of a penny.

220–1. *contemned*] scorned.

221. *toss your handkerchiefs*] i.e. tie your money in a handkerchief and toss
it to me and I will return the purchase the same way.

222. *be advertised*] take note.

225. *shall please it*] which will please that heroic spirit, that brave soul.

226. pistolet] a Venetian coin worth about six shillings; the Spanish coin
of the same name was worth about eighteen shillings.

228. *prevented*] anticipated, gone first and thus thwarted.

233. *mean*] lowly.

238. *to*] compared to. (Also in 242.)

firmed her gums, filled her skin, coloured her hair; from   245
her derived to Helen, and at the sack of Troy unfortu-
nately lost; till now, in this our age, it was as happily
recovered by a studious antiquary, out of some ruins of
Asia, who sent a moiety of it to the court of France (but
much sophisticated), wherewith the ladies there now   250
colour their hair. The rest, at this present, remains with
me, extracted to a quintessence, so that, wherever it but
touches, in youth it perpetually preserves, in age restores
the complexion; seats your teeth, did they dance like
virginal jacks, firm as a wall; makes them white as ivory,   255
that were black as—

ACT 2   SCENE 3

[*Enter*] CORVINO.

Corvino. Blood of the devil, and my shame! Come down here,
                    He beats away the mountebank, etc.
                    [*and Celia leaves the window*].
      Come down! No house but mine to make your scene?
      Signor Flamineo, will you down, sir? Down!
      What, is my wife your *Franciscina*, sir?
      No windows on the whole Piazza here   5
      To make your properties but mine? But mine?

---

245. *filled*] (1) filled out, plumped; (2) filed, smoothed, polished (?).

249. *moiety*] part.

250. *sophisticated*] adulterated.

252. *quintessence*] refined extract; the elixir or philosopher's stone. See 133n. above.

254. *did they*] even if they were to.

255. *virginal jacks*] i.e. the plucking devices in the action of a virginal or small spinet.

2.3.1. *Blood of*] F reads 'Spite o'', which is entirely intelligible, but the Q reading given here allows Corvino to conclude Scoto's speech: 'black as— Blood of the devil, and my shame!'

2.] Street scenes with stage 'houses' facing on to a public area were common in Roman comedy and in Italian neoclassical comedy; window scenes were similarly common in the *commedia dell'arte*.

3–4. Flamineo . . . Franciscina] a young lover and the saucy serving wench in the *commedia dell'arte*.

6. *properties*] (1) stage set; (2) personal belongings.

  Heart! Ere tomorrow I shall be new christened
  And called the *Pantalone di Besogniosi*
  About the town. [*Exit* CORVINO; *the* Crowd *disperses*.]
Peregrine.   What should this mean, Sir Pol?
Sir Politic. Some trick of state, believe it. I will home.   10
Peregrine. It may be some design on you.
Sir Politic.   I know not.
  I'll stand upon my guard.
Peregrine.   It is your best, sir.
Sir Politic. This three weeks all my advices, all my letters,
  They have been intercepted.
Peregrine.   Indeed, sir?
  Best have a care.
Sir Politic.   Nay, so I will.   [*Exit*.]
Peregrine.   This knight,   15
  I may not lose him, for my mirth, till night. [*Exit*.]

ACT 2 SCENE 4

     [*Enter*] VOLPONE [*and*] MOSCA.

Volpone. Oh, I am wounded!
Mosca.   Where, sir?
Volpone.   Not without;
  Those blows were nothing, I could bear them ever.
  But angry Cupid, bolting from her eyes,
  Hath shot himself into me like a flame,
  Where now he flings about his burning heat,   5
  As in a furnace an ambitious fire
  Whose vent is stopped. The fight is all within me.

---

 8. Pantalone] the avaricious old Venetian husband in the *commedia dell'arte*. Corvino includes the title *'di Besogniosi'*, 'of the beggars', to emphasize his fear of being mocked for poverty as well as cuckoldry.
 12. *your best*] your wisest course of action.
 16.] I wouldn't lose this dolt for anything as a subject of my mirth for the whole day.

 2.4. Location: a street in Venice.
 1. *without*] externally.
 3. *bolting*] shooting bolts or arrows.
 6. *ambitious*] rising, swelling.
 7. *stopped*] blocked.

         I cannot live except thou help me, Mosca;
         My liver melts, and I, without the hope
         Of some soft air from her refreshing breath,   10
         Am but a heap of cinders.
Mosca.   'Las, good sir!
         Would you had never seen her.
Volpone.   Nay, would thou
         Hadst never told me of her.
Mosca.   Sir, 'tis true;
         I do confess I was unfortunate
         And you unhappy; but I'm bound in conscience,   15
         No less than duty, to effect my best
         To your release of torment, and I will, sir.
Volpone. Dear Mosca, shall I hope?
Mosca.   Sir, more than dear,
         I will not bid you to despair of aught
         Within a human compass.
Volpone.   Oh, there spoke   20
         My better angel. Mosca, take my keys,
         Gold, plate, and jewels—all's at thy devotion;
         Employ them how thou wilt. Nay, coin me too,
         So thou in this but crown my longings. Mosca?
Mosca. Use but your patience.
Volpone.   So I have.
Mosca.   I doubt not   25
         To bring success to your desires.
Volpone.   Nay, then,
         I not repent me of my late disguise.

---

   8. *except*] unless.

   9. *liver*] thought to be the seat of love and violent passions.

   10. *air*] Volpone longs for that which would consume him all the more
quickly, since air feeds a fire.

   18. *Sir . . . dear*] my very dear sir.

   20. *Within . . . compass*] that can be accomplished by human action.

   21.] At 1.3.40, Mosca brags of being the custodian of Volpone's keys, but
see 5.5.12 and 5.11.12 where Mosca's possession of the keys is spoken of as
something unusual. Cf. 1.3.40n.

   22. *devotion*] disposal; with ironic overtones of 'loyalty' and 'worship'.

   23. *coin me*] turn me into money. (Coining, in the sense of counterfeiting
coins with official images over them, was illegal.)

   24. *crown*] perfect; with a pun on the preceding 'coin'.

Mosca. If you can horn him, sir, you need not.
Voplone. True.
    Besides, I never meant him for my heir.
    Is not the colour o' my beard and eyebrows   30
    To make me known?
Mosca.   No jot.
Volpone.   I did it well.
Mosca. So well, would I could follow you in mine
    With half the happiness! And yet, I would
    Escape your epilogue.
Volpone.   But were they gulled
    With a belief that I was Scoto?
Mosca.   Sir,   35
    Scoto himself could hardly have distinguished!
    I have not time to flatter you now; we'll part,
    And, as I prosper, so applaud my art.   *[Exeunt.]*

ACT 2   SCENE 5

[Enter] CORVINO *[and]* CELIA.

Corvino. Death of mine honour, with the city's fool?
    A juggling, tooth-drawing, prating mountebank?
    And at a public window? Where, whilst he
    With his strained action and his dole of faces
    To his drug-lecture draws your itching ears,   5
    A crew of old, unmarried, noted lechers
    Stood leering up like satyrs? And you smile
    Most graciously, and fan your favours forth,

---

28. *horn*] cuckold.

30. *colour*] i.e. red, the fox's colour.

32–3. *So . . . happiness*] You disguised yourself so successfully that I could wish myself half as successful in the art of fooling.

34. *epilogue*] i.e. the beating given by Corvino at 2.3.1.1.

37. *flatter*] (1) please with a belief (that your disguise was entirely successful); (2) compliment insincerely.

2.5. Location: Corvino's house, through 2.7.

2. *tooth-drawing*] one of the mountebanks' major services.

4. *strained action*] overemphatic gesture.

 dole of faces] repertory of grimaces and mugging, or possibly, of masks. As Scoto, Volpone has used a broader acting style.

8. *fan . . . forth*] literally, distribute your regard or approval; perhaps with an actual fan.

To give your hot spectators satisfaction!
What, was your mountebank their call? Their whistle?   10
Or were you enamoured on his copper rings,
His saffron jewel with the toad-stone in 't,
Or his embroidered suit with the cope-stitch,
Made of a hearse cloth? Or his old tilt-feather?
Or his starched beard? Well, you shall have him, yes!   15
He shall come home and minister unto you
The fricace for the mother. Or, let me see,
I think you'd rather mount? Would you not mount?
Why, if you'll mount, you may; yes truly, you may—
And so you may be seen down to th' foot.   20
Get you a cittern, Lady Vanity,
And be a dealer with the Virtuous Man;
Make one. I'll but protest myself a cuckold,
And save your dowry. I am a Dutchman, I!

---

10. *call . . . whistle*] bird lures.

11. *copper rings*] cheap substitutes for gold.

12. *saffron*] yellow, imitation gold.

toad-stone] agate-like stone supposed to have been taken from a toad's head and to have medicinal and magical properties.

13. *cope-stitch*] a stitch like that used in embroidering the straight edge of a cope or ecclesiastical gown.

14. *hearse cloth*] heavy cloth draped over a coffin.

tilt-feather] plume like that worn on jousting helmets in the tilt-yard.

15. *starched*] stiffened with gum or egg-white in a fashionable shape.

17. *fricace . . . mother*] massage for hysteria, believed to originate in the womb; hence, sexual caresses. Cf. *fricatrice* (4.2.55), meaning 'whore'.

18–20.] Corvino acidly suggests that Celia might like to get up on the mountebank's platform, where she could be seen from head to foot, and indeed under her skirts. With suggestion too of the woman-on-top position in sex.

21. *cittern*] stringed instrument often used by street performers, and associated with prostitutes.

Lady Vanity] a dissipated female character in a morality play like that presented in the play within the play of *The Book of Sir Thomas More*, 4.1 (c. 1590–1601).

22.] And solicit sex with the hero of a morality play like *Enough Is as Good as a Feast* (c. 1559–1570), in which a major character is called Heavenly Man.

23. *Make one*] (1) join their company; (2) make a deal; (3) copulate.

protest] declare.

24. *save your dowry*] An unfaithful wife forfeited her dowry to the wronged husband. Corvino says that he will at least have the comfort of Celia's money, but see 5.12.142–4.

24–9. *I am . . . justice*] i.e. (sarcastically) I must be a phlegmatic Dutchman. If you thought me a fiercely jealous Italian man, you wouldn't dare do

For if you thought me an Italian,   25
You would be damned ere you did this, you whore!
Thou'dst tremble to imagine that the murder
Of father, mother, brother, all thy race,
Should follow as the subject of my justice.
Celia. Good sir, have patience!
Corvino. [*Drawing a dagger*]   What couldst thou propose   30
Less to thyself than, in this heat of wrath
And stung with my dishonour, I should strike
This steel into thee, with as many stabs
As thou wert gazed upon with goatish eyes?
Celia. Alas, sir, be appeased! I could not think   35
My being at the window should more now
Move your impatience than at other times.
Corvino. No? Not to seek and entertain a parley
With a known knave? Before a multitude?
You were an actor, with your handkerchief,   40
Which he most sweetly kissed in the receipt,
And might, no doubt, return it with a letter,
And 'point the place where you might meet—your
      sister's,
Your mother's, or your aunt's might serve the turn.
Celia. Why, dear sir, when do I make these excuses?   45
Or ever stir abroad but to the church?
And that so seldom—
Corvino.   Well, it shall be less;
And thy restraint before was liberty
To what I now decree. And therefore mark me.
First, I will have this bawdy light dammed up;   50
And, till 't be done, some two or three yards off

what you've just done; you'd know that an Italian husband would kill your whole family for revenge.
31. *to thyself*] as appropriate punishment for yourself.
34. *goatish*] lecherous.
38. *entertain a parley*] hold conference with.
40. *actor*] not only 'participant' but 'someone putting on a performance'.
43. *'point*] appoint.
44. *aunt's*] slang for 'bawd'.
serve the turn] (1) answer the purpose; (2) provide sexual service.
49. *To*] compared to.
50. *bawdy light*] window inciting to immorality.

I'll chalk a line, o'er which if thou but chance
To set thy desp'rate foot, more hell, more horror,
More wild, remorseless rage shall seize on thee
Than on a conjuror that had heedless left   55
His circle's safety ere his devil was laid.
Then, [*Showing her a chastity belt*] here's a lock which I
    will hang upon thee;
And, now I think on 't, I will keep thee backwards:
Thy lodging shall be backwards, thy walks backwards,
Thy prospect—all be backwards, and no pleasure   60
That thou shalt know but backwards. Nay, since you
    force
My honest nature, know it is your own
Being too open makes me use you thus.
Since you will not contain your subtle nostrils
In a sweet room, but they must snuff the air   65
Of rank and sweaty passengers—   *Knock within.*
                          One knocks!
Away, and be not seen, pain of thy life;
Not look toward the window; if thou dost—
                          [*Celia starts to leave.*]
Nay, stay, hear this: let me not prosper, whore,
But I will make thee an anatomy,   70
Dissect thee mine own self, and read a lecture

---

53. *desp'rate*] reckless, irreclaimable.

55–6. *conjuror . . . laid*] Magicians were supposed to be able to raise spirits with impunity so long as they drew, and stayed within, a magic circle or pentagram till the spirit was 'laid' back in hell. With bawdy suggestion of raising up a 'spirit' (semen, and the male sexual member) in a circle; cf. 2.6.65–6 and *R&J*, 2.1.24–30.

58–61. *backwards . . . backwards*] literally, at the rear of the house; but with a suggestion of anal sex, continued in 63, 'open' and 'use'. Sodomy was considered an Italian vice and particularly associated with Venetian transvestites; see Lady Pol's suspicions of Peregrine at 4.2.51ff.

60. *prospect*] (1) view; (2) expectations.

64. *subtle*] (1) cunning; (2) dainty (used sarcastically).

65. *sweet*] sweet-smelling (rooms were perfumed at this time).

66. *passengers*] passers by.

67. *pain . . . life*] on pain of death.

69–70. *let . . . will*] i.e. may heaven strike me down, you whore, if I do not.

70. *anatomy*] (1) corpse for dissection; (2) subject for moral analysis.

Upon thee to the city, and in public.
Away!   [*Exit* CELIA.]
    Who's there?

             [*Enter* Servant.]

Servant.   'Tis Signor Mosca, sir.

ACT 2   SCENE 6

Corvino. Let him come in.   [*Exit* Servant.]
            His master's dead! There's yet
Some good to help the bad.

           [*Enter* MOSCA.]

            My Mosca, welcome!
I guess your news.
Mosca.   I fear you cannot, sir.
Corvino. Is 't not his death?
Mosca.   Rather the contrary.
Corvino. Not his recovery?
Mosca.   Yes, sir.
Corvino.   I am cursed,   5
I am bewitched; my crosses meet to vex me.
How? How? How? How?
Mosca.   Why, sir, with Scoto's oil.
Corbaccio and Voltore brought of it,
Whilst I was busy in an inner room—
Corvino. Death! That damned mountebank! But for the law,   10
Now, I could kill the rascal. 'T cannot be
His oil should have that virtue. Ha' not I
Known him a common rogue, come fiddling in
To th' *osteria*, with a tumbling whore,
And, when he has done all his forced tricks, been glad   15

2.6.6. *crosses*] afflictions.
  8. *of it*] some of it.
 10. *But for*] were it not for.
 12. *virtue*] efficacy.
 14. osteria] inn.
  tumbling whore] (1) female acrobat; (2) prostitute.
 15. *forced*] (1) lacking in spontaneity, strained, artificial; (2) enforced by poverty.

Of a poor spoonful of dead wine, with flies in 't?
It cannot be. All his ingredients
Are a sheep's gall, a roasted bitch's marrow,
Some few sod earwigs, pounded caterpillars,
A little capon's grease, and fasting spittle;   20
I know 'em to a dram.
Mosca.   I know not, sir;
But some on 't, there, they poured into his ears,
Some in his nostrils, and recovered him,
Applying but the fricace.
Corvino.   Pox o' that fricace!
Mosca. And since, to seem the more officious   25
And flatt'ring of his health, there they have had,
At extreme fees, the college of physicians
Consulting on him, how they might restore him,
Where one would have a cataplasm of spices,
Another a flayed ape clapped to his breast,   30
A third would have 't a dog, a fourth an oil
With wildcats' skins. At last they all resolved
That to preserve him was no other means
But some young woman must be straight sought out,
Lusty, and full of juice, to sleep by him;   35
And to this service, most unhappily
And most unwillingly, am I now employed,
Which here I thought to pre-acquaint you with,
For your advice, since it concerns you most,
Because I would not do that thing might cross   40
Your ends, on whom I have my whole dependence, sir.

---

16. *dead*] stale.

19. *sod*] boiled.

20. *fasting spittle*] i.e. the spittle of a starving man, perhaps Scoto himself.

21. *to a dram*] i.e. down to the smallest detail or amount.

24. *fricace*] massage, as at 2.5.17.

Pox o'] i.e. a plague on. (*Pox* is, literally, syphilis.)

25. *officious*] zealous, helpful.

26. *flatt'ring of*] delusively encouraging about.

29. *cataplasm*] poultice.

34-5.] This cure was attempted for the ageing King David in 1 Kings 1.1–4.

34. *straight*] immediately.

35. *Lusty*] (1) full of health; (2) lustful.

40–1. *cross . . . ends*] thwart your purposes.

Yet, if I do it not, they may delate
My slackness to my patron, work me out
Of his opinion; and there all your hopes,
Ventures, or whatsoever, are all frustrate.   45
I do but tell you, sir. Besides, they are all
Now striving who shall first present him. Therefore—
I could entreat you, briefly, conclude somewhat.
Prevent 'em if you can.
Corvino.   Death to my hopes!
This is my villainous fortune! Best to hire   50
Some common courtesan?
Mosca.   Ay, I thought on that, sir.
But they are all so subtle, full of art,
And age again doting and flexible,
So as—I cannot tell—we may perchance
Light on a quean may cheat us all.
Corvino.   'Tis true.   55
Mosca. No, no; it must be one that has no tricks, sir,
Some simple thing, a creature made unto it;
Some wench you may command. Ha' you no
    kinswoman?
Godso—Think, think, think, think, think, think, think,
    sir.
One o' the doctors offered there his daughter.   60
Corvino. How!
Mosca.   Yes, Signor Lupo, the physician.
Corvino. His daughter?
Mosca.   And a virgin, sir. Why, alas,
He knows the state of 's body, what it is:

---

42. *delate*] report, denounce.
44. *opinion*] good opinion.
47. *present him*] i.e. present him with a young woman.
48. *conclude somewhat*] decide on something.
49. *Prevent*] forestall, and thus stop.
53. *again*] in addition, moreover.
55. *quean*] whore.
57. *a creature . . . it*] (1) a woman fit for the task; (2) a dependant who can be forced to do it.
59. *Godso*] an oath, from 'by God's soul', but sounding like *cazzo*, Italian for 'penis'.
61. *Lupo*] Italian for 'wolf'; applied here to a rapacious doctor. 'Wolf' is also a medical term for an ulcer.

That nought can warm his blood, sir, but a fever,
Nor any incantation raise his spirit.   65
A long forgetfulness hath seized that part.
Besides, sir, who shall know it? Some one or two—
Corvino. I pray thee give me leave. [*He walks aside, pondering.*]
    If any man
But I had had this luck—The thing in 'tself
I know is nothing.—Wherefore should not I   70
As well command my blood and my affections
As this dull doctor? In the point of honour,
The cases are all one, of wife and daughter.
Mosca. [*Aside*] I hear him coming.
Corvino. [*Aside*]   She shall do 't. 'Tis done.
'Slight, if this doctor, who is not engaged,   75
Unless 't be for his counsel (which is nothing),
Offer his daughter, what should I that am
So deeply in? I will prevent him. Wretch!
Covetous wretch! [*To Mosca*] Mosca, I have determined.
Mosca. How, sir?
Corvino.   We'll make all sure. The party you wot of   80
Shall be mine own wife, Mosca.
Mosca.   Sir, the thing—
But that I would not seem to counsel you—
I should have motioned to you at the first.
And, make your count, you have cut all their throats.
Why, 'tis directly taking a possession!   85
And in his next fit, we may let him go.

_____

65–6.] The image is of raising a diabolical spirit and also of sexual erection
no longer possible. 'Spirit' is both semen and the male member; cf. 2.5.55–
6 and note.

71. *my blood . . . affections*] (1) my own passions; (2) a member of my close
family.

74. *coming*] coming around.

75. *'Slight*] by God's light; an oath.

is not engaged] has not staked anything, is not deeply involved.

80. *wot*] know.

83. *motioned*] proposed.

84. *make your count*] (1) you may count on it; (2) when you count your
gains (?).

cut . . . throats] i.e. outsmarted them all (as in 'cutthroat competition').

85. *taking a possession*] enjoying a thing either by the owner himself or by
another in his name.

'Tis but to pull the pillow from his head,
And he is throttled; 't had been done before
But for your scrupulous doubts.
Corvino.　　　　　　　　　　　　Ay, a plague on 't;
　My conscience fools my wit! Well, I'll be brief,　　　90
　And so be thou, lest they should be before us.
　Go home, prepare him, tell him with what zeal
　And willingness I do it; swear it was
　On the first hearing, as thou mayst do truly,
　Mine own free motion.
Mosca.　　　　　　　　　Sir, I warrant you　　　95
　I'll so possess him with it that the rest
　Of his starved clients shall be banished all,
　And only you received. But come not, sir,
　Until I send, for I have something else
　To ripen for your good; you must not know 't.　　100
Corvino. But do not you forget to send, now.
Mosca.　　　　　　　　　　　　Fear not.
　　　　　　　　　　　　　　　　　[*Exit.*]

ACT 2　SCENE 7

Corvino. Where are you, wife? My Celia? Wife!

　　　　　[*Enter* CELIA, *crying.*]

　　　　　　　　　　What, blubbering?
　Come, dry those tears. I think thou thought'st me in
　　earnest?
　Ha? By this light, I talked so but to try thee.
　Methinks the lightness of the occasion
　Should ha' confirmed thee. Come, I am not jealous.　　5
Celia. No?
Corvino.　Faith, I am not, I, nor never was;
　It is a poor, unprofitable humour.

---

90. *fools my wit*] makes a fool of my common sense.
95. *Mine . . . motion*] my own voluntary proposition.
96. *possess*] impress, persuasively influence.

2.7.3. *try*] test.
5. *confirmed*] assured.

Do not I know, if women have a will
They'll do 'gainst all the watches o' the world?
And that the fiercest spies are tamed with gold?   10
Tut, I'm confident in thee, thou shalt see 't;
And see, I'll give thee cause too, to believe it.
Come, kiss me. [*Celia kisses him.*] Go, and make thee
    ready straight
In all thy best attire, thy choicest jewels;
Put 'em all on, and with 'em thy best looks.   15
We are invited to a solemn feast
At old Volpone's, where it shall appear
How far I am free from jealously or fear.   [*Exeunt.*]

---

8. *will*] (1) inclination; (2) sexual appetite.
9.] they'll take a lover despite all the watchfulness of the world.
10. *spies*] i.e. persons employed by husbands to guard their wives.
16. *solemn feast*] formal banquet.

Act 3

[*Enter*] MOSCA.

Mosca. I fear I shall begin to grow in love
    With my dear self and my most prosp'rous parts,
    They do so spring and burgeon; I can feel
    A whimsy i' my blood. I know not how,
    Success hath made me wanton. I could skip   5
    Out of my skin, now, like a subtle snake,
    I am so limber. Oh, your parasite
    Is a most precious thing, dropped from above,
    Not bred 'mongst clods and clotpolls here on earth.
    I muse the mystery was not made a science,   10
    It is so liberally professed! Almost
    All the wise world is little else, in nature,
    But parasites or sub-parasites. And yet
    I mean not those that have your bare town-art,
    To know who's fit to feed 'em; have no house,   15
    No family, no care, and therefore mould

3.1. Location: the piazza.

2. *parts*] abilities, talents; sexual organs (?).

3. *burgeon*] thrive; swell or grow larger.

4. *whimsy*] giddiness; whim. (With erotic suggestiveness, continued in 'wanton', 'limber', etc.)

5. *wanton*] reckless, insolent, sportive, self-indulgent, amorous.

6. *subtle*] (1) cunning; (2) elusive.

8. *dropped from above*] heaven-sent.

9. *clotpolls*] blockheads, dolts.

10. *mystery*] skill, trade.

science] one of the branches required for a degree in 'Liberal Arts'.

11. *liberally*] (1) freely; (2) referring to 'science' (10).

professed] practised as a profession; taught.

14. *your . . . town-art*] i.e. the crude skill of the typical city-dwelling sponger—you know the sort I mean.

15. *To . . . 'em*] who can easily identify suitable victims to sponge off.

16–17. *mould . . . sense*] make up stories calculated to win the sympathy of such easily gulled citizens. To 'bait' is to cater for, entice, indulge.

Tales for men's ears, to bait that sense, or get
Kitchen-invention and some stale receipts
To please the belly and the groin; nor those,
With their court-dog-tricks, that can fawn and fleer,   20
Make their revenue out of legs and faces,
Echo my lord, and lick away a moth—
But your fine, elegant rascal, that can rise
And stoop almost together, like an arrow,
Shoot through the air as nimbly as a star,   25
Turn short as doth a swallow, and be here,
And there, and here, and yonder, all at once,
Present to any humour, all occasion,
And change a visor swifter than a thought!
This is the creature had the art born with him,   30
Toils not to learn it, but doth practise it
Out of most excellent nature, and such sparks
Are the true parasites, others but their zanies.

ACT 3   SCENE 2

[Enter] BONARIO.

Mosca. *[Aside]* Who's this? Bonario? Old Corbaccio's son?
The person I was bound to seek. *[To him]* Fair sir,

17–19. *or get . . . groin*] or else provide themselves with some old cooking recipes and similar whorish tricks calculated to appeal to gluttony and sexual appetite (since food can act as an aphrodisiac, and since 'stale' can mean 'whore').

20. *court-dog-tricks*] courtier-like begging and sycophancy, calculated to impress men more important than mere citizens.

fleer] smile or smirk obsequiously.

21–2.] earn their keep by their obsequious bows and smirks, flatter a courtier by calling him 'my lord' and flicking away specks of dust (mote, 'moth') from his clothing even with their tongues. ('Moth' also suggests an insect-parasite, like Mosca.)

25. *star*] i.e. meteor or shooting star.

28.] ready to gratify any whim or mood.

29. *visor*] mask, hence facial expression or role.

30.] This then is the parasite who is born to the art of flattering.

32. *nature*] innate ability.

33. *zanies*] clownish imitators.

3.2. Location: the piazza still.

2. *bound*] on my way.

You are happ'ly met.

Bonario.   That cannot be by thee.

Mosca. Why, sir?

Bonario.   Nay, pray thee know thy way and leave me;   5
          I would be loath to interchange discourse
          With such a mate as thou art.

Mosca.   Courteous sir,
          Scorn not my poverty.

Bonario.   Not I, by heaven;
          But thou shalt give me leave to hate thy baseness.

Mosca. Baseness?

Bonario.   Ay. Answer me, is not thy sloth
          Sufficient argument? Thy flattery?   10
          Thy means of feeding?

Mosca.   Heaven be good to me!
          These imputations are too common, sir,
          And eas'ly stuck on virtue when she's poor.
          You are unequal to me, and howe'er
          Your sentence may be righteous, yet you are not,   15
          That, ere you know me, thus proceed in censure.
          St Mark bear witness 'gainst you, 'tis inhuman.

                                        [*He weeps.*]

Bonario. [*Aside*] What? Does he weep? The sign is soft and
          good.
          I do repent me that I was so harsh.

Mosca. 'Tis true that, swayed by strong necessity,   20
          I am enforced to eat my careful bread
          With too much obsequy; 'tis true, beside,
          That I am fain to spin mine own poor raiment

---

3. *happ'ly*] by good chance.

4. *pray . . . way*] please go about your business.

6. *mate*] fellow (used contemptuously).

11. *means of feeding*] i.e. parasitism.

14. *unequal*] (1) unjust; (2) above me in station.

15. *sentence*] judgement; stated opinion.

are not] are not just.

18–19, 35.] Mosca may hear these 'asides', even though they are not directed to him.

21. *careful*] full of care, i.e. hard won.

22. *obsequy*] obsequiousness, humility.

23. *fain*] compelled; but with an ironic suggestion of 'eager' (?).

23–4. *spin . . . observance*] make my living (literally, clothe myself) solely by means of dutiful service.

Out of my mere observance, being not born
To a free fortune; but that I have done   25
Base offices in rending friends asunder,
Dividing families, betraying counsels,
Whispering false lies, or mining men with praises,
Trained their credulity with perjuries,
Corrupted chastity, or am in love   30
With mine own tender ease, but would not rather
Prove the most rugged and laborious course
That might redeem my present estimation,
Let me here perish in all hope of goodness.

Bonario. [*Aside*] This cannot be a personated passion!   35
    [*To him*] I was to blame, so to mistake thy nature;
    Pray thee forgive me, and speak out thy business.

Mosca. Sir, it concerns you; and though I may seem
    At first to make a main offence in manners
    And in my gratitude unto my master,   40
    Yet for the pure love which I bear all right
    And hatred of the wrong, I must reveal it.
    This very hour your father is in purpose
    To disinherit you—

Bonario.   How!

Mosca.   And thrust you forth
    As a mere stranger to his blood. 'Tis true, sir.   45
    The work no way engageth me but as
    I claim an interest in the general state
    Of goodness and true virtue, which I hear
    T' abound in you, and for which mere respect,
    Without a second aim, sir, I have done it.   50

Bonario. This tale hath lost thee much of the late trust
    Thou hadst with me; it is impossible.
    I know not how to lend it any thought,

---

28. *mining*] undermining.
29. *Trained*] led on.
32. *Prove*] experience, undertake.
35. *personated passion*] impersonated or false emotion.
39. *main*] major, serious.
46. *engageth*] concerns.
49. *for . . . respect*] only for this reason.
50. *Without . . . aim*] without ulterior motive.
51–2. *the late . . . me*] the confidence I put in you just a minute ago.
53.] it is inconceivable to me (that).

My father should be so unnatural.

Mosca. It is a confidence that well becomes 55
    Your piety; and formed, no doubt, it is
    From your own simple innocence, which makes
    Your wrong more monstrous and abhorred. But, sir,
    I now will tell you more. This very minute
    It is, or will be, doing; and if you 60
    Shall be but pleased to go with me, I'll bring you—
    I dare not say where you shall see, but—where
    Your ear shall be a witness of the deed;
    Hear yourself written bastard and professed
    The common issue of the earth.

Bonario.   I'm mazed! 65

Mosca. Sir, if I do it not, draw your just sword,
    And score your vengeance on my front and face;
    Mark me your villain. You have too much wrong,
    And I do suffer for you, sir. My heart
    Weeps blood in anguish—

Bonario.   Lead. I follow thee. 70

                        [Exeunt.]

ACT 3   SCENE 3

       [Enter] VOLPONE, NANO, ANDROGYNO,
            [and] CASTRONE.

Volpone. Mosca stays long, methinks.—Bring forth your
    sports
    And help to make the wretched time more sweet.

Nano. Dwarf, fool, and eunuch, well met here we be.
    A question it were now, whether of us three,

---

56. *piety*] filial obligation (Latin *pietas*).

57. *simple*] pure (but with an undertone of 'simpleminded').

65. *The common . . . earth*] of obscure or unknown parentage (Latin *terrae filius*).

    mazed] dazed, stupefied.

67. *score*] mark up, record.

    front] forehead. Bonario actually does this later (see 3.8.3–5, 4.5.83–4).

3.3. Location: Volpone's house.
4. *whether*] which.

Being, all, the known delicates of a rich man,   5
    In pleasing him claim the precedency can?
Castrone. I claim for myself.
Androgyno.   And so doth the fool.
Nano. 'Tis foolish indeed; let me set you both to school.
    First for your dwarf: he's little and witty,
        And everything, as it is little, is pretty;   10
    Else why do men say to a creature of my shape,
        So soon as they see him, 'It's a pretty little ape'?
    And why a pretty 'ape'? But for pleasing imitation
        Of greater men's action, in a ridiculous fashion.
    Beside, this feat body of mine doth not crave   15
        Half the meat, drink, and cloth one of your bulks will
            have.
    Admit your fool's face be the mother of laughter,
        Yet, for his brain, it must always come after;
    And though that do feed him, it's a pitiful case
        His body is beholding to such a bad face.   20
                              (*One knocks.*)
Volpone. Who's there? My couch! Away! Look, Nano, see!
    Give me my caps first.—Go, inquire.
                [*Exeunt* NANO, CASTRONE, *and* ANDROGYNO.]
                [*Volpone gets into bed.*] Now Cupid
    Send it be Mosca, and with fair return!

                    [*Re-enter* NANO.]

Nano. It is the beauteous madam—
Volpone.   Would-be—is it?
Nano. The same.

---

5. *Being . . . delicates*] being all of us, as we are, the acknowledged favourites.

15. *Beside*] besides.
feat] dainty.

16. *bulks*] bodies of large proportion.

18. *for*] as for.
come after] be lesser.

19. *that*] i.e. laughter.
feed him] earn his keep.

20. *beholding*] beholden, indebted.

22–3. *Cupid / Send*] may Cupid grant that.

23. *fair return*] good results, profit; specifically, a good report of Corvino's response.

Volpone.   Now torment on me! Squire her in,   25
        For she will enter or dwell here for ever.
        Nay, quickly, that my fit were past!   [*Exit* NANO.]
                                        I fear
        A second hell too, that my loathing this
        Will quite expel my appetite to the other.
        Would she were taking now her tedious leave!   30
        Lord, how it threats me, what I am to suffer!

ACT 3   SCENE 4

        [*Enter*] NANO [*with*] LADY [POLITIC WOULD-BE].

Lady Politic. [*To Nano*] I thank you, good sir. Pray you signify
        Unto your patron I am here.—This band
        Shows not my neck enough.—I trouble you, sir;
        Let me request you bid one of my women
        Come hither to me. [*Nano goes to the door.*] In good faith,
            I'm dressed   5
        Most favourably today! It is no matter;
        'Tis well enough.

                        [*Enter* 1 Woman.]

                        Look, see, these petulant things,
        How they have done this!
Volpone. [*Aside*]   I do feel the fever
        Ent'ring in at mine ears. Oh, for a charm
        To fright it hence!

---

        25. *Squire*] escort.
        26. *here*] i.e. in the waiting room.
        27. *that . . . past*] so that my painful experience might be over.
        29. *the other*] i.e. Celia.

        3.4.0.1.] Volpone's being in bed presumably allows him to remain unob-
served by Lady Pol until 39, or else she is simply absorbed in her fatuous
concern with her appearance.
        2. *band*] neckband, collar.
        3. *Shows . . . enough*] Venetian dresses were notorious for their low neck-
lines, exposing the breasts.
        5–6. *I'm . . . matter*] i.e. I look like a wreck! Oh, well, what would you
expect.
        7. *things*] i.e. servant women; or the uncooperative curls.

Lady Politic. [*To 1 Woman*] Come nearer. Is this curl   10
   In his right place? Or this? Why is this higher
   Than all the rest? You ha' not washed your eyes yet?
   Or do they not stand even i' your head?
   Where's your fellow? Call her.   [*Exit 1 Woman.*]
Nano. [*Aside*]   Now, St Mark
   Deliver us! Anon she'll beat her women   15
   Because her nose is red.

          [*Re-enter 1 with 2 Woman.*]

Lady Politic.   I pray you, view
   This tire, forsooth. Are all things apt, or no?
2 Woman. One hair a little, here, sticks out, forsooth.
Lady Politic. Does 't so, forsooth! [*To 1 Woman*] And where
     was your dear sight
   When it did so, forsooth? What now! Bird-eyed?   20
   [*To 2 Woman*] And you too? Pray you both approach
     and mend it.   [*They fuss over her.*]
   Now, by that light, I muse you're not ashamed!
   I, that have preached these things so oft unto you,
   Read you the principles, argued all the grounds,
   Disputed every fitness, every grace,   25
   Called you to counsel of so frequent dressings—
Nano. [*Aside*] More carefully than of your fame or honour.
Lady Politic. Made you acquainted what an ample dowry
   The knowledge of these things would be unto you,
   Able, alone, to get you noble husbands   30
   At your return—and you thus to neglect it!

---

11. *his*] its.

12. *You . . . yet?*] i.e. Haven't you even washed the sleep out of your eyes yet, you lazy thing?

13. *even*] focused, balanced.

17. *tire*] headdress, coiffeur. Venetian courtesans of this period wore two curls standing up like horns above the forehead.

20. *forsooth*] Lady Pol caustically repeats the woman's insipid oath in 18.
Bird-eyed?] i.e. Are you looking startled or fearful, with the eyes of a bird sensing danger?

22. *by that light*] by the light of heaven (an oath).
muse] wonder, am surprised.

27. *fame*] reputation.

31. *return*] i.e. return to England.

Besides, you seeing what a curious nation
Th' Italians are, what will they say of me?
'The English lady cannot dress herself.'
Here's a fine imputation to our country! 35
Well, go your ways, and stay i' the next room.
This fucus was too coarse too; it's no matter.
[*To Nano*] Good sir, you'll give 'em entertainment?
[*Exit* NANO *with* Women.]
Volpone. [*Aside*] The storm comes toward me.
Lady Politic. [*Approaching the bed*] How does my Volp?
Volpone. Troubled with noise; I cannot sleep. I dreamt 40
That a strange fury entered now my house
And with the dreadful tempest of her breath
Did cleave my roof asunder.
Lady Politic. Believe me, and I
Had the most fearful dream, could I remember 't—
Volpone. [*Aside*] Out on my fate! I ha' giv'n her the occasion 45
How to torment me: she will tell me hers.
Lady Politic. Methought the golden mediocrity,
Polite, and delicate—
Volpone. Oh, if you do love me,
No more; I sweat and suffer at the mention
Of any dream. Feel how I tremble yet. 50
Lady Politic. Alas, good soul! The passion of the heart.
Seed-pearl were good now, boiled with syrup of apples,
Tincture of gold, and coral, citron pills,

---

32. *curious*] fastidious, particular, discriminating.

37. *fucus*] cosmetic, paste.

39. *Volp*] a brazenly familiar diminutive suggesting, even more plainly
than 'Volpone', the Latin *vulpis*, fox.

47. *golden mediocrity*] Lady Pol's over-reaching Latinate vocabulary results in a travestied form of Horace's 'golden mean'.

51–63.] Lady Pol officiously offers cures for 'passion of the heart', whether
that affliction be heartburn or palpitations or depression: seed-pearl as a
heart stimulant, syrup of apples for heart and stomach ailments, tincture
of gold as *aurum potabile* (see I.4.73 and note), coral to strengthen the heart
and drive away melancholia, elecampane or horse-heal as a stimulant,
myrobalanes (plum-like fruit) as a tonic, burnt silk for smallpox, amber
(ambergris) to disguise the flavour of bitter medicines, muscadel wine to
dissolve medicines, saffron and cloves as spices used in medicines, musk and
bugloss (borage) as heart stimulants, mint as a general strengthener, barley-
meal to thicken the preparation, and scarlet cloths used to apply poultices.

Your elecampane root, myrobalanes—
Volpone. [*Aside*] Ay me, I have ta'n a grasshopper by the wing!   55
Lady Politic. Burnt silk, and amber. You have muscadel
    Good i' the house—
Volpone.   You will not drink and part?
Lady Politic. No, fear not that. I doubt we shall not get
    Some English saffron—half a dram would serve;
    Your sixteen cloves, a little musk, dried mints,   60
    Bugloss, and barley-meal—
Volpone. [*Aside*]   She's in again.
    Before, I feigned diseases; now I have one.
Lady Politic. And these applied with a right scarlet cloth—
Volpone. [*Aside*] Another flood of words! A very torrent!
Lady Politic. Shall I, sir, make you a poultice?
Volpone.   No, no, no.   65
    I'm very well; you need prescribe no more.
Lady Politic. I have, a little, studied physic; but now
    I'm all for music, save i' the forenoons
    An hour or two for painting. I would have
    A lady, indeed, t' have all letters and arts,   70
    Be able to discourse, to write, to paint,
    But principal, as Plato holds, your music—
    And so does wise Pythagoras, I take it—
    Is your true rapture, when there is concent
    In face, in voice, and clothes, and is, indeed,   75
    Our sex's chiefest ornament.
Volpone.   The poet

55.] i.e. Alas, I have unwittingly incited Lady Pol to do something she was quite prepared to do even without encouragement.

72–3.] Plato recommends music, in *The Republic*, to inspire courage and moderation. On Pythagoras and music, see 1.2.26–7 and note.

74. *concent*] harmony.

76–81. *The poet . . . Hadria*] Euripides, Sophocles, Homer, and St Paul all express the commonplace that silence is a woman's best grace. Lady Pol's fatuous guesses are all chronologically way off target in attempting to name a poet 'As old in time as Plato'; they range in date from Dante Alighieri (1265–1321) and Francisco Petrarca (1304–74) to Giovanni Battista Guarini (1537–1612), author of *Il Pastor Fido* (86). Torquato Tasso wrote *Jerusalem Delivered*, Ludovico Ariosto *Orlando Furioso*. Pietro Aretino was best known for his pornographic sonnets, as Lady Pol notes at 96–7. Cieco di Hadria, 'the blind man of Adria', Luigi Groto (1541–85), is a distinctly minor name in this company; Lady Pol (and Jonson) are showing off.

As old in time as Plato, and as knowing,
Says that your highest female grace is silence.
Lady Politic. Which o' your poets? Petrarch? Or Tasso? Or
    Dante?
    Guarini? Ariosto? Aretine?   80
    Cieco di Hadria? I have read them all.
Volpone. [*Aside*] Is everything a cause to my destruction?
Lady Politic. I think I ha' two or three of 'em about me.
Volpone. [*Aside*] The sun, the sea, will sooner both stand still
    Than her eternal tongue! Nothing can scape it.   85
Lady Politic. [*Producing a book*] Here's *Pastor Fido*—
Volpone. [*Aside*]   Profess obstinate silence;
    That's now my safest.
Lady Politic.   All our English writers,
    I mean such as are happy in th' Italian,
    Will deign to steal out of this author mainly,
    Almost as much as from Montaignié.   90
    He has so modern and facile a vein,
    Fitting the time and catching the court ear!
    Your Petrarch is more passionate, yet he,
    In days of sonneting, trusted 'em with much.
    Dante is hard, and few can understand him.   95
    But, for a desperate wit, there's Aretine!
    Only his pictures are a little obscene—
    You mark me not?
Volpone.   Alas, my mind's perturbed.
Lady Politic. Why, in such cases, we must cure ourselves,
    Make use of our philosophy—
Volpone.   Ohimè!   100
Lady Politic. And, as we find our passions do rebel,
    Encounter 'em with reason, or divert 'em

---

88. *happy . . . Italian*] able to command the Italian tongue.

90. *Montaignié*] Michel de Montaigne, whose *Essays* were translated by John Florio in 1603. Pronounced here in four syllables.

91. *facile*] fluent.

94. *trusted . . . much*] entrusted to later poets an impressive literary heritage.

96. *desperate*] outrageous.

97.] Aretino's pornographic *Sonnetti Lussuriosi*, 1523 (see 76–81 n. above), were written as a commentary on sixteen obscene drawings by Giulio Romano, referred to also at 3.7.60 below.

100. Ohimè!] Italian for 'Alas!' Q reads 'O'ay mee', F 'O'y me'.

By giving scope unto some other humour
Of lesser danger, as in politic bodies
There's nothing more doth overwhelm the judgement   105
And clouds the understanding than too much
Settling and fixing and, as 'twere, subsiding
Upon one object. For the incorporating
Of these same outward things into that part
Which we call mental leaves some certain faeces   110
That stop the organs, and, as Plato says,
Assassinates our knowledge.

Volpone. [*Aside*]   Now, the spirit
Of patience help me!

Lady Politic.   Come, in faith, I must
Visit you more a-days, and make you well.
Laugh and be lusty.

Volpone. [*Aside*]   My good angel save me!   115

Lady Politic. There was but one sole man in all the world
With whom I e'er could sympathize; and he
Would lie you often three, four hours together
To hear me speak, and be sometime so rapt
As he would answer me quite from the purpose,   120
Like you—and you are like him, just. I'll discourse,
An 't be but only, sir, to bring you asleep,
How we did spend our time and loves together,
For some six years.

Volpone.   Oh, oh, oh, oh, oh, oh!

Lady Politic. For we were *coaetanei*, and brought up—   125

Volpone. Some power, some fate, some fortune rescue me!

---

104. *politic bodies*] sagacious persons. Lady Pol is garbling the common-place comparison of man the microcosm and the state, or body politic.

107.] separating, congealing, and precipitating. Lady Pol applies technical terms of alchemy to the notion of bodily 'humour' in a pretentious diagnosis of Volpone's professed mental perturbation.

110. *faeces*] dregs.

111. *Plato*] Lady Pol drags Plato in here at random.

114. *more a-days*] more often.

115. *lusty*] merry; healthful; lustful.

118. *lie you*] lie.

119. *rapt*] enraptured; carried away by strong emotion; buried in thought. Perhaps with overtones of 'raped'.

120. *from the purpose*] off the point.

125. coaetanei] of the same age (Latin).

ACT 3   SCENE 5

[*Enter*] MOSCA.

Mosca. God save you, madam.
Lady Politic.   Good sir.
Volpone.   Mosca? Welcome!
    Welcome to my redemption.
Mosca.   Why, sir?
Volpone. [*Aside to Mosca*]   Oh,
    Rid me of this my torture quickly, there,
    My madam with the everlasting voice!
    The bells in time of pestilence ne'er made   5
    Like noise, or were in that perpetual motion!
    The cockpit comes not near it. All my house
    But now steamed like a bath with her thick breath.
    A lawyer could not have been heard, nor scarce
    Another woman, such a hail of words   10
    She has let fall. For hell's sake, rid her hence.
Mosca. [*Aside*] Has she presented?
Volpone. [*Aside*]   Oh, I do not care;
    I'll take her absence upon any price,
    With any loss.
Mosca. [*To Lady Politic*] Madam—
Lady Politic.   I ha' brought your patron
    A toy, a cap here, of mine own work—
Mosca.   'Tis well.   15
    I had forgot to tell you I saw your knight
    Where you'd little think it—
Lady Politic.   Where?
Mosca.   Marry,
    Where yet, if you make haste, you may apprehend him,
    Rowing upon the water in a gondole
    With the most cunning courtesan of Venice.   20

    3.5.5–6.] Church bells in London rang almost continuously for the dead in
times of plague, of which there had been a severe visitation in 1603.

    7. *cockpit*] Several cockpits attested to the popularity of this fashionable
and noisy sport.

    12. *presented*] given a present.

    15. *toy*] trifle.

    work] embroidery.

    19. *gondole*] gondola.

Lady Politic. Is 't true?
Mosca.   Pursue 'em, and believe your eyes.
    Leave me to make your gift.   [*Exit* LADY POLITIC.]
                      I knew 'twould take,
    For lightly, they that use themselves most licence
    Are still most jealous.
Volpone.   Mosca, hearty thanks
    For thy quick fiction and delivery of me.   25
    Now, to my hopes, what sayst thou?

          [*Re-enter* LADY POLITIC.]

Lady Politic.   But do you hear, sir?
Volpone. [*Aside*] Again! I fear a paroxysm.
Lady Politic.   Which way
    Rowed they together?
Mosca.   Toward the Rialto.
Lady Politic. I pray you, lend me your dwarf.
Mosca.   I pray you, take him.
                    [*Exit* LADY POLITIC.]
    Your hopes, sir, are like happy blossoms: fair,   30
    And promise timely fruit, if you will stay
    But the maturing. Keep you at your couch.
    Corbaccio will arrive straight with the will;
    When he is gone, I'll tell you more.   [*Exit.*]
Volpone.   My blood,
    My spirits are returned; I am alive;   35
    And, like your wanton gamester at primero,
    Whose thought had whispered to him 'not go less',
    Methinks I lie, and draw—for an encounter.
          [*He draws the curtains across his bed.*]

---

    23. *lightly*] commonly; here with the suggestion too of 'wantonly'. *Licence*
has the same resonance: (1) liberty to act; (2) licentiousness.
    24. *still*] always.
    26. *hopes*] i.e. hopes of seducing Celia.
    28. *Rialto*] commercial centre of Venice.
    36. *wanton gamester*] (1) reckless gambler; (2) lecherous woman-chaser.
primero] a card game rather like poker.
    37. *not go less*] in primero, to lay the highest wager possible.
    38.] terms from primero given here a sexual ambivalence: 'lie', lay or place
the bet; 'draw', draw a card; 'encounter', have the cards match for a winning
suit. *Draw* suggests that Volpone draws the curtains to hide himself, lying in
wait for the encounter.

Act 3   Scene 6

[*Enter*] MOSCA [*with*] BONARIO.

Mosca. [*Indicating a hiding place*] Sir, here concealed, you
    may hear all. But pray you
    Have patience, sir.   *One knocks.*
               The same's your father knocks.
    I am compelled to leave you.
                    [*He goes towards the knocking.*]
Bonario.   Do so. Yet
    Cannot my thought imagine this a truth.
                      [*Bonario conceals himself.*]

Act 3   Scene 7

MOSCA [*admits*] CORVINO [*and*] CELIA.

Mosca. Death on me! You are come too soon. What meant
    you?
    Did not I say I would send?
Corvino.   Yes, but I feared
    You might forget it, and then they prevent us.
Mosca. Prevent? [*Aside*] Did e'er man haste so for his horns?
    A courtier would not ply it so for a place.   5
    [*To Corvino*] Well, now there's no helping it, stay here;
    I'll presently return.   [*Mosca goes to Bonario.*]
Corvino.   Where are you, Celia?
    You know not wherefore I have brought you hither?
Celia. Not well, except you told me.
Corvino.   Now I will:
    Hark hither.   [*They talk apart.*]
Mosca. (*To Bonario*) Sir, your father hath sent word   10
    It will be half an hour ere he come;
    And therefore, if you please to walk the while
    Into that gallery—at the upper end

    3.7.3. *prevent*] act before (Latin *praevenire*), thwart.
    4. *horns*] cuckold's horns.
    5. *place*] position at court.
    9. *except . . . me*] (1) except what you have already told me; (2) unless you
were to tell me.

There are some books to entertain the time;
And I'll take care no man shall come unto you, sir.   15
Bonario. Yes, I will stay there. [*Aside*] I do doubt this fellow.
                                                              [*Exit.*]
Mosca. There, he is far enough; he can hear nothing.
    And for his father, I can keep him off.
              [*Mosca goes to Volpone's bed, opens the curtains,
                                  and whispers to him.*]
Corvino. [*To Celia*] Nay, now, there is no starting back, and
        therefore
    Resolve upon it; I have so decreed.   20
    It must be done. Nor would I move 't afore,
    Because I would avoid all shifts and tricks
    That might deny me.
Celia.   Sir, let me beseech you,
    Affect not these strange trials. If you doubt
    My chastity, why, lock me up for ever;   25
    Make me the heir of darkness. Let me live
    Where I may please your fears, if not your trust.
Corvino. Believe it, I have no such humour, I.
    All that I speak I mean; yet I am not mad,
    Not horn-mad, see you? Go to, show yourself   30
    Obedient, and a wife.
Celia.   O heaven!
Corvino.   I say it,
    Do so.
Celia.   Was this the train?
Corvino.   I've told you reasons:
    What the physicians have set down; how much
    It may concern me; what my engagements are;

---

21. *move*] urge, suggest.

22. *shifts*] evasions, stratagems.

24. *Affect*] (1) seek to obtain, insist on; (2) make a pretence of insisting on.

  strange trials] i.e. extraordinary tests (of my chastity).

27. *please*] satisfy.

30. *horn-mad*] (1) sexually jealous; (2) eager to be cuckolded.

32. *train*] trick, trap.

33. *set down*] declared in written (medical) opinion.

34. *engagements*] commitments, as gifts to Volpone or perhaps as financial commitments in general.

My means, and the necessity of those means 35
For my recovery. Wherefore, if you be
Loyal and mine, be won; respect my venture.
Celia. Before your honour?
Corvino.　　　　　　　　　Honour! Tut, a breath.
There's no such thing in nature; a mere term
Invented to awe fools. What is my gold 40
The worse for touching? Clothes, for being looked on?
Why, this 's no more. An old, decrepit wretch,
That has no sense, no sinew; takes his meat
With others' fingers; only knows to gape
When you do scald his gums; a voice; a shadow; 45
And what can this man hurt you?
Celia.　　　　　　　　　Lord! What spirit
Is this hath entered him?
Corvino.　　　　　　　　And for your fame,
That's such a jig; as if I would go tell it,
Cry it, on the Piazza! Who shall know it
But he that cannot speak it, and this fellow 50
Whose lips are i' my pocket, save yourself?
If you'll proclaim 't, you may. I know no other
Should come to know it.
Celia.　　　　　　　Are heaven and saints then nothing?
Will they be blind, or stupid?
Corvino.　　　　　　　　　　How?

---

35. *means*] opportunity or course of action by which an object can be obtained; less probably, 'financial resources'.

36. *recovery*] getting back the value of the commitments already made, and a regaining of financial security in a larger sense.

43. *sense*] sensory perception or capability.

47. *him*] Corvino.

for your fame] as for your reputation.

48. *jig*] farce, trifle, joke of an excuse.

49. *Cry*] advertise.

50. *he*] Volpone.

this fellow] Mosca.

51. *Whose . . . pocket*] whose silence I have bought.

save] except.

53. *Should*] who would have opportunity to.

53-4. *Are . . . stupid?*] i.e. You say that no others will come to know this shameful thing, but the heavens and saints are neither unobservant or unable to understand what this would mean.

Celia.   Good sir,
    Be jealous still: emulate them, and think   55
    What hate they burn with toward every sin.
Corvino. I grant you, if I thought it were a sin
    I would not urge you. Should I offer this
    To some young Frenchman or hot Tuscan blood
    That had read Aretine, conned all his prints,   60
    Knew every quirk within lust's labyrinth,
    And were professed critic in lechery,
    And I would look upon him and applaud him,
    This were a sin; but here 'tis contrary,
    A pious work, mere charity, for physic,   65
    And honest polity to assure mine own.
Celia. O heaven! Canst thou suffer such a change?
Volpone. [*Aside to Mosca*] Thou art mine honour, Mosca,
        and my pride,
    My joy, my tickling, my delight! Go, bring 'em.
Mosca. [*Advancing*] Please you draw near, sir.
Corvino.   Come on! What?   70
                                    [*Celia resists.*]
    You will not be rebellious? By that light—
                            [*He drags her to the bed.*]
Mosca. [*To Volpone*] Sir, Signor Corvino here is come to see
        you—
Volpone. Oh!
Mosca.   And, hearing of the consultation had
    So lately for your health, is come to offer,
    Or rather, sir, to prostitute—
Corvino.   Thanks, sweet Mosca.   75
Mosca. Freely, unasked, or unentreated—

---

57. *I grant you*] I concede you that point.
60.] See 3.4.97 and note.
conned] learned by heart.
62. *professed critic*] connoisseur, qualified specialist.
63. *And I would*] and if I were to.
65. *mere . . . physic*] simply a charitable cure.
66.] an honourable device to make sure the recovery of my investments
and Volpone's legacy.
75. *prostitute*] offer with complete and self-denying devotion; with an
obvious ironic play on the more usual meaning.

Corvino.   Well.

Mosca. As the true, fervent instance of his love,
    His own most fair and proper wife, the beauty
    Only of price in Venice—

Corvino.   'Tis well urged.

Mosca. To be your comfortress, and to preserve you.   80

Volpone. Alas, I'm past already! Pray you, thank him
    For his good care and promptness. But, for that,
    'Tis a vain labour, e'en to fight 'gainst heaven,
    Applying fire to a stone, [*Coughing*] Uh! Uh! Uh! Uh!
    Making a dead leaf grow again. I take   85
    His wishes gently, though; and you may tell him
    What I've done for him. Marry, my state is hopeless!
    Will him to pray for me, and t' use his fortune
    With reverence when he comes to 't.

Mosca. [*To Corvino*]   Do you hear, sir?
    Go to him with your wife.

Corvino. [*To Celia*]   Heart of my father!   90
    Wilt thou persist thus? Come, I pray thee, come.
    Thou seest 'tis nothing, Celia. By this hand,
    I shall grow violent. Come, do 't, I say.

Celia. Sir, kill me rather. I will take down poison,
    Eat burning coals, do anything—

Corvino.   Be damned!   95
    Heart! I will drag thee hence home by the hair,
    Cry thee a strumpet through the streets, rip up
    Thy mouth unto thine ears, and slit thy nose,
    Like a raw rochet!—Do not tempt me; come,
    Yield; I am loath—Death! I will buy some slave   100
    Whom I will kill, and bind thee to him, alive,

---

76. *Well*] Corvino modestly accepts Mosca's accolade, and indicates his approval.

78. *proper*] (1) comely; (2) respectable; (3) exclusively his; (4) suitable.

79. *Only of price*] of unique worth.

81. *past*] beyond cure.

82. *for that*] as for that.

86. *gently*] kindly.

90. *Heart . . . father!*] an oath: by my father's heart.

95. *Eat . . . coals*] commit suicide by swallowing fire, like Brutus's wife, Portia, a paragon of married chastity (see *JC*, 4.3.155).

99. *rochet*] a type of fish, the red gurnard.

100-1. *I . . . alive*] Cf. Tarquin's threat to Lucrece in Shakespeare's *The Rape of Lucrece*, 515-17.

And at my window hang you forth, devising
Some monstrous crime, which I, in capital letters,
Will eat into thy flesh with aquafortis
And burning cor'sives, on this stubborn breast.   105
Now, by the blood thou hast incensed, I'll do 't!
Celia. Sir, what you please, you may; I am your martyr.
Corvino. Be not thus obstinate; I ha' not deserved it.
Think who it is entreats you. Pray thee, sweet;
Good faith, thou shalt have jewels, gowns, attires,   110
What thou wilt think and ask. Do but go kiss him.
Or touch him, but. For my sake. At my suit.
This once. [*She refuses.*] No? Not? I shall remember this.
Will you disgrace me thus? D' you thirst my undoing?
Mosca. Nay, gentle lady, be advised.
Corvino.   No, no.   115
She has watched her time. God's precious, this is scurvy,
'Tis very scurvy; and you are—
Mosca.   Nay, good sir.
Corvino. An errant locust, by heaven, a locust. Whore,
Crocodile, that hast thy tears prepared,
Expecting how thou'lt bid 'em flow!
Mosca.   Nay, pray you, sir.   120
She will consider.
Celia.   Would my life would serve
To satisfy—
Corvino.   'Sdeath! If she would but speak to him,
And save my reputation, 'twere somewhat;
But spitefully to affect my utter ruin!
Mosca. Ay, now you've put your fortune in her hands.   125
Why, i' faith, it is her modesty; I must quit her.

---

104. *aquafortis*] nitric acid, used in etching.
105. *cor'sives*] corrosives.
111. *What . . . ask*] whatever you can think to ask for.
116. *watched her time*] i.e. waited for her chance to play this dirty trick.
God's precious] an oath: by God's (Christ's) precious blood.
118. *errant*] wandering, promiscuous; suggesting also 'arrant'.
locust] i.e. a plague, like the plagues of ancient Egypt in Genesis, capable of eating up Corvino's fortune.
120. *Expecting*] waiting to see, calculating.
121. *consider*] reconsider.
122. *'Sdeath*] by this (God's) death. (An oath).
124. *affect*] seek to attain.
126. *quit*] acquit, clear.

If you were absent, she would be more coming;
I know it, and dare undertake for her.
What woman can before her husband? Pray you,
Let us depart and leave her here.
Corvino.   Sweet Celia,   130
Thou mayst redeem all yet; I'll say no more.
If not, esteem yourself as lost.
                    [*She begins to leave with him.*]
                         —Nay, stay there.
                    [*Exeunt* CORVINO *and* MOSCA.]
Celia. O God, and his good angels! Whither, whither,
Is shame fled human breasts, that with such ease
Men dare put off your honours and their own?   135
Is that which ever was a cause of life
Now placed beneath the basest circumstance,
And modesty an exile made, for money?
                    He [*Volpone*] *leaps off from his couch.*
Volpone. Ay, in Corvino, and such earth-fed minds,
That never tasted the true heav'n of love.   140
Assure thee, Celia, he that would sell thee,
Only for hope of gain, and that uncertain,
He would have sold his part of Paradise
For ready money, had he met a copeman.
Why art thou mazed to see me thus revived?   145
Rather applaud thy beauty's miracle;
'Tis thy great work, that hath, not now alone,
But sundry times raised me in several shapes,
And but this morning, like a mountebank,
To see thee at thy window. Ay, before   150

---

127. *coming*] forthcoming; sexually responsive.

129. *can*] can do it, engage in sex.

135. *your honours*] the honour enjoined by God and his angels.

136. *that . . . life*] (1) honourable wedlock, the only source of life in its truest sense; (2) sex.

137.] now subordinated to the lowest of concerns.

144. *copeman*] (1) merchant (with the implication of 'devil'); (2) someone as base as himself (?).

145. *mazed*] amazed, bewildered.

147. *not now alone*] not only just now.

148. *raised . . . shapes*] with suggestion of erotic arousal.

149. *but*] only.

I would have left my practice for thy love,
In varying figures I would have contended
With the blue Proteus or the hornèd flood.
Now art thou welcome.

Celia.   Sir!
Volpone.   Nay, fly me not.
Nor let thy false imagination   155
That I was bedrid make thee think I am so;
Thou shalt not find it. I am, now, as fresh,
As hot, as high, and in as jovial plight
As when, in that so celebrated scene
At recitation of our comedy   160
For entertainment of the great Valois,
I acted young Antinous, and attracted
The eyes and ears of all the ladies present,
T' admire each graceful gesture, note, and footing.

                                        [*He sings.*]

SONG

Come, my Celia, let us prove,   165
While we can, the sports of love.
Time will not be ours for ever;
He, at length, our good will sever.
Spend not then his gifts in vain.
Suns that set may rise again;   170

---

151. *practice*] constant or habitual endeavour; with overtones of 'scheming'.

152. *figures*] shapes, disguises.

153. *blue Proteus*] god of the wine-dark sea.

hornèd flood] The river-god Achelous, son of Oceanus, changed himself into a serpent, a bull, and a man with the head of an ox when he fought with Hercules for the favour of Dejanira (Ovid, *Met.*, 8.31–7). The horns suggest virility.

158. *jovial*] Jove-like, both regal and amorous. (Cf. Epilogue 6.)

160–1.] at performance of our play (in Venice, 1574) before Henry of Valois, the future Henry III of France.

162. *Antinous*] the wooer of Penelope in Homer's *Odyssey*, who figures as a paragon of courtly love in John Davies's *Orchestra* (1596); or, less probably, the beautiful youth who was minion to the Emperor Hadrian.

164. *footing*] dance step.

165–82.] The song is based on Catullus's Ode 5, but lines 175–82 are interpolated by Volpone (and Jonson).

165. *prove*] experience, try.

168. *our good will sever*] will end our well-being.

But if once we lose this light,
'Tis with us perpetual night.
Why should we defer our joys?
Fame and rumour are but toys.
Cannot we delude the eyes   175
Of a few poor household spies?
Or his easier ears beguile,
Thus removèd by our wile?
'Tis no sin love's fruits to steal,
But the sweet thefts to reveal: 180
To be taken, to be seen,
These have crimes accounted been.

Celia. Some serene blast me, or dire lightning strike
    This my offending face!

Volpone.   Why droops my Celia?
    Thou hast in place of a base husband found   185
    A worthy lover. Use thy fortune well,
    With secrecy and pleasure. See, behold
    What thou art queen of; [*Showing her the treasure*] not
        in expectation,
    As I feed others, but possessed and crowned.
    See, here, a rope of pearl, and each more orient   190
    Than that the brave Egyptian queen caroused.
    Dissolve and drink 'em. See, a carbuncle
    May put out both the eyes of our St Mark;

---

174. *toys*] trifles.

177–8.] i.e. or craftily deprive some easily deluded person (such as
Corvino) of the ability to hear our secret talk.

179–82.] i.e. The only crime is to be caught, not the stealing (of sexual
pleasure) itself.

181. *taken*] caught in the act.

183. *serene*] a fine mist of rain falling after sunset in hot countries, here
regarded as noxious.

184. *offending*] To Celia, her beauty offends because it provokes lust.

188. *expectation*] i.e. mere promises of future reward.

190. *orient*] rare and fine, as at 1.5.9.

191.] i.e. than that which Cleopatra caused to be dissolved in vinegar, for
her to drink off in a competition of extravagance with Mark Antony.

192–3. *a carbuncle . . . Mark*] a ruby capable of outshining two famous
Venetian rubies. (Two such carbuncles, one in the Treasury and one lodged
in the Doge's crown, may have been known as 'St Mark's eyes'.)

A diamond would have bought Lollia Paulina
When she came in like starlight, hid with jewels   195
That were the spoils of provinces. Take these,
And wear, and lose 'em; yet remains an earring
To purchase them again, and this whole state.
A gem but worth a private patrimony
Is nothing; we will eat such at a meal.   200
The heads of parrots, tongues of nightingales,
The brains of peacocks and of ostriches
Shall be our food, and, could we get the phoenix,
Though nature lost her kind, she were our dish.
Celia. Good sir, these things might move a mind affected   205
With such delights; but I, whose innocence
Is all I can think wealthy, or worth th' enjoying,
And which, once lost, I have nought to lose beyond it,
Cannot be taken with these sensual baits.
If you have conscience—
Volpone.   'Tis the beggar's virtue.   210
If thou hast wisdom, hear me, Celia.
Thy baths shall be the juice of July-flowers,
Spirit of roses and of violets,
The milk of unicorns, and panthers' breath
Gathered in bags and mixed with Cretan wines.   215

194–6. *A diamond . . . provinces*] a diamond that would have been able to buy the famous consort of Caligula, glittering with precious jewels ransacked from provinces that the Romans had conquered. (The beautiful Lollia Paulina was divorced by Caligula in A.D. 39, was foiled by Agrippina in an attempt to marry Claudius, and was driven into exile and suicide in A.D. 49.)

198. *state*] costly display; possibly also, the Venetian state.

201–2.] The details are from the banquets of the decadent emperor Heliogabalus.

203. *phoenix*] a unique mythical bird that was thought to incinerate itself every five hundred years and rise from its own ashes.

204. *Though . . . kind*] i.e. even if it became extinct.

207. *wealthy*] valuable.

212. *July-flowers*] gillyflowers, clove-scented pinks.

213. *Spirit*] distillations.

214. *milk of unicorns*] The mythical unicorn was associated with virginity and was chaste.

panthers' breath] The panther was supposed to attract its victims with its breath, then destroy them.

Our drink shall be preparèd gold and amber,
Which we will take until my roof whirl round
With the vertigo; and my dwarf shall dance,
My eunuch sing, my fool make up the antic,
Whilst we, in changèd shapes, act Ovid's tales,   220
Thou like Europa now and I like Jove,
Then I like Mars and thou like Erycine;
So of the rest, till we have quite run through
And wearied all the fables of the gods.
Then will I have thee in more modern forms,   225
Attirèd like some sprightly dame of France,
Brave Tuscan lady, or proud Spanish beauty;
Sometimes unto the Persian Sophy's wife,
Or the Grand Signor's mistress; and, for change,
To one of our most artful courtesans,   230
Or some quick Negro, or cold Russian;
And I will meet thee in as many shapes,
Where we may so transfuse our wand'ring souls
Out at our lips and score up sums of pleasures,
[*He sings.*] That the curious shall not know   235
        How to tell them as they flow,
        And the envious, when they find
        What their number is, be pined.
Celia. [*Struggling*] If you have ears that will be pierced—or
    eyes
That can be opened—a heart may be touched—   240
Or any part that yet sounds man about you—

---

219. *antic*] grotesque dance or pageant.
220. *Ovid's tales*] i.e. the *Metamorphoses*.
221.] Zeus disguised himself as a bull to woo Europa.
222. *Erycine*] i.e. Venus, who had a temple on Mount Eryx in Sicily. The
affair of Ares and Aphrodite (Mars and Venus) is described in Homer's
Odyssey, Book 8.
224. *wearied*] exhausted, completely used up.
228. *Sophy*] Shah, or ruler.
229. *Grand Signor*] Sultan of Turkey.
231. *quick*] lively (with a sexual connotation here).
233. *transfuse*] cause to flow from one to another.
235–8.] This song, like that at 2.7.165–82, is from Catullus, Ode 5.
236. *tell*] count.
238. *pined*] vexed, pained.
241. *sounds man*] proclaims you a man.

If you have touch of holy saints—or heaven—
Do me the grace to let me scape.—If not,
Be bountiful and kill me.—You do know
I am a creature hither ill betrayed   245
By one whose shame I would forget it were.—
If you will deign me neither of these graces,
Yet feed your wrath, sir, rather than your lust—
It is a vice comes nearer manliness—
And punish that unhappy crime of nature,   250
Which you miscall my beauty—flay my face,
Or poison it with ointments for seducing
Your blood to this rebellion.—Rub these hands
With what may cause an eating leprosy,
E'en to my bones and marrow—anything   255
That may disfavour me, save in my honour—
And I will kneel to you, pray for you, pay down
A thousand hourly vows, sir, for your health—
Report, and think you virtuous—
Volpone.   Think me cold,
Frozen, and impotent, and so report me?   260
That I had Nestor's hernia, thou wouldst think.
I do degenerate and abuse my nation
To play with opportunity thus long.
I should have done the act, and then have parleyed.
Yield, or I'll force thee.
Celia.   O, just God!
Volpone.   In vain—   265
    He [Bonario] leaps out from where Mosca had placed him.
Bonario. Forbear, foul ravisher, libidinous swine!
Free the forced lady or thou diest, impostor.
But that I am loath to snatch thy punishment
Out of the hand of justice, thou shouldst yet
Be made the timely sacrifice of vengeance   270
Before this altar and this dross, thy idol.
                                    [He indicates the treasure.]

---

253. *rebellion*] rebellion of the flesh.
256. *disfavour*] disfigure.
261. *Nestor's hernia*] The aged Nestor served as one of the Greek commanders against Troy. The hernia suggests impotence.
262. *my nation*] i.e. the Italians' reputation for irresistible virility.

Lady, let's quit the place; it is the den
Of villainy. Fear nought, you have a guard;
And he ere long shall meet his just reward.

> [*Exit with* CELIA.]

Volpone. Fall on me, roof, and bury me in ruin;   275
Become my grave, that wert my shelter! Oh,
I am unmasked, unspirited, undone,
Betrayed to beggary, to infamy—

ACT 3   SCENE 8

> [*Enter*] MOSCA [*bleeding*].

Mosca. Where shall I run, most wretched shame of men,
To beat out my unlucky brains?
Volpone.   Here, here.
What! Dost thou bleed?
Mosca.   Oh, that his well-driv'n sword
Had been so courteous to have cleft me down
Unto the navel, ere I lived to see   5
My life, my hopes, my spirits, my patron, all
Thus desperately engagèd by my error!
Volpone. Woe on thy fortune!
Mosca.   And my follies, sir.
Volpone. Th' hast made me miserable.
Mosca.   And myself, sir.
Who would have thought he would have hearkened so?   10
Volpone. What shall we do?
Mosca.   I know not. If my heart
Could expiate the mischance, I'd pluck it out.
Will you be pleased to hang me, or cut my throat?
And I'll requite you, sir. Let's die like Romans,
Since we have lived like Grecians.   *They knock without.*

---

274. *he*] Volpone.
277. *unspirited*] dejected, deflated, with suggestion of detumescence.

3.8.3. *Dost . . . bleed?*] Mosca has been wounded in the face (see 4.5.83–4).
7. *engagèd*] involved, entangled.
10. *he*] Bonario.
hearkened] eavesdropped.
14. *like Romans*] i.e. falling on our swords.
15. *like Grecians*] i.e. in dissipated revelry.

Volpone.   Hark, who's there?   15
   I hear some footing: officers, the *Saffi*,
   Come to apprehend us! I do feel the brand
   Hissing already at my forehead; now,
   Mine ears are boring.
Mosca.   To your couch, sir; you
   Make that place good, however. [*Volpone lies down.*]
     Guilty men   20
   Suspect what they deserve still. [*He opens the door.*]
     Signor Corbaccio!

ACT 3   SCENE 9

   [*Enter*] CORBACCIO, [*with*] VOLTORE [*behind, unseen*].

Corbaccio. Why, how now, Mosca?
Mosca.   Oh, undone, amazed, sir.
   Your son, I know not by what accident,
   Acquainted with your purpose to my patron
   Touching your will and making him your heir,
   Entered our house with violence, his sword drawn,   5
   Sought for you, called you wretch, unnatural,
   Vowed he would kill you.
Corbaccio.   Me?
Mosca.   Yes, and my patron.
Corbaccio. This act shall disinherit him indeed.
   Here is the will.   [*He gives the will to Mosca.*]
Mosca.   'Tis well, sir.

---

16. *footing*] footsteps.
Saffi] bailiffs.
17–19. *brand . . . boring*] Branding, and cropping (rather than piercing) of ears, were common punishments.
19–20. *you . . . however*] (1) you must maintain the role of invalid, whatever happens (or 'at least'); (2) that role suits you, at least.
21. *Suspect*] anticipate with dread.

3.9.1. *amazed*] confused, stupefied.
2. *accident*] happenstance.
4. *Touching*] concerning.
8. *disinherit him indeed*] i.e. disinherit Bonario permanently, not just as a ruse to trick Volpone.

Corbaccio. Right and well.
  Be you as careful now for me.
Mosca. My life, sir, 10
  Is not more tendered; I am only yours.
Corbaccio. How does he? Will he die shortly, think'st thou?
Mosca. I fear
  He'll outlast May.
Corbaccio. Today?
Mosca. No, last out May, sir!
Corbaccio. Couldst thou not gi' him a dram?
Mosca. Oh, by no means, sir.
Corbaccio. Nay, I'll not bid you.
Voltore. [*Coming forward*] This is a knave, I see. 15
Mosca. [*Aside*] How! Signor Voltore! Did he hear me?
Voltore. Parasite!
Mosca. Who's that? Oh, sir, most timely welcome—
Voltore. Scarce
  To the discovery of your tricks, I fear.
  You are his only? And mine also? Are you not?
Mosca. Who? I, sir? [*They speak privately.*]
Voltore. You, sir. What device is this 20
  About a will?
Mosca. A plot for you, sir.
Voltore. Come,
  Put not your foists upon me; I shall scent 'em.
Mosca. Did you not hear it?
Voltore. Yes, I hear Corbaccio
  Hath made your patron, there, his heir.
Mosca. 'Tis true,
  By my device, drawn to it by my plot, 25
  With hope—
Voltore. Your patron should reciprocate?
  And you have promised?

---

10. *careful*] solicitous.
11. *tendered*] cared for tenderly, cherished.
14. *dram*] dose of poison.
15. *This*] i.e. Mosca.
17–18. *Scarce . . . tricks*] scarcely in time to discover what you are up to.
20. *device*] ruse, trick.
22. *foists*] (1) dishonest tricks; (2) fusty smells, farts (hence, 'scent 'em').

Mosca.   For your good I did, sir.
    Nay, more, I told his son, brought, hid him here,
    Where he might hear his father pass the deed,
    Being persuaded to it by this thought, sir,   30
    That the unnaturalness, first, of the act,
    And then his father's oft disclaiming in him—
    Which I did mean t' help on—would sure enrage him
    To do some violence upon his parent,
    On which the law should take sufficient hold,   35
    And you be stated in a double hope.
    Truth be my comfort and my conscience,
    My only aim was to dig you a fortune
    Out of these two old, rotten sepulchres—
Voltore. I cry thee mercy, Mosca.
Mosca.   Worth your patience   40
    And your great merit, sir. And see the change!
Voltore. Why, what success?
Mosca.   Most hapless! You must help, sir.
    Whilst we expected th' old raven, in comes
    Corvino's wife, sent hither by her husband—
Voltore. What, with a present?
Mosca.   No, sir, on visitation—   45
    I'll tell you how anon—and, staying long,
    The youth he grows impatient, rushes forth,
    Seizeth the lady, wounds me, makes her swear—
    Or he would murder her, that was his vow—
    T' affirm my patron to have done her rape,   50
    Which how unlike it is, you see! And hence
    With that pretext he's gone t' accuse his father,
    Defame my patron, defeat you—
Voltore.   Where's her husband?
    Let him be sent for straight.
Mosca.   Sir, I'll go fetch him.
Voltore. Bring him to the Scrutineo.

---

    32. *disclaiming in*] disinheriting or disowning of.
    36.] and you be established in a hope of inheriting two fortunes, of
Corbaccio and Volpone (provided Corbaccio dies first).
    41. *change*] i.e. change for the worse.
    42. *success*] result, sequel.
    hapless] unfortunate.
    55. *Scrutineo*] law court in the Venetian Senate House.

Mosca.   Sir, I will.   55
Voltore. This must be stopped.
Mosca.   Oh, you do nobly, sir.
　　Alas, 'twas laboured all, sir, for your good;
　　Nor was there want of counsel in the plot.
　　But fortune can, at any time, o'erthrow
　　The projects of a hundred learnèd clerks, sir.   60
Corbaccio. [*Striving to hear*] What's that?
Voltore. [*To Corbaccio*]   Will 't please you, sir, to go along?
　　　　　　　　　　[*Exeunt* VOLTORE *and* CORBACCIO.]
Mosca. [*To Volpone*] Patron, go in and pray for our success.
Volpone. [*Rising*] Need makes devotion; heaven your labour
　　bless!   [*Exeunt.*]

---

　58. *want of counsel*] lack of deliberation, sagacity.
　60. *clerks*] scholars.

Act 4

[*Enter* SIR] POLITIC [*and*] PEREGRINE.

Sir Politic. I told you, sir, it was a plot; you see
　　　　What observation is! You mentioned me
　　　　For some instructions. I will tell you, sir,
　　　　Since we are met here in this height of Venice,
　　　　Some few particulars I have set down　　　　　　　　5
　　　　Only for this meridian, fit to be known
　　　　Of your crude traveller, and they are these.
　　　　I will not touch, sir, at your phrase, or clothes,
　　　　For they are old.
Peregrine.　　　　　　　　Sir, I have better.
Sir Politic.　　　　　　　　　　　　Pardon,
　　　　I meant as they are themes.
Peregrine.　　　　　　　　　　　Oh, sir, proceed.　　　　10
　　　　I'll slander you no more of wit, good sir.

4.1. Location: the piazza.

1. *it*] i.e. the mountebank incident in 2.2; cf. 2.3.10.

2. *observation*] taking methodical note of phenomena.

2–3. *You . . . instructions*] You suggested that I might be able to give you some tips.

4. *height*] latitude, part of the world; or referring to the Rialto, or Venice's splendour; see 2.1.12 and note. Multiple possible meanings continue in *meridian* (6), though its main significance is merely 'this part of the world'.

7. *crude*] unpolished, inexperienced.

7, 8, 12 etc. *your*] The same impersonal use as at 2.1.74; see also 4.1.30, 33, 60, 113, etc. An affectation of travellers.

8.] I will not say anything critical about the idioms of language that travellers use, or the ways they dress.

9. *old*] familiar, well known; old-fashioned.

Sir . . . better] Peregrine's joke is to pretend to take Sir Pol's remark as criticism of his clothes.

10. *themes*] general topics.

11.] 'Never again will I misrepresent you for the sake of being witty'; but with a second meaning that Sir Pol presumably does not understand: 'Never again will I accuse you of being witty'.

Sir Politic. First, for your garb, it must be grave and serious,
    Very reserved and locked; not tell a secret
    On any terms, not to your father; scarce
    A fable but with caution. Make sure choice   15
    Both of your company and discourse; beware
    You never speak a truth—
Peregrine.   How!
Sir Politic.   Not to strangers,
    For those be they you must converse with most;
    Others I would not know, sir, but at distance,
    So as I still might be a saver in 'em.   20
    You shall have tricks, else, passed upon you hourly.
    And then, for your religion, profess none,
    But wonder at the diversity of all;
    And, for your part, protest, were there no other
    But simply the laws o' th' land, you could content you.   25
    Nick Machiavel and Monsieur Bodin both
    Were of this mind. Then must you learn the use
    And handling of your silver fork at meals,
    The metal of your glass—these are main matters

---

12. *for your garb*] as for the bearing and demeanour that a traveller should adopt. *Garb* also suggests appearance and dress.

13. *locked*] reticent, guarded.

not] do not.

14. *On any terms*] under any circumstances.

15. *fable*] moral tale or fictional story.

19. *Others*] i.e. non-'strangers', fellow countrymen.

20.] so that I might always save myself trouble (and expense?) from them. 'Saver' is a gambling term for one who escapes loss but makes no gain. 'Tricks' (21) continues the metaphor of gambling.

24–5.] and declare that as far as you're concerned, it would be fine if there were only a single official state religion.

26–7. *Nick . . . mind*] Jean Bodin (1530–96), in his *Six Livres de la République*, advocates religious toleration on the pragmatic grounds that attempts to impose uniformity are doomed to fail and merely disrupt the state. Niccolò Machiavelli (1469–1527) makes no such argument, though his subordinating of all values to political expediency in *The Prince* was mistakenly taken to advocate a kind of toleration. Sir Pol reveals his glib ignorance by lumping them together and by the affectedly familiar 'Nick Machiavel'.

28. *fork*] Forks were still uncommon in England at this time.

29. *metal*] (1) mettle, quality; (2) molten substance used in manufacture. QF spell 'mettall'.

main] of first importance.

With your Italian—and to know the hour   30
When you must eat your melons and your figs.
Peregrine. Is that a point of state too?
Sir Politic.   Here it is;
For your Venetian, if he see a man
Preposterous in the least, he has him straight;
He has. He strips him. I'll acquaint you, sir.   35
I now have lived here, 'tis some fourteen months;
Within the first week of my landing here
All took me for a citizen of Venice,
I knew the forms so well—
Peregrine. [*Aside*]   And nothing else.
Sir Politic. I had read Contarine, took me a house,   40
Dealt with my Jews to furnish it with movables—
Well, if I could but find one man, one man
To mine own heart, whom I durst trust, I would—
Peregrine. What? What, sir?
Sir Politic.   Make him rich, make him a fortune.
He should not think again. I would command it.   45
Peregrine. As how?
Sir Politic.   With certain projects that I have,
Which I may not discover.
Peregrine. [*Aside*]   If I had
But one to wager with, I would lay odds, now,

---

31. *melons . . . figs*] Both these fruits were considered aphrodisiacs, though Sir Pol may not intend this.

34. *Preposterous*] (1) literally, 'in the wrong order'; (2) acting unconventionally; (3) perverse, unnatural, sodomitical, 'ass backwards'.

has him] has him at a disadvantage; with sexual undertone, continued in 'strips him' in 35.

35. *strips him*] i.e. exposes him to ridicule; but see previous note.

I 'll . . . you] Let me tell you.

39. *nothing else*] i.e. all form and no substance.

40. *Contarine*] Cardinal Gaspare Contarini's *De Magistratibus et Republica Venetorium* (1589), translated in 1599 by Lewis Lewkenor as *The Commonwealth and Government of Venice*.

41. *my Jews*] the Jewish moneylenders from whom I borrow at interest.

movables] movable furniture, as distinct from 'fixtures'.

45. *think again*] consider the matter twice.

command it] arrange matters in his behalf; have matters at my disposal.

46. *projects*] speculations, quasi-scientific experiments.

47. *discover*] reveal.

48. *But one*] someone (other than Sir Pol).

       He tells me instantly.

Sir Politic.   One is (and that
       I care not greatly who knows) to serve the state   50
       Of Venice with red herrings for three years,
       And at a certain rate, from Rotterdam,
       Where I have correspondence. [*He shows a letter.*]
         There's a letter
       Sent me from one o' th' States, and to that purpose;
       He cannot write his name, but that's his mark.   55

Peregrine. [*Examining the seal*] He is a chandler?

Sir Politic.   No, a cheesemonger.
       There are some other too with whom I treat
       About the same negotiation,
       And I will undertake it; for 'tis thus—
       I'll do 't with ease; I've cast it all. Your hoy   60
       Carries but three men in her and a boy,
       And she shall make me three returns a year;
       So, if there come but one of three, I save;
       If two, I can defalk. But this is, now,
       If my main project fail.

Peregrine.   Then you have others?   65

Sir Politic. I should be loath to draw the subtle air
       Of such a place without my thousand aims.
       I'll not dissemble, sir; where'er I come,
       I love to be considerative, and 'tis true
       I have at my free hours thought upon   70

---

    51. *red herrings*] smoked herrings.

    53. *correspondence*] business dealings and correspondence by mail; but with a suggestion too of illicit dealings.

    54. *States*] men of the States-General, the governing assembly in the United Netherlands.

    56. *chandler*] retailer of provisions, originally a dealer in candles. (Peregrine is presumably mocking the greasiness of the paper.)

    57. *other*] others.
    treat] deal.

    60. *cast it all*] figured it all out, reckoned the total.
    Your hoy] the average-sized small vessel used for short hauls along the coast.

    62. *returns*] round trips.

    63–4. *if . . . defalk*] if only one such venture out of three actually succeeds, I can at least come out even; if two, I can pay off some of my other expenses.

    66. *draw . . . air*] breathe the atmosphere of scheming.

    69. *considerative*] enterprisingly analytic.

Some certain goods unto the state of Venice,
Which I do call my cautions, and, sir, which
I mean, in hope of pension, to propound
To the Great Council, then unto the Forty,
So to the Ten. My means are made already—   75
Peregrine. By whom?
Sir Politic.   Sir, one that, though his place b' obscure,
Yet he can sway, and they will hear him. He's
A *commandatore.*
Peregrine.   What, a common sergeant?
Sir Politic. Sir, such as they are put it in their mouths
What they should say sometimes, as well as greater.   80
I think I have my notes to show you—   [*Searching*]
Peregrine.   Good, sir.
Sir Politic. But you shall swear unto me, on your gentry,
Not to anticipate—
Peregrine.   I, sir?
Sir Politic.   Nor reveal
A circumstance—My paper is not with me.
Peregrine. Oh, but you can remember, sir.
Sir Politic.   My first is   85
Concerning tinder-boxes. You must know
No family is here without its box.
Now, sir, it being so portable a thing,
Put case that you or I were ill affected
Unto the state; sir, with it in our pockets,   90

---

71. *goods*] benefits.

72. *cautions*] precautionary measures.

74–5. *Great . . . Ten*] The complex ruling hierarchy of Venice consisted of the Great Council, made up of traditional patrician families, from which the Senate was elected; the 'Forty', a court of appeal drawn from the Senate; and the 'Ten', an all-powerful committee of public safety.

75. *means*] i.e. means of access to the ruling hierarchy.

78. commandatore] an officer charged with the arrest or summoning to court of offenders—a ridiculously minor official for such a purpose.

79–80.] i.e. Such arresting officers, like more important people, may sometimes tell the government what to think and do.

82. *gentry*] honour as a gentleman.

86. *tinder-boxes*] boxes to hold flint and steel and flammable material needed to start a fire.

89. *Put case*] suppose for example.

89–90. *ill . . . Unto*] ill disposed towards.

Might not I go into the Arsenale?
Or you? Come out again? And none the wiser?
Peregrine. Except yourself, sir.
Sir Politic.   Go to, then. I therefore
    Advertise to the state how fit it were
    That none but such as were known patriots,   95
    Sound lovers of their country, should be suffered
    T' enjoy them in their houses, and even those
    Sealed at some office and at such a bigness
    As might not lurk in pockets.
Peregrine.   Admirable!
Sir Politic. My next is, how t' inquire and be resolved   100
    By present demonstration whether a ship
    Newly arrived from Sorìa, or from
    Any suspected part of all the Levant,
    Be guilty of the plague; and, where they use
    To lie out forty, fifty days, sometimes   105
    About the Lazaretto for their trial,
    I'll save that charge and loss unto the merchant
    And in an hour clear the doubt.
Peregrine.   Indeed, sir?
Sir Politic. Or—I will lose my labour.
Peregrine.   My faith, that's much.
Sir Politic. Nay, sir, conceive me. 'Twill cost me in onions   110
    Some thirty *livres*—

---

91. *Arsenale*] a shipyard and depot for storing munitions] in Venice, rigorously guarded but, in Sir Pol's view, still vulnerable to anyone with a tinder-box in his pocket. Pronounced in four syllables.

94. *Advertise*] make known, warn. Stressed on the middle syllable.

97. *them*] tinder-boxes.

98. *Sealed*] licensed. Sir Pol's zany scheme is to register tinder-boxes.

100–1. *resolved . . . demonstration*] satisfied by on-the-spot inspection. Venice was known for its quarantining of incoming ships.

102. *Soria*] the Italian form of Syria.

103. *Levant*] countries of the Middle East.

106. *Lazaretto*] pest-house; there were two on islands in the Gulf of Venice.

110–25.] Onions were popularly thought to offer protection against the plague. Sir Pol's ludicrous scheme of onions, waterworks, and bellows may also be suggestive of the male sexual organ, urination, and flatulence.

110. *conceive*] understand.

111. livres] French coins.

Peregrine.   Which is one pound sterling.
Sir Politic. Beside my waterworks. For this I do, sir:
    First, I bring in your ship 'twixt two brick walls—
    But those the state shall venture. On the one
    I strain me a fair tarpaulin, and in that   115
    I stick my onions, cut in halves; the other
    Is full of loopholes, out at which I thrust
    The noses of my bellows; and those bellows
    I keep, with waterworks, in perpetual motion
    (Which is the easi'st matter of a hundred).   120
    Now, sir, your onion, which doth naturally
    Attract th' infection, and your bellows blowing
    The air upon him, will show instantly,
    By his changed colour, if there be contagion,
    Or else remain as fair as at the first.   125
    Now 'tis known, 'tis nothing.
Peregrine.   You are right, sir.
Sir Politic. I would I had my note.
Peregrine.   Faith, so would I.
    But you ha' done well for once, sir.
Sir Politic. [*Searching his pockets again*] Were I false,
    Or would be made so, I could show you reasons
    How I could sell this state now to the Turk,   130
    Spite of their galleys, or their—
Peregrine.   Pray you, Sir Pol.
Sir Politic. I have 'em not about me.
Peregrine.   That I feared.
    They're there, sir?   [*He indicates a book of Sir Pol's.*]
Sir Politic.   No, this is my diary,

---

114. *venture*] invest in, pay for.

115. *strain me*] stretch.

120.] i.e. which is as easy as can be. Attaining perpetual motion was a popular will-o'-the-wisp at the time, and Sir Pol is fatuously overconfident.

126. *Now . . . nothing*] i.e. Now that I've made known to you this amazing invention, it seems obvious. Peregrine ironically takes the phrase at face value.

127. *I would I had*] I wish I could find. Sir Pol is still searching.

128. *false*] traitorous.

129. *Or . . . so*] or could be persuaded to be so.

130. *the Turk*] the Ottoman empire, with which Venice was at war for dominance in the Mediterranean.

Wherein I note my actions of the day.
Peregrine. Pray you, let's see, sir. What is here?   [*He reads.*]
          'Notandum,   135
     A rat hath gnawn my spur leathers; notwithstanding,
     I put on new and did go forth; but first
     I threw three beans over the threshold. *Item,*
     I went and bought two toothpicks, whereof one
     I burst immediately in a discourse   140
     With a Dutch merchant 'bout *ragion' del stato.*
     From him I went and paid a *moccenigo*
     For piecing my silk stockings; by the way
     I cheapened sprats, and at St Mark's I urined.'
     Faith, these are politic notes!
Sir Politic.   Sir, I do slip   145
     No action of my life, thus, but I quote it.
Peregrine. Believe me, it is wise!
Sir Politic.   Nay, sir, read forth.

ACT 4   SCENE 2

[*Enter, at a distance,*] LADY [POL], NANO, [*and the two*] Women.

Lady Politic. [*To Nano*] Where should this loose knight be,
     trow? Sure, he's housed.

---

135. Notandum] a thing worthy of note.
136–8.] Sir Pol betrays a superstitious fear of venturing forth in the face of
ominous signs, and so he performs precautionary rituals. *Spur leathers* are
laces for attaching spurs to boots.
137. *new*] new laces.
139. *toothpicks*] fashionable accoutrements; cf. 2.1.80.
141. ragion' del stato] reasons of state, political affairs.
142. moccenigo] a small coin, as at 2.2.216.
143. *piecing*] mending.
144. *cheapened*] bargained for.
145. *slip*] allow to pass.
146. *quote*] note.
147. *forth*] on.

4.2.1. *loose*] lascivious; roving.
trow?] do you suppose?
housed] indoors, i.e. in a bawdy house, with the 'courtesan' of 3.5.20.

Nano. Why, then he's fast.

Lady Politic.   Ay, he plays both with me.

    I pray you, stay. This heat will do more harm

    To my complexion than his heart is worth.

    I do not care to hinder, but to take him.—   5

    How it comes off!   [*Rubbing her cheeks*]

1 Woman. [*Pointing*]   My master's yonder.

Lady Politic.   Where?

2 Woman. With a young gentleman.

Lady Politic.   That same's the party!

    In man's apparel. [*To Nano*] Pray you, sir, jog my knight.

    I will be tender to his reputation,

    However he demerit.

Sir Politic. [*Seeing her*]   My lady!

Peregrine.   Where?   10

Sir Politic. 'Tis she indeed; sir, you shall know her. She is,

    Were she not mine, a lady of that merit

    For fashion and behaviour, and for beauty,

    I durst compare—

Peregrine.   It seems you are not jealous,

    That dare commend her.

Sir Politic.   Nay, and for discourse—   15

Peregrine. Being your wife, she cannot miss that.

Sir Politic. [*Introducing Peregrine*]   Madam,

    Here is a gentleman; pray you, use him fairly.

    He seems a youth, but he is—

Lady Politic.   None!

---

    2. *fast*] quick-moving; secure from detection; caught.

    both] i.e. 'fast and loose', playing on Nano's 'fast'. See 1.2.8 and note.

    4. *complexion*] applied cosmetics.

    5.] I do not want to prevent him, but take him in the act.

    6. *it*] the *fucus* of 3.4.37.

    8. *In man's apparel*] Lady Pol thinks that Peregrine is one of the transvestites for which Venice was notorious.

    10. *demerit*] does not deserve (my care for his reputation).

    12. *Were . . . mine*] i.e. even if it is I, her husband, who says these things of her.

    16.] A wife of a man like you could not help being talkative.

    18. *None!*] Lady Pol reiterates her suspicion that Peregrine is a transvestite.

Sir Politic.   Yes, one
   Has put his face as soon into the world—
Lady Politic. You mean, as early? But today?
Sir Politic.   How's this!   20
Lady Politic. Why, in this habit, sir; you apprehend me.
   Well, Master Would-be, this doth not become you.
   I had thought the odour, sir, of your good name
   Had been more precious to you, that you would not
   Have done this dire massacre on your honour—   25
   One of your gravity and rank besides!
   But knights, I see, care little for the oath
   They make to ladies—chiefly their own ladies.
Sir Politic. Now, by my spurs, the symbol of my knighthood—
Peregrine. [*Aside*] Lord, how his brain is humbled for an
      oath!   30
Sir Politic. I reach you not.
Lady Politic.   Right, sir, your polity
   May bear it through thus. [*To Peregrine*] Sir, a word
      with you.
   I would be loath to contest publicly
   With any gentlewoman, or to seem
   Froward, or violent, as *The Courtier* says;   35
   It comes too near rusticity in a lady,
   Which I would shun by all means. And, however
   I may deserve from Master Would-be, yet
   T' have one fair gentlewoman thus be made
   Th' unkind instrument to wrong another,   40

   19.] who has put himself forward into the world at so early an age. (But
Lady Pol misinterprets this to mean that the supposed courtesan has only
recently disguised 'herself' as Peregrine.)

   20. *But*] only.

   21.] i.e. Why, in this masculine attire—you understand my meaning.

   30. *humbled*] brought low—down to his spurs.

   31. *reach*] understand.

   31–2. *your . . . thus*] your cunning may try to bluff it out.

   32–66.] Lady Pol comically addresses or refers to the supposed transves-
tite courtesan (Peregrine) as both 'Sir' (32, 66) and 'she' (41), 'Her' (63), and
'gentlewoman' (34).

   35. *Froward*] refractory, ill-humoured.

   The Courtier] Baldassare Castiglione's definitive courtesy book was
translated into English by Thomas Hoby in 1561. The sentiment here is
found in Book 3.

   40. *unkind*] (1) unnatural; (2) not kindly.

And one she knows not, ay, and to persever,
In my poor judgement is not warranted
From being a solecism in our sex,
If not in manners.
Peregrine. [*Laughing*]   How is this?
Sir Politic.   Sweet madam,
Come nearer to your aim.
Lady Politic.   Marry, and will, sir.   45
Since you provoke me with your impudence
And laughter of your light land-siren here,
Your Sporus, your hermaphrodite—
Peregrine.   What's here?
Poetic fury and historic storms!
Sir Politic. The gentleman, believe it, is of worth,   50
And of our nation.
Lady Politic.   Ay, your Whitefriars nation!
Come, I blush for you, Master Would-be, I,
And am ashamed you should ha' no more forehead
Than thus to be the patron, or St George,
To a lewd harlot, a base fricatrice,   55
A female devil in a male outside.
Sir Politic. [*To Peregrine*]   Nay,
An you be such a one, I must bid adieu
To your delights. The case appears too liquid.

---

41. *persever*] pronounced per-SEV-er.

42. *warranted*] guaranteed.

43. *solecism*] breach of decorum.

47. *light land-siren*] lecherous whore. The sirens were mermaids who lured men to their destruction, and as half-woman, half-sea creature they are like transvestites.

48. *Sporus*] a favourite of Nero, who had him castrated, dressed him as a woman, and married him in 67 A.D.

49. *historic storms*] noteworthy outbursts.

51. *Whitefriars nation*] i.e. denizen of a district in London exempt from city control and hence a sanctuary for criminals, prostitutes, debtors, and the like.

52. *I*] QF's 'I' could represent 'ay'.

53. *forehead*] modesty, capacity for blushing.

54. *St George*] England's patron saint and hence the prototype of patrons, especially those who protect maidens in distress.

55. *fricatrice*] massage-parlour whore. Cf. 2.5.17, 2.6.24.

57. *An*] if.

58. *liquid*] manifest. Possibly Lady Would-be is crying.

Lady Politic. Ay, you may carry 't clear, with your state
　　　face!
　　　But for your carnival concupiscence,　　　　　　　　　60
　　　Who here is fled for liberty of conscience
　　　From furious persecution of the marshal,
　　　Her will I disc'ple.　　　　　　　　　[*Exit* SIR POL.]
Peregrine.　　　　　　　This is fine, i' faith!
　　　And do you use this often? Is this part
　　　Of your wit's exercise, 'gainst you have occasion?　　65
　　　Madam—
Lady Politic.　Go to, sir.
Peregrine.　　　　　　　Do you hear me, lady?
　　　Why, if your knight have set you to beg shirts,
　　　Or to invite me home, you might have done it
　　　A nearer way by far.
Lady Politic.　　　　　　This cannot work you
　　　Out of my snare.
Peregrine.　　　　　Why, am I in it, then?　　　　70
　　　Indeed, your husband told me you were fair,
　　　And so you are; only your nose inclines—
　　　That side that's next the sun—to the queen-apple.
Lady Politic. This cannot be endured by any patience.

---

59. *state face*] hypocritical countenance and demeanour.

59–63] Sir Pol may leave any time between 59 and 63; Lady Pol's speech seems shot after him as he flees.

60. *carnival concupiscence*] (1) lechery appropriate to carnival time; (2) lecherous whore.

61. *for . . . conscience*] i.e. in order to be free to practise unlicensed behaviour.

62. *marshal*] prison officer.

63. *disc'ple*] discipline.

64. *use this*] act in this way.

65. *'gainst . . . occasion*] whenever you find the opportunity.

67. *beg shirts*] Peregrine may suggest, ironically, that Lady Pol seems enamoured of his clothes, since she has talked of transvestism so pointedly. Perhaps she is tugging at his supposed 'disguise' in her wish to discipline and punish, or prevent escape.

69. *nearer*] more direct.

69–70. *work . . . snare*] let you escape from me. (But Peregrine acidly pretends to think that she speaks of a sexual trap.)

73. *queen-apple*] a large red apple. Presumably an indication of Lady Pol's large parrot-like 'beak'.

ACT 4   SCENE 3

[*Enter*] MOSCA.

Mosca. What's the matter, madam?
Lady Politic.   If the Senate
    Right not my quest in this, I will protest 'em
    To all the world no aristocracy.
Mosca. What is the injury, lady?
Lady Politic.   Why, the callet
    You told me of, here I have ta'en disguised.   5
Mosca. Who? This? What means your ladyship? The creature
    I mentioned to you is apprehended now
    Before the Senate. You shall see her—
Lady Politic.   Where?
Mosca. I'll bring you to her. This young gentleman,
    I saw him land this morning at the port.   10
Lady Politic. Is 't possible? How has my judgement
        wandered!—
    Sir, I must, blushing, say to you I have erred,
    And plead your pardon.
Peregrine.   What, more changes yet?
Lady Politic. I hope you ha' not the malice to remember
    A gentlewoman's passion. If you stay   15
    In Venice here, please you to use me, sir—
Mosca. Will you go, madam?
Lady Politic.   Pray you, sir, use me. In faith,
    The more you see me, the more I shall conceive
    You have forgot our quarrel.
                [*Exeunt* LADY POL, MOSCA, NANO, *and* Women.]
Peregrine.   This is rare!
    Sir Politic Would-be? No, Sir Politic Bawd!   20

4.3.2. *quest*] petition.
protest] publicly proclaim.
4. *callet*] whore.
13. *What . . . yet?*] Possibly an aside.
16. *use me*] i.e. let me be socially useful to you (but with a sexual connotation as well).
18. *see*] This F reading in place of Q's 'use' might be a compositorial
error, but might also be a deliberate revision to avoid repeating 'use me' a
third time.
conceive] understand (but again with sexual suggestion).

To bring me thus acquainted with his wife!
Well, wise Sir Pol, since you have practised thus
Upon my freshmanship, I'll try your salt-head,
What proof it is against a counterplot.   [*Exit.*]

Act 4   Scene 4

[*Enter*] VOLTORE, CORBACCIO, CORVINO, [*and*] MOSCA.

Voltore. Well, now you know the carriage of the business,
Your constancy is all that is required
Unto the safety of it.
Mosca.   Is the lie
Safely conveyed amongst us? Is that sure?
Knows every man his burden?
Corvino.   Yes.
Mosca.   Then shrink not.   5
Corvino. [*Aside to Mosca*] But knows the advocate the
      truth?
Mosca.   Oh, sir,
By no means. I devised a formal tale
That salved your reputation. But be valiant, sir.
Corvino. I fear no one but him, that this his pleading
Should make him stand for a co-heir—
Mosca.   Co-halter!   10
Hang him! We will but use his tongue, his noise,

---

23. *freshmanship*] inexperience.
salt-head] (1) experienced head (contrasting the 'salt' of pickling prepara-
tions with the 'fresh' of 'freshmanship'); (2) bawdy disposition.
24. *What proof*] how invulnerable.

4.4. Location: the Scrutineo, or court of law, in the Doge's palace.
1. *carriage*] management, conduct.
3-4. *Is . . . us?*] Are we agreed upon the lie that we all are going to tell?
5. *burden*] (1) refrain in a song, hence, part in the song we're all going to
sing; (2) assignment, responsibility.
6. *the truth*] i.e. that Corvino *did* try to prostitute Celia.
7. *formal*] elaborate, circumstantial.
8. *salved*] saved.
But] only.
9. *him*] Voltore, the 'advocate' of 6.
10. *Co-halter*] A 'halter' was a hangman's rope.

As we do Croaker's here.   [*He indicates Corbaccio.*]
Corvino.   Ay, what shall he do?
Mosca. When we ha' done, you mean?
Corvino.   Yes.
Mosca.   Why, we'll think:
    Sell him for mummia; he's half dust already.
    (*To Voltore*) [*Aside, indicating Corvino*] Do you not smile
      to see this buffalo,   15
    How he doth sport it with his head? [*To himself*] I should,
    If all were well and past. (*To Corbaccio*) [*aloud*] Sir, only
      you
    Are he that shall enjoy the crop of all,
    And these not know for whom they toil.
Corbaccio.   Ay, peace!
Mosca. (*To Corvino*) [*Aside*] But you shall eat it. [*To himself*]
    Much! (*Then to Voltore again*) Worshipful sir,   20
    Mercury sit upon your thund'ring tongue,
    Or the French Hercules, and make your language
    As conquering as his club, to beat along,
    As with a tempest, flat, our adversaries!
    [*To him aside*] But much more yours, sir.
Voltore.   Here they come; ha' done.   25

---

12. *Croaker's*] i.e. this croaking raven's, Corbaccio's.

14. *mummia*] powdered mummy, regarded as medicinal and magical.

15–16. *this buffalo . . . head*] i.e. this large horned cuckold.

16–17. *I should . . . past*] This may be Mosca's aside to Voltore still, or to himself.

19. *peace!*] hush! Corbaccio fears that Mosca speaks too loudly in his attempt to be heard by this deaf old man.

20. *Much!*] ironic: 'Not at all'; 'So you would like to think'. Probably Mosca says this aside to himself, but cf. 16–17n. above.

20–4. *Worshipful . . . adversaries*] This is probably spoken aloud to Voltore, not as an aside.

21. *Mercury*] the god of eloquence but also of theft.

22. *French Hercules*] i.e. Celtic Hercules, the supposed originator of the Celts in Gaul (France) while returning from his tenth labour, at which time, according to Lucian's *Herakles*, he was a weak old man but so eloquent that his speech was like chains of gold and amber binding the listeners' ears to his tongue.

23. *along*] at full length.

25. *But . . . sir*] i.e. Though the others consider you merely their advocate, you and I hope to win everything for yourself.

ha' done] be quiet, stop talking.

Mosca. I have another witness if you need, sir,
    I can produce.
Voltore.   Who is it?
Mosca.   Sir, I have her.

ACT 4   SCENE 5

    [*Enter*] *four* Avocatori, BONARIO, CELIA, Notario,
        Commandatori [*and other court officials*].

1 Avocatore. The like of this the Senate never heard of.
2 Avocatore. 'Twill come most strange to them when we
        report it.
4 Avocatore. The gentlewoman has been ever held
        Of unreprovèd name.
3 Avocatore.   So the young man.
4 Avocatore. The more unnatural part that of his father.   5
2 Avocatore. More of the husband.
1 Avocatore.   I not know to give
        His act a name, it is so monstrous!
4 Avocatore. But the impostor, he is a thing created
        T' exceed example!
1 Avocatore.   And all after-times!
2 Avocatore. I never heard a true voluptuary   10
        Described but him.
3 Avocatore.   Appear yet those were cited?
Notario. All but the old magnifico, Volpone.
1 Avocatore. Why is not he here?
Mosca.   Please your fatherhoods,
        Here is his advocate. Himself's so weak,
        So feeble—

---

26. *another witness*] i.e. Lady Pol.

4.5.6. *More . . . husband*] i.e. It is even more unnatural for Corvino to
have done the thing he stands accused of. (The *avocatori* prejudge the case at
first in favour of Celia and Bonario, since they are well reputed.)

8. *the impostor*] Volpone. (The *avocatori* have received charges accusing
Volpone of pretending illness in order to deceive Celia and Bonario; see
previous note.)

9. *example*] precedent.
after-times] future possibilities.

11. *those were cited*] those who have been summoned to appear in court.

13. *fatherhoods*] correct form to address the *avocatori*, which Volpone later
mocks (5.2.33–7).

4 Avocatore.   What are you?

Bonario. [*Interrupting*]   His parasite,   15
    His knave, his pander! I beseech the court
    He may be forced to come, that your grave eyes
    May bear strong witness of his strange impostures.

Voltore. Upon my faith and credit with your virtues,
    He is not able to endure the air.   20

2 Avocatore. Bring him, however.

3 Avocatore.   We will see him.

4 Avocatore. [*To Officers*]   Fetch him.
                    [*Exeunt* Officers.]

Voltore. Your fatherhoods' fit pleasures be obeyed,
    But sure the sight will rather move your pities
    Than indignation. May it please the court,
    In the meantime, he may be heard in me.   25
    I know this place most void of prejudice,
    And therefore crave it, since we have no reason
    To fear our truth should hurt our cause.

3 Avocatore.   Speak free.

Voltore. Then know, most honoured fathers, I must now
    Discover to your strangely abusèd ears   30
    The most prodigious and most frontless piece
    Of solid impudence and treachery
    That ever vicious nature yet brought forth
    To shame the state of Venice. This lewd woman
        [*Indicating Celia*],
    That wants no artificial looks or tears   35
    To help the visor she has now put on,
    Hath long been known a close adulteress
    To that lascivious youth there [*Indicating Bonario*]; not
      suspected,
    I say, but known, and taken in the act

---

18. *strange*] unnatural.

19. *credit . . . virtues*] good name and trust in your virtuous eyes.

27. *it*] a hearing.

30. *Discover*] reveal.

abusèd] deceived, imposed upon.

31. *frontless*] shameless, unblushing.

32. *solid*] complete, through-and-through.

35. *wants*] lacks. (Celia is weeping; see 4.6.2–3.)

36. *visor*] mask (of innocence); perhaps the halfmask that Venetian ladies wore in public.

37. *close*] secret.

With him; and by this man, the easy husband
    [*Indicating Corvino*],   40
Pardoned; whose timeless bounty makes him now
Stand here, the most unhappy, innocent person
That ever man's own goodness made accused.
For these, not knowing how to owe a gift
Of that dear grace but with their shame, being placed   45
So above all powers of their gratitude,
Began to hate the benefit, and, in place
Of thanks, devise t' extirp the memory
Of such an act. Wherein I pray your fatherhoods
To observe the malice, yea, the rage of creatures   50
Discovered in their evils, and what heart
Such take even from their crimes. But that anon
Will more appear. This gentleman, the father
    [*Indicating Corbaccio*],
Hearing of this foul fact, with many others
Which daily struck at his too tender ears,   55
And grieved in nothing more than that he could not
Preserve himself a parent (his son's ills
Growing to that strange flood), at last decreed
To disinherit him.
1 Avocatore.   These be strange turns!
2 Avocatore. The young man's fame was ever fair and
    honest.   60
Voltore. So much more full of danger is his vice,

---

40. *easy*] (1) good-natured, lenient; (2) credulous.

41. *timeless*] limitless; also perhaps suggesting 'untimely, ill-advised'.

43.] that ever had his own goodness twisted against him.

44–9. *For . . . act*] i.e. For Celia and Bonario, not knowing how to acknowledge, except by feeling shame, the great kindnesses so infinitely exceeding their ability to be grateful, began to hate their benefactor, and, instead of giving thanks, acted in such a way as to obliterate all memory of the goodness done them.

51. *heart*] audacity, boldness.

54. *fact*] deed, crime.

55. *too tender*] overly solicitous and sensitive (ironic, in view of Corbaccio's deafness).

57. *Preserve himself*] i.e. remain
ills] evils.

58. *strange flood*] abnormal profusion; perhaps also with a sense of 'unfamilial' (?).

59. *turns*] turns of event.

That can beguile so under shade of virtue.
But, as I said, my honoured sires, his father
Having this settled purpose (by what means
To him betrayed, we know not), and this day   65
Appointed for the deed, that parricide
(I cannot style him better), by confederacy
Preparing this his paramour to be there,
Entered Volpone's house (who was the man,
Your fatherhoods must understand, designed   70
For the inheritance), there sought his father.
But with what purpose sought he him, my lords?
I tremble to pronounce it, that a son
Unto a father, and to such a father,
Should have so foul, felonious intent: 75
It was to murder him! When, being prevented
By his more happy absence, what then did he?
Not check his wicked thoughts; no, now new deeds
(Mischief doth ever end where it begins)
An act of horror, fathers! He dragged forth   80
The agèd gentleman, that had there lain bedrid
Three years and more, out of his innocent couch,
Naked, upon the floor; there left him; wounded
His servant in the face; and, with this strumpet,
The stale to his forged practice, who was glad   85
To be so active (I shall here desire
Your fatherhoods to note but my collections,
As most remarkable), thought at once to stop
His father's ends, discredit his free choice
In the old gentleman, redeem themselves   90

---

65. *him*] Bonario.

67. *style him better*] address or refer to him (Bonario) with a more suitable title.

77. *his more happy*] Corbaccio's fortunate.

he] Bonario.

79.] Wickedness ever breeds more wickedness.

82. *of*] QF's 'off' could mean 'of' or perhaps 'off'.

85. *stale . . . practice*] whore used as a decoy in his fraudulent scheme.

86. *active*] (1) active as a co-conspirator; (2) sexually active.

87. *collections*] conclusions, inferences.

89. *ends*] aims, purposes.

90. *In . . . gentleman*] i.e. of Volpone as his heir.

redeem] free from a charge, exculpate.

By laying infamy upon this man,
To whom, with blushing, they should owe their lives.
1 Avocatore. What proofs have you of this?
Bonario.   Most honoured fathers,
  I humbly crave there be no credit given
  To this man's mercenary tongue.
2 Avocatore.   Forbear.   95
Bonario. His soul moves in his fee.
3 Avocatore.   Oh, sir!
Bonario.   This fellow,
  For six *sols* more, would plead against his Maker.
1 Avocatore. You do forget yourself.
Voltore.   Nay, nay, grave fathers,
  Let him have scope. Can any man imagine
  That he will spare 's accuser, that would not   100
  Have spared his parent?
1 Avocatore.   Well, produce your proofs.
Celia. I would I could forget I were a creature!
Voltore. [*Calling a witness*] Signor Corbaccio!
4 Avocatore.   What is he?
Voltore.   The father.
2 Avocatore. Has he had an oath?
Notario.   Yes.
Corbaccio. [*Coming forth*]   What must I do now?
Notario. Your testimony's craved.
Corbaccio. [*Mishearing*]   Speak to the knave?   105
  I'll ha' my mouth first stopped with earth. My heart
  Abhors his knowledge; I disclaim in him.
1 Avocatore. But for what cause?
Corbaccio.   The mere portent of nature.
  He is an utter stranger to my loins.

---

91. *this man*] Corvino.
96. *moves*] lives.
97. sols] French coins worth a halfpenny each; with a pun on 'soul' in 96.
100. *spare 's*] spare his.
102. *creature*] (1) one of God's creatures; (2) a dependent (on Corvino).
107. *his knowledge*] knowledge of him.
disclaim in] disclaim, deny kinship in.
108. *The mere . . . nature*] i.e. He is nothing but a freak.

Bonario. Have they made you to this?
Corbaccio.   I will not hear thee,   110
    Monster of men, swine, goat, wolf, parricide!
    Speak not, thou viper.
Bonario.   Sir, I will sit down,
    And rather wish my innocence should suffer
    Than I resist the authority of a father.
Voltore. [*Calling a witness*] Signor Corvino!
2 Avocatore.   This is strange!
1 Avocatore.   Who's this?   115
Notario. The husband.
4 Avocatore.   Is he sworn?
Notario.   He is.
3 Avocatore.   Speak, then.
Corvino. This woman, please your fatherhoods, is a whore
    Of most hot exercise, more than a partridge,
    Upon record—
1 Avocatore.   No more.
Corvino.   Neighs like a jennet.
Notario. Preserve the honour of the court.
Corvino.   I shall,   120
    And modesty of your most reverend ears.
    And yet I hope that I may say these eyes
    Have seen her glued unto that piece of cedar,
    That fine, well-timbered gallant; and that here
        [*Indicating his forehead*]
    The letters may be read, thorough the horn,   125

---

110. *made you*] brought you.

118. *partridge*] birds regarded as lecherous.

119. *Upon record*] as is well known.

jennet] a mare (in heat) of a Spanish breed of horse.

120. *Preserve . . . court*] i.e. Speak decorously; avoid scandalous talk that might discredit these proceedings. (The first *Avocatore*'s 'No more' in the previous line registers the same sort of pious humbug shock.)

121. *And modesty*] and I will preserve the modesty.

123. *cedar*] a tall tree, like a 'well-timbered gallant' in 124; with a suggestion in the latter phrase of 'well-built' and 'well-hung'.

125.] i.e. the signs of the cuckold may be read on Corvino's forehead, much as letters can be read through the thin semi-transparent sheet of horn used as a protective cover on a child's 'horn-book' or primer featuring the letters of the alphabet.

That make the story perfect.

Mosca. [*Aside to Corvino*]   Excellent, sir!

Corvino. [*Aside to Mosca*] There is no shame in this,
    now, is there?

Mosca. [*Aside*]   None.

Corvino. [*To the court*] Or if I said I hoped that she were
    onward
    To her damnation, if there be a hell
    Greater than whore and woman—a good Catholic   130
    May make the doubt.

3 Avocatore.   His grief hath made him frantic.

1 Avocatore. Remove him hence.   *She* [*Celia*] *swoons.*

2 Avocatore.   Look to the woman.

Corvino.   Rare!
    Prettily feigned! Again!

4 Avocatore.   Stand from about her.

1 Avocatore. Give her the air.

3 Avocatore. [*To Mosca*]   What can you say?

Mosca.   My wound,
    May 't please your wisdoms, speaks for me, received   135
    In aid of my good patron, when he missed
    His sought-for father, when that well-taught dame
    Had her cue given her to cry out a rape.

Bonario. Oh, most laid impudence! Fathers—

3 Avocatore.   Sir, be silent.
    You had your hearing free; so must they theirs.   140

2 Avocatore. I do begin to doubt th' imposture here.

4 Avocatore. This woman has too many moods.

Voltore.   Grave fathers,
    She is a creature of a most professed
    And prostituted lewdness.

---

126. *perfect*] complete.

127.] Corvino is referring merely to the warning he received against lewd
speech at 120, but Mosca's reply recognizes the deeper irony of Corvino's
shameful behaviour in parading himself (falsely) as a cuckold before the
world in order to win a legacy.

128. *onward*] well on the way.

136. *he*] Bonario.

139. *laid*] carefully plotted.

140. *free*] free from interruption.

Corvino.   Most impetuous,
    Unsatisfied, grave fathers!
Voltore.   May her feignings   145
    Not take your wisdoms! But this day she baited
    A stranger, a grave knight, with her loose eyes
    And more lascivious kisses. [*Indicating Mosca*] This man
      saw 'em
    Together on the water in a gondola.
Mosca. Here is the lady herself that saw 'em too,   150
    Without, who then had in the open streets
    Pursued them but for saving of her knight's honour.
1 Avocatore. Produce that lady.
2 Avocatore.   Let her come. [*Exit* MOSCA.]
4 Avocatore.   These things,
    They strike with wonder!
3 Avocatore.   I am turned a stone!

ACT 4   SCENE 6

      [*Enter*] MOSCA [*with*] LADY [POL].

Mosca. Be resolute, madam.
Lady Politic. [*Indicating Celia*] Ay, this same is she.
    Out, thou chameleon harlot! Now thine eyes
    Vie tears with the hyena. Dar'st thou look
    Upon my wrongèd face? [*To Avocatori*] I cry your
      pardons.
    I fear I have forgettingly transgressed   5
    Against the dignity of the court—
2 Avocatore.   No, madam.

---

  145. *Unsatisfied*] insatiable.
  146. *take*] take in, deceive.
  But . . . baited] only this day she enticed.
  151. *Without*] i.e. waiting outside the court.
  154. *turned a stone*] turned to stone—the literal sense of a*ston*ished.

  4.6.2. *chameleon*] deceiving; literally, a lizard capable of changing colour to suit its surroundings.
  3. *Vie . . . hyena*] Lady Pol means to accuse Celia of using crocodile tears to inveigle a victim. The hyena was supposed to entice by its human-sounding voice.
  4. *cry*] beg.

Lady Politic. And been exorbitant—
2 Avocatore.   You have not, lady.
4 Avocatore. These proofs are strong.
Lady Politic.   Surely, I had no purpose
    To scandalise your honours, or my sex's.
3 Avocatore. We do believe it.
Lady Politic.   Surely, you may believe it.   10
2 Avocatore. Madam, we do.
Lady Politic.   Indeed, you may; my breeding
    Is not so coarse—
4 Avocatore.   We know it.
Lady Politic.   To offend
    With pertinacy—
3 Avocatore.   Lady—
Lady Politic.   Such a presence;
    No, surely.
1 Avocatore.   We well think it.
Lady Politic.   You may think it.
1 Avocatore. Let her o'ercome. [*To Bonario and Celia*] What
    witnesses have you   15
    To make good your report?
Bonario.   Our consciences.
Celia. And heaven, that never fails the innocent.
4 Avocatore. These are no testimonies.
Bonario.   Not in your courts,
    Where multitude and clamour overcomes.
1 Avocatore. Nay, then you do wax insolent.

    VOLPONE *is brought in, as impotent.* [*Lady Pol embraces him.*]

Voltore.   Here, here,   20
    The testimony comes that will convince
    And put to utter dumbness their bold tongues.
    See here, grave fathers, here's the ravisher,
    The rider on men's wives, the great impostor,

---

7. *exorbitant*] i.e. immoderate in speaking.
13. *pertinacy*] pertinacity, perverse obstinacy in airing views.
presence] presence-chamber or courtroom.
15. *o'ercome*] prevail, have the last word.
19. *multitude*] force of numbers.
20 SD. impotent] feeble, wholly disabled.
embraces him] See 5.2.97.

The grand voluptuary! Do you not think   25
These limbs should affect venery? Or these eyes
Covet a concubine? Pray you, mark these hands:
Are they not fit to stroke a lady's breasts?
Perhaps he doth dissemble?
Bonario.   So he does.
Voltore. Would you ha' him tortured?
Bonario.   I would have him proved.   30
Voltore. Best try him, then, with goads, or burning irons;
Put him to the *strappado*. I have heard
The rack hath cured the gout. Faith, give it him,
And help him of a malady; be courteous.
I'll undertake, before these honoured fathers,   35
He shall have yet as many left diseases
As she has known adulterers, or thou strumpets.
O my most equal hearers, if these deeds,
Acts of this bold and most exorbitant strain,
May pass with suff'rance, what one citizen   40
But owes the forfeit of his life, yea, fame
To him that dares traduce him? Which of you
Are safe, my honoured fathers? I would ask,
With leave of your grave fatherhoods, if their plot
Have any face or colour like to truth?   45
Or if, unto the dullest nostril here,
It smell not rank and most abhorrèd slander?

---

26. *affect venery*] hunger after sex, perform sexually.

30. *proved*] tested.

32. strappado] a torture in which the victim is hauled aloft by a rope tied to his hands behind his back and then is jerked up and down.

33. *rack*] another torture instrument on which the victim is stretched and pulled apart.

34. *help*] cure.

36.] he will be left with as many diseases.

37. *known*] (1) recognized; (2) known carnally, copulated with.
thou] Bonario.

38. *equal*] impartial.

39. *exorbitant strain*] outrageous kind.

40. *suff'rance*] allowance.

40–2. *what . . . him?*] what citizen of Venice does not stand in danger of losing his life and reputation to anyone that dares slander him?

45.] has any appearance or resemblance of truth.

47. *smell not*] smells not of.

I crave your care of this good gentleman,
Whose life is much endangered by their fable;
And as for them, I will conclude with this,   50
That vicious persons, when they're hot and fleshed
In impious acts, their constancy abounds.
Damned deeds are done with greatest confidence.

1 Avocatore. Take 'em to custody, and sever them.
                    [CELIA *and* BONARIO *are led out separately.*]
2 Avocatore. 'Tis pity two such prodigies should live.   55
1 Avocatore. Let the old gentleman be returned with care.
  I'm sorry our credulity wronged him.
                    [*Exeunt* Officers *with* VOLPONE.]
4 Avocatore. These are two creatures!
3 Avocatore.   I have an earthquake in me!
2 Avocatore. Their shame, even in their cradles, fled their
  faces.
4 Avocatore. [*To Voltore*] You've done a worthy service to
  the state, sir,   60
  In their discovery.
1 Avocatore.   You shall hear ere night
What punishment the court decrees upon 'em.
Voltore. We thank your fatherhoods.
          [*Exeunt* Avocatori, Notario, Commandatori,
                  and other court officials.]
                 How like you it?
Mosca.   Rare!
I'd ha' your tongue, sir, tipped with gold for this;
I'd ha' you be the heir to the whole city;   65
The earth I'd have want men, ere you want living.
They're bound t' erect your statue in St Mark's.
Signor Corvino, I would have you go
And show yourself, that you have conquered.
Corvino.   Yes.
Mosca. [*Aside to him*] It was much better that you should
  profess   70

---

51. *fleshed*] (1) inflamed, incited; (2) initiated.
52. *constancy*] (evil) resolution.
55. *prodigies*] monsters.
58. *creatures*] brutes, monsters.
66. *want living*] lack a livelihood.

Yourself a cuckold thus than that the other
Should have been proved.
Corvino.   Nay, I considered that.
Now it is her fault.
Mosca.   Then it had been yours.
Corvino. True. I do doubt this advocate still.
Mosca.   I' faith,
You need not; I dare ease you of that care.   75
Corvino. I trust thee, Mosca.
Mosca.   As your own soul, sir.

> [*Exit* CORVINO.]

Corbaccio.   Mosca!
Mosca. [*Going to him*] Now for your business, sir.
Corbaccio.   How? Ha' you business?
Mosca. Yes, yours, sir.
Corbaccio.   Oh, none else?
Mosca.   None else, not I.
Corbaccio. Be careful then.
Mosca.   Rest you with both your eyes, sir.
Corbaccio. Dispatch it.
Mosca.   Instantly.
Corbaccio.   And look that all,   80
Whatever, be put in: jewels, plate, moneys,
Household stuff, bedding, curtains.
Mosca.   Curtain rings, sir.
Only the advocate's fee must be deducted.
Corbaccio. I'll pay him now; you'll be too prodigal.
Mosca. Sir, I must tender it.
Corbaccio.   Two *chequins* is well?   85
Mosca. No, six, sir.
Corbaccio.   'Tis too much.
Mosca.   He talked a great while;
You must consider that, sir.
Corbaccio. [*Giving money*]   Well, there's three—
Mosca. I'll give it him.

---

71. *the other*] i.e. the attempted pandering of Celia to Volpone.
74. *do doubt*] mistrust.
79. *Rest . . . eyes*] Sleep easy, don't worry.
81. *put in*] i.e. included in the inventory.
85. *tender*] give.

Corbaccio.   Do so, and there's for thee.   [*Exit.*]

Mosca. [*Aside*] Bountiful bones! What horrid, strange offence
 Did he commit 'gainst nature in his youth,   90
 Worthy this age? [*To Voltore*] You see, sir, how I work
 Unto your ends; take you no notice.

Voltore.   No,
 I'll leave you.

Mosca.   All is yours,   [*Exit* VOLTORE.]
    —the devil and all,
 Good advocate! [*To Lady Pol*] Madam, I'll bring you
  home.

Lady Politic. No, I'll go see your patron.

Mosca.   That you shall not.   95
 I'll tell you why: my purpose is to urge
 My patron to reform his will, and for
 The zeal you've shown today, whereas before
 You were but third or fourth, you shall be now
 Put in the first, which would appear as begged   100
 If you were present. Therefore—

Lady Politic.   You shall sway me.
        [*Exeunt.*]

---

88. *there's for thee*] presumably a very small tip.

89. *Bountiful bones!*] ironically connecting Corbaccio's stinginess with his cadaverousness.

91. *Worthy this age*] deserving of such a dreadful old age.

92. *take . . . notice*] (1) leave everything to me; (2) don't worry whether I might seem to be conspiring with others; (3) don't fret about the small fee you just received.

93. *the devil and all*] the whole confounded lot; all or everything bad (spoken, of course, out of Voltore's hearing).

97. *reform*] rewrite, revise.

101. *sway*] persuade.

Act 5

[Enter] VOLPONE *[attended]*.

Volpone. Well, I am here, and all this brunt is passed.
    I ne'er was in dislike with my disguise
    Till this fled moment. Here 'twas good, in private;
    But in your public—*cavè* whilst I breathe.
    'Fore God, my left leg 'gan to have the cramp,   5
    And I appre'nded straight some power had struck me
    With a dead palsy. Well, I must be merry
    And shake it off. A many of these fears
    Would put me into some villainous disease,
    Should they come thick upon me. I'll prevent 'em.   10
    Give me a bowl of lusty wine to fright
    This humour from my heart. Hum, hum, hum!
                                     He drinks.
    'Tis almost gone already; I shall conquer.
    Any device, now, of rare, ingenious knavery
    That would possess me with a violent laughter   15
    Would make me up again. So, so, so, so. *Drinks again.*
    This heat is life; 'tis blood by this time.—Mosca!

5.1. Location: Volpone's house.

1. *brunt*] crisis, confusion.

3. *fled*] past.

4. *cavè*] beware (Latin). Perhaps a warning to himself, or else a request to Androgyno to keep a lookout while he relaxes. Androgyno may be onstage to hand him the bowl of wine he asks for at 11. (Nano and Castrone are summoned later, at 5.2.58.)

5. *'gan*] began.

6. *appre'nded straight*] apprehended, felt, perceived at once.

7. *dead palsy*] palsy producing complete insensibility or immobility (foreshadowing Volpone's final punishment, 5.12.118–24).

13. *conquer*] i.e. conquer my 'humour' (12) or fear.

16. *make . . . again*] restore me.

17. *heat*] flushed euphoria caused by intoxication (or being 'foxed').
    'tis blood] The wine is like a transfusion of new energy.

ACT 5   SCENE 2

[Enter] MOSCA.

Mosca. How now, sir? Does the day look clear again?
    Are we recovered and wrought out of error
    Into our way, to see our path before us?
    Is our trade free once more?
Volpone.   Exquisite Mosca!
Mosca. Was it not carried learnedly?
Volpone.   And stoutly.   5
    Good wits are greatest in extremities.
Mosca. It were a folly beyond thought to trust
    Any grand act unto a cowardly spirit.
    You are not taken with it enough, methinks?
Volpone. Oh, more than if I had enjoyed the wench!   10
    The pleasure of all womankind's not like it.
Mosca. Why, now you speak, sir. We must here be fixed;
    Here we must rest. This is our masterpiece;
    We cannot think to go beyond this.
Volpone.   True,
    Thou'st played thy prize, my precious Mosca.
Mosca.   Nay, sir,   15
    To gull the court—
Volpone.   And quite divert the torrent
    Upon the innocent.
Mosca.   Yes, and to make
    So rare a music out of discords—
Volpone.   Right.
    That yet to me 's the strangest (how thou'st borne it!),
    That these, being so divided 'mongst themselves,   20
    Should not scent somewhat, or in me or thee,
    Or doubt their own side.

5.2.4. *Exquisite*] (1) consummately excellent; (2) careful, painstaking.
5. *stoutly*] resolutely, bravely.
9. *taken with*] pleased with, thrilled by.
15. *thy prize*] *your* best trick. (Volpone intends to go further.)
16. *gull*] deceive, dupe.
17–18. *make . . . discords*] i.e. persuade the rival dupes to act in concert.
19. *how thou'st borne it*] how you managed it.
21. *or . . . or*] either . . . or.
22. *Or . . . side*] or suspect their own (temporary) allies.

Mosca.   True. They will not see 't;
    Too much light blinds 'em, I think. Each of 'em
    Is so possessed and stuffed with his own hopes
    That anything unto the contrary,   25
    Never so true or never so apparent,
    Never so palpable, they will resist it—
Volpone. Like a temptation of the devil.
Mosca.   Right, sir.
    Merchants may talk of trade, and your great signors
    Of land that yields well, but if Italy   30
    Have any glebe more fruitful than these fellows,
    I am deceived. Did not your advocate rare?
Volpone. Oh—'My most honoured fathers, my grave fathers,
    Under correction of your fatherhoods,
    What face of truth is here? If these strange deeds   35
    May pass, most honoured fathers'—I had much ado
    To forbear laughing.
Mosca.   'T seemed to me you sweat, sir.
Volpone. In troth, I did a little.
Mosca.   But confess, sir,
    Were you not daunted?
Volpone.   In good faith, I was
    A little in a mist, but not dejected;   40
    Never but still myself.
Mosca.   I think it, sir.
    Now, so truth help me, I must needs say this, sir,
    And out of conscience, for your advocate:
    He's taken pains, in faith, sir, and deserved,
    In my poor judgement (I speak it under favour,   45
    Not to contrary you, sir), very richly—
    Well—to be cozened.

---

    24. *possessed*] taken over as if by demonic possession.
    31. *glebe*] earth, cultivated ground.
    32. *rare*] rarely, excellently.
    37. *sweat*] sweated (with fear).
    39. *daunted*] intimidated. Volpone replies in 39–40 that he was confused ('in a mist') but not cast down or afraid ('dejected').
    41. *I think it*] I believe you.
    45. *under favour*] with permission.
    46. *contrary*] contradict.
    47. *cozened*] cheated.

Volpone.   Troth, and I think so too,
   By that I heard him in the latter end.
Mosca. Oh, but before, sir. Had you heard him first
   Draw it to certain heads, then aggravate,   50
   Then use his vehement figures—I looked still
   When he would shift a shirt; and doing this
   Out of pure love, no hope of gain—
Volpone.   'Tis right.
   I cannot answer him, Mosca, as I would,
   Not yet; but for thy sake, at thy entreaty,   55
   I will begin e'en now to vex 'em all,
   This very instant.
Mosca.   Good, sir.
Volpone.   Call the dwarf
   And eunuch forth.
Mosca. [*Calling*]   Castrone! Nano!

[*Enter* CASTRONE *and* NANO.]

Nano.   Here.
Volpone. Shall we have a jig now?
Mosca.   What you please, sir.
Volpone.   Go,
   Straight give out about the streets, you two,   60
   That I am dead; do it with constancy,
   Sadly, do your hear? Impute it to the grief
   Of this late slander.   [*Exeunt* CASTRONE *and* NANO.]
Mosca.   What do you mean, sir?

48.] by what I heard him say towards the end of his courtroom oration. (Volpone entered in time to hear only the end of Voltore's presentation.)

49. *Oh . . . sir*] i.e. Oh, but Voltore deserves to be tricked just as fully for what he said before you entered.

50. *heads*] chief points of discourse.

aggravate] intensify, exaggerate.

51. *vehement figures*] forceful figures of speech and gestures.

52. *When . . . shirt*] to see him work himself into such a sweat that he would have to change his shirt.

54. *answer*] repay.

59. *jig*] a clownish dance and song that often followed the main play on the Elizabethan stage.

61. *with constancy*] (1) with conviction; (2) with straight faces.

62. *Sadly*] gravely.

63. *mean*] intend.

Volpone.   Oh,
 I shall have instantly my vulture, crow,
 Raven, come flying hither on the news   65
 To peck for carrion, my she-wolf and all,
 Greedy and full of expectation—
Mosca. And then to have it ravished from their mouths?
Volpone. 'Tis true. I will ha' thee put on a gown
 And take upon thee as thou wert mine heir;   70
 Show 'em a will. Open that chest and reach
 Forth one of those that has the blanks. I'll straight
 Put in thy name.
Mosca. [*Getting him a blank will*] It will be rare, sir.
Volpone.   Ay,
 When they e'en gape, and find themselves deluded—
Mosca. Yes.
Volpone. And thou use them scurvily. Dispatch.   75
 Get on thy gown.
Mosca. [*Dressing*] But what, sir, if they ask
 After the body?
Volpone. Say it was corrupted.
Mosca. I'll say it stunk, sir; and was fain t' have it
 Coffined up instantly and sent away.
Volpone. Anything; what thou wilt. Hold, here's my will.   80
 Get thee a cap, a count-book, pen and ink,
 Papers afore thee; sit as thou wert taking
 An inventory of parcels. I'll get up
 Behind the curtain, on a stool, and hearken;
 Sometime peep over, see how they do look,   85
 With what degrees their blood doth leave their faces.
 Oh, 'twill afford me a rare meal of laughter!

---

66. *she-wolf*] i.e. Lady Pol (though she is usually seen as a parrot).

70. *take upon thee as*] act as though.

72. *blanks*] spaces left for the legatees' names to be filled in.

78. *was fain*] I was obliged.

81. *cap*] as worn by clerks.

count-book] account book.

83. *parcels*] lots, items.

84. *curtain*] probably the 'traverse' mentioned at 5.3.8.1, a curtain hung over a stage door or 'discovery space' or some such arrangement; not the bedcurtains, since Volpone intends to stand on a stool in his place of concealment.

Mosca. Your advocate will turn stark dull upon it.
Volpone. It will take off his oratory's edge.
Mosca. But your *clarissimo*, old round-back, he   90
    Will crump you like a hog-louse with the touch.
Volpone. And what Corvino?
Mosca.   Oh, sir, look for him
    Tomorrow morning with a rope and a dagger
    To visit all the streets; he must run mad.
    My lady too, that came into the court   95
    To bear false witness for your worship—
Volpone.   Yes,
    And kissed me 'fore the fathers, when my face
    Flowed all with oils—
Mosca.   And sweat, sir. Why, your gold
    Is such another med'cine, it dries up
    All those offensive savours. It transforms   100
    The most deformèd, and restores 'em lovely
    As 'twere the strange poetical girdle. Jove
    Could not invent t' himself a shroud more subtle
    To pass Acrisius' guards. It is the thing
    Makes all the world her grace, her youth, her beauty.   105
Volpone. I think she loves me.
Mosca.   Who? The lady, sir?

---

88. *stark dull*] completely insensible, catatonic. Volpone answers (89) to 'dull' as meaning 'blunt'.

90. clarissimo] Venetian grandee.

round-back] the stooped Corbaccio.

91.] will curl up for you as a woodlouse does when it is touched. The woodlouse, a kind of small crustacean found in old wood and under stones, rolls itself into a ball when endangered.

93. *rope and a dagger*] symbols of suicidal madness.

99. *such . . . med'cine*] such an effective medicine.

102. *As . . . girdle*] as if gold were Venus's girdle (mentioned in Homer's *Iliad*, 14.214–17), interwoven with intricately wrought emblems of love, desire, and dalliance.

103. *shroud*] cloak of disguise.

104. *To . . . guards*] i.e. to evade those who were ordered by King Acrisius to guard his daughter Danaë in a brazen tower. Jove disguised himself as a shower of gold. In Lucian's *The Dream*, Lucian's cock suggests that some of the golden shower was used to corrupt Acrisius's guards.

105. *Makes*] that provides.

106. *she . . . The lady*] Volpone may be dreaming of Celia, but Mosca seems to take the remark as referring to Lady Pol.

She's jealous of you.
Volpone.   Dost thou say so?

[*Knocking offstage*]

Mosca.   Hark,
There's some already.
Volpone.   Look.
Mosca. [*Looking out*]   It is the vulture;
He has the quickest scent.
Volpone.   I'll to my place,
Thou to thy posture.   [*He conceals himself.*]
Mosca.   I am set.
Volpone.   But, Mosca,   110
Play the artificer now; torture 'em rarely.

ACT 5   SCENE 3

[*Enter*] VOLTORE.

Voltore. How now, my Mosca?
Mosca. [*Writing*]   'Turkey carpets, nine—'
Voltore. Taking an inventory? That is well.
Mosca. 'Two suits of bedding, tissue—'
Voltore.   Where's the will?
Let me read that the while.

[*Enter* Servants, *carrying* CORBACCIO *in a chair.*]

Corbaccio.   So, set me down,
And get you home.   [*Exeunt* Servants.]
Voltore.   Is he come now to trouble us?   5
Mosca. 'Of cloth of gold, two more—'
Corbaccio.   Is it done, Mosca?

---

107. *jealous of you*] (1) devotedly wishing to care for you (out of a sense of wanting to ingratiate herself with you, and out of amorous desire as well); (2) envious of your attentions to others.

110. *posture*] imposture, pretence.

111. *artificer*] (1) skilled craftsman; (2) trickster.

5.3.1. *Turkey carpets*] used as table and wall coverings in that period.

3. *suits . . . tissue*] i.e. sets of bed covers and hangings, here woven with cloth or silver thread. (The full name, 'tissue of cloth of gold', is completed in 6.)

4. *the while*] i.e. while you complete the inventory.

Mosca. 'Of several velvets, eight—'
Voltore.   I like his care.
Corbaccio. Dost thou not hear?

[*Enter* CORVINO.]

Corvino.   Ha! Is th' hour come, Mosca?
                    Volpone peeps from behind a traverse.
Volpone. [*Aside*] Ay, now they muster.
Corvino.   What does the advocate here,
    Or this Corbaccio?
Corbaccio.   What do these here?

[*Enter* LADY POL.]

Lady Politic.   Mosca!   10
    Is his thread spun?
Mosca.   'Eight chests of linen—'
Volpone. [*Aside*]   Oh,
    My fine Dame Would-be too!
Corvino.   Mosca, the will,
    That I may show it these and rid 'em hence.
Mosca. 'Six chests of diaper, four of damask—' There!
                         [*He gives Corvino the will.*]
Corbaccio. Is that the will?
Mosca.   'Down-beds and bolsters—'
Volpone. [*Aside*]   Rare!   15
    Be busy still. Now they begin to flutter;
    They never think of me. Look, see, see, see!
    How their swift eyes run over the long deed
    Unto the name, and to the legacies,
    What is bequeathed them there—
Mosca.   'Ten suits of hangings—'   20
Volpone. [*Aside*] Ay, i' their garters, Mosca. Now their hopes

---

7. *several velvets*] separate velvet hangings.

8.1. traverse] a screen or curtain. See 5.2.84 and note.

11. *Is . . . spun?*] i.e. Have the Three Fates spun, measured, and cut the thread of life? Is Volpone dead?

14. *diaper*] linen woven in a diamond-shaped pattern.

damask] a twilled linen fabric richly figured in the weaving with designs, used chiefly for table linen.

20. *suits of hangings*] sets of tapestries.

21. *i' their garters*] playing on the jeering invitation to commit suicide: 'Hang yourself in your own garters'.

    Are at the gasp.

Voltore.   Mosca the heir!

Corbaccio.   What's that?

Volpone. [*Aside*] My advocate is dumb. Look to my merchant:
    He has heard of some strange storm, a ship is lost,
    He faints. My lady will swoon. Old glazen-eyes,   25
    He hath not reached his despair yet.

Corbaccio. [*Getting possession of the will*] All these
    Are out of hope; I'm sure the man.

Corvino.   But Mosca—

Mosca. 'Two cabinets—'

Corvino.   Is this in earnest?

Mosca.   'One
    Of ebony—'

Corvino.   Or do you but delude me?

Mosca. 'The other, mother of pearl'—I am very busy.   30
    Good faith, it is a fortune thrown upon me—
    'Item, one salt of agate'—not my seeking.

Lady Politic. Do you hear, sir?

Mosca.   'A perfumed box'—Pray you, forbear;
    You see I am troubled—'made of an onyx'—

Lady Politic.   How?

Mosca. Tomorrow, or next day, I shall be at leisure   35
    To talk with you all.

Corvino.   Is this my large hope's issue?

Lady Politic. Sir, I must have a fairer answer.

Mosca.   Madam!
    Marry, and shall: pray you, fairly quit my house.
    Nay, raise no tempest with your looks, but hark you:
    Remember what your ladyship offered me   40
    To put you in an heir; go to, think on 't;

---

22. *gasp*] last gasp (before death).

25. *glazen-eyes*] wearing thick glasses. Corbaccio needs them to read the will (see 63).

32. *salt*] salt-cellar.

33. *perfumed box*] container for perfume.

34. *troubled*] busy; but also suggesting 'vexed'.

36. *issue*] outcome.

38. *fairly*] (1) plainly, positively (responding to 'fairer' in the previous line); (2) in the spirit of fair play, quietly (leading into 39).

40–3. *Remember . . . you*] The implication is that Lady Pol has offered Mosca her favours; cf. 4.6.101.

41. *put you in*] put your name in as.

And what you said e'en your best madams did
For maintenance; and why not you? Enough!
Go home and use the poor Sir Pol, your knight, well,
For fear I tell some riddles. Go, be melancholic.   45
                                        [*Exit* LADY POL.]
Volpone. [*Aside*] O my fine devil!
Corvino.   Mosca, pray you a word.
Mosca. Lord! Will not you take your dispatch hence yet?
    Methinks, of all, you should have been th' example.
    Why should you stay here? With what thought? What
        promise?
    Hear you: do not you know I know you an ass?   50
    And that you would most fain have been a wittol
    If fortune would have let you? That you are
    A declared cuckold, on good terms? This pearl,
    You'll say, was yours? Right. This diamond?
    I'll not deny 't, but thank you. Much here else?   55
    It may be so. Why, think that these good works
    May help to hide your bad. I'll not betray you.
    Although you be but extraordinary
    And have it only in title, it sufficeth.
    Go home; be melancholic too, or mad.   60
                                        [*Exit* CORVINO.]
Volpone. [*Aside*] Rare, Mosca! How his villainy becomes him!
Voltore. [*Aside*] Certain he doth delude all these for me.
Corbaccio. [*Finally reading the will*] Mosca the heir!
Volpone. [*Aside*]   Oh, his four eyes have found it.
Corbaccio. I am cozened, cheated, by a parasite slave.
    Harlot, thou'st gulled me.
Mosca.   Yes, sir. Stop your mouth,   65

---

43. *For maintenance*] in order to survive comfortably.
45. *riddles*] secrets.
48.] It seems to me that you, Corvino, should have set an example for the others by leaving first.
51. *wittol*] willing cuckold.
53. *on good terms*] fair and square, without a doubt.
58–9.] i.e. Although you are unusual in being a cuckold in name only, not in fact, let that suffice; I won't give away your secret.
63. *four eyes*] referring to the bespectacled Corbaccio.
65. *Harlot*] rascal, villain.

Or I shall draw the only tooth is left.
Are not you he, that filthy, covetous wretch
With the three legs, that here, in hope of prey,
Have, any time this three year, snuffed about
With your most grov'ling nose, and would have hired   70
Me to the pois'ning of my patron, sir?
Are not you he that have today in court
Professed the disinheriting of your son?
Perjured yourself? Go home, and die, and stink.
If you but croak a syllable, all comes out.   75
Away, and call your porters! Go, go stink.
                                        [*Exit* CORBACCIO.]
Volpone. [*Aside*] Excellent varlet!
Voltore.   Now, my faithful Mosca,
    I find thy constancy—
Mosca.   Sir?
Voltore.   Sincere.
Mosca. [*Writing*]   'A table
    Of porphyry'—I mar'l you'll be thus troublesome.
Voltore. Nay, leave off now, they are gone.
Mosca.   Why, who are you?   80
    What? Who did send for you? Oh, cry you mercy,
    Reverend sir! Good faith, I am grieved for you,
    That any chance of mine should thus defeat
    Your (I must needs say) most deserving travails;
    But I protest, sir, it was cast upon me,   85
    And I could almost wish to be without it,
    But that the will o' th' dead must be observed.
    Marry, my joy is that you need it not;
    You have a gift, sir (thank your education)
    Will never let you want while there are men   90
    And malice to breed causes. Would I had
    But half the like, for all my fortune, sir!

---

68. *three legs*] the third being Corbaccio's cane.
69–70. *snuffed . . . nose*] Corbaccio must have a perpetual sniffle.
79. *porphyry*] a dark red, semiprecious stone.
mar'l] marvel.
83. *chance*] luck.
91. *causes*] lawsuits.
91–2. *Would . . . fortune*] I wish that I, even though I have done well just
now, were half as wealthy as you.

If I have any suits (as I do hope,
Things being so easy and direct, I shall not)
I will make bold with your obstreperous aid,   95
Conceive me—for your fee, sir. In meantime,
You that have so much law I know ha' the conscience
Not to be covetous of what is mine.
Good sir, I thank you for my plate; 'twill help
To set up a young man. Good faith, you look   100
As you were costive; best go home and purge, sir.
                                        [*Exit* VOLTORE.]
Volpone. [*Coming from behind the curtain*] Bid him eat
          lettuce well! My witty mischief,
Let me embrace thee. Oh, that I could now
Transform thee to a Venus! Mosca, go,
Straight take my habit of *clarissimo*,   105
And walk the streets; be seen, torment 'em more.
We must pursue as well as plot. Who would
Have lost this feast?
Mosca.   I doubt it will lose them.
Volpone. Oh, my recovery shall recover all.
That I could now but think on some disguise   110
To meet 'em in, and ask 'em questions!
How I would vex 'em still at every turn!
Mosca. Sir, I can fit you.
Volpone.   Canst thou?
Mosca.   Yes, I know

---

94. *Things . . . direct*] since the terms of the will seem so simple and not challengeable.

95. *obstreperous*] vociferous, noisy.

96. *Conceive . . . fee*] 'it's understood, I'll pay your usual fee, of course'. This is not only patronizing, it also rubs in the fact that Voltore was not paid properly for his recent pleading.

97. *have . . . law*] understand the law so well.

99. *plate*] Voltore's gift to Volpone in 1.3.

101. *costive*] constipated.

102. *lettuce*] often used as a laxative.

105. *habit of* clarissimo] clothing worn by a Venetian gentleman.

108. *I doubt . . . them*] (1) I doubt it will get rid of them; (2) I fear it will lose them as our dupes. Volpone understands the latter meaning; see next note.

109.] Oh, but my appearance of being alive and well again will bring them all back as scheming petitioners.

One o' the *commandatori*, sir, so like you;
Him will I straight make drunk, and bring you his
    habit.   115
Volpone. A rare disguise, and answering thy brain!
    Oh, I will be a sharp disease unto 'em.
Mosca. Sir, you must look for curses—
Volpone.   Till they burst;
    The Fox fares ever best when he is cursed.   [*Exeunt.*]

ACT 5   SCENE 4

    [*Enter*] PEREGRINE, [*disguised, and*] *three* Merchants.

Peregrine. Am I enough disguised?
1 Merchant.   I warrant you.
Peregrine. All my ambition is to fright him only.
2 Merchant. If you could ship him away, 'twere excellent.
3 Merchant. To Zante or to Aleppo?
Peregrine.   Yes, and have 's
    Adventures put i' th' *Book of Voyages*,   5
    And his gulled story registered for truth!
    Well, gentlemen, when I am in awhile,
    And that you think us warm in our discourse,
    Know your approaches.
1 Merchant.   Trust it to our care.
                         [*Exeunt* Merchants.]

    [*Peregrine knocks. A* Woman *comes to the door.*]

---

114. commandatori] sergeants of the law courts, as at 4.1.78.
115. *habit*] clothing. The tipsy Volpone misses Mosca's irony here.
118. *Till they burst*] let them pronounce curses till they burst.

5.4. Location: in Venice's streets.
1. *warrant*] assure.
4. *Zante*] an island off the west coast of Greece, then a Venetian
possession.
Aleppo] an important inland trading centre in Syria.
have 's] have his.
5. Book of Voyages] such as Hakluyt's *Principal Navigations* (1589 *et seq.*).
6. *his gulled story*] the story of his gulling.
registered] recorded.
7. *in awhile*] entered into conversation with Sir Pol awhile, or entered into
his house.
9. *Know your approaches*] know that it is time for you to approach us.

Peregrine. Save you, fair lady. Is Sir Pol within?   10
Woman. I do not know, sir.
Peregrine.   Pray you, say unto him
    Here is a merchant upon earnest business
    Desires to speak with him.
Woman.   I will see, sir.
Peregrine.   Pray you.
                                        [*Exit* Woman.]
        I see the family is all female here.

                [*Re-enter* Woman.]

Woman. He says, sir, he has weighty affairs of state   15
    That now require him whole; some other time
    You may possess him.
Peregrine.   Pray you, say again,
    If those require him whole, these will exact him
    Whereof I bring him tidings.   [*Exit* Woman.]
                    What might be
    His grave affair of state now? How to make   20
    Bolognian sausages here in Venice, sparing
    One o' th' ingredients?

                [*Re-enter* Woman.]

Woman.   Sir, he says he knows
    By your word 'tidings' that you are no statesman,
    And therefore wills you stay.
Peregrine.   Sweet, pray you return him:
    I have not read so many proclamations   25
    And studied them for words as he has done,

---

10. *Save*] God save.

12. *earnest*] serious, important.

16. *require him whole*] require his whole attention.

17. *possess him*] (1) give him your information; (2) see him, have his company.

18. *exact him*] enforce his attention.

21. *sparing*] omitting.

23. *'tidings'*] Sir Pol's pedantic point seems to be that a true statesman (i.e. government agent) would say 'intelligence', 'advertisement', 'relations', and other terms that Sir Pol himself has employed.

24. *wills you stay*] i.e. insists that you can just wait until he is ready.
return him] take back this reply to him.

25-6.] Said sarcastically: I haven't studied government publications to acquire bureaucratic jargon, as Sir Pol has done.

But—Here he deigns to come.

[*Enter* SIR POL. *The* Woman *stands aside*.]

Sir Politic.   Sir, I must crave
Your courteous pardon. There hath chanced today
Unkind disaster 'twixt my lady and me,
And I was penning my apology   30
To give her satisfaction as you came now.
Peregrine. Sir, I am grieved I bring you worse disaster.
The gentleman you met at th' port today,
That told you he was newly arrived—
Sir Politic.   Ay, was
A fugitive punk?
Peregrine.   No, sir, a spy, set on you,   35
And he has made relation to the Senate
That you professed to him to have a plot
To sell the state of Venice to the Turk.
Sir Politic. Oh, me!
Peregrine.   For which warrants are signed by this time
To apprehend you and to search your study   40
For papers—
Sir Politic.   Alas, sir, I have none but notes
Drawn out of playbooks—
Peregrine.   All the better, sir.
Sir Politic. And some essays. What shall I do?
Peregrine.   Sir, best
Convey yourself into a sugar chest,
Or, if you could lie round, a frail were rare;   45
And I could send you aboard.
Sir Politic.   Sir, I but talked so
For discourse sake, merely.   *They knock without.*

---

29. *Unkind*] (1) unaccustomed, untoward; (2) devoid of amiability.
31. *give her satisfaction*] as though responding to a challenge; the term is from the protocol of duelling.
35. *punk*] prostitute.
37–8.] At 4.1.128–30, Sir Pol mentions the danger of being suspected of selling state secrets to the Ottoman empire.
42. *playbooks*] printed plays.
43. *essays*] perhaps those of Montaigne, mentioned at 3.4.90.
45. *lie round*] curl up.
frail] rush basket for figs and raisins.
47. *For discourse sake*] for the sake of conversation.

Peregrine.　　　　　　　　　　Hark, they are there.

Sir Politic. I am a wretch, a wretch!

Peregrine.　　　　　　　　　　What will you do, sir?
　　Ha' you ne'er a currant-butt to leap into?
　　They'll put you to the rack; you must be sudden.　　　　50

Sir Politic. Sir, I have an engine—

3 Merchant. [*Offstage*]　　　　Sir Politic Would-be!

2 Merchant. [*Offstage*] Where is he?

Sir Politic.　　　　　　That I have thought upon beforetime.

Peregrine. What is it?

Sir Politic.　　　　　—I shall ne'er endure the torture!—
　　Marry, it is, sir, of a tortoise shell,
　　Fitted for these extremities. Pray you, sir, help me.　　55
　　[*Getting into the shell*] Here I've a place, sir, to put back
　　　　my legs
　　(Please you to lay it on, sir), with this cap
　　And my black gloves. I'll lie, sir, like a tortoise
　　Till they are gone.

Peregrine.　　　　　　　And call you this an engine?

Sir Politic. Mine own device.—Good sir, bid my wife's
　　women　　　　　　　　　　　　　　　　　　　　　　60
　　To burn my papers.
　　　　　　　　[*Peregrine signals to the* Woman, *who exits.*]

　　　　　　　　They [*the three* Merchants] *rush in.*

1 Merchant.　　　　　　　Where's he hid?

3 Merchant.　　　　　　　　　　　We must,
　　And will, sure, find him.

2 Merchant.　　　　　　　Which is his study?

1 Merchant.　　　　　　　　　　　　　　What
　　Are you, sir?

Peregrine.　　　I'm a merchant that came here
　　To look upon this tortoise.

---

49. *currant-butt*] cask for holding currants or currant wine.

50. *sudden*] quick.

51. *engine*] device, contrivance.

55. *Fitted . . . extremities*] designed for such emergencies.

60. *device*] (1) invention; (2) emblem.

61 SD.] Alternatively, the Woman might exit at 27.1, in which case Peregrine might here go out briefly to speak with the Woman and then return at
62, after 'his study'.

3 Merchant.   How?
1 Merchant.   St Mark!
    What beast is this?
Peregrine.   It is a fish.
2 Merchant.   Come out here!   65
Peregrine. Nay, you may strike him, sir, and tread upon him.
    He'll bear a cart.
1 Merchant.   What, to run over him?
Peregrine.   Yes.
3 Merchant. Let's jump upon him.
2 Merchant.   Can he not go?
Peregrine.   He creeps, sir.
1 Merchant. Let's see him creep.
Peregrine.   No, good sir, you will hurt him.
2 Merchant. Heart, I'll see him creep, or prick his guts.   70
                [They call mockingly to Sir Pol.]
3 Merchant. Come out here!
Peregrine.   Pray you, sir, creep a little.
1 Merchant.   Forth!
2 Merchant. Yet further.
Peregrine.   Good sir, creep!
2 Merchant. *[To the others]*   We'll see his legs.
        They pull off the shell and discover him.
3 Merchant. Godso, he has garters!
1 Merchant.   Ay, and gloves!
2 Merchant.   Is this
    Your fearful tortoise?
Peregrine. *[Throwing off his disguise]* Now, Sir Pol, we are even.
    For your next project I shall be prepared.   75
    I am sorry for the funeral of your notes, sir.
1 Merchant. 'Twere a rare motion to be seen in Fleet Street!
2 Merchant. Ay, i' the term.

---

    68. *go*] move.
    72.1. *discover*] disclose, expose.
    73. *Godso*] See 2.6.59n.
    74. *fearful*] (1) frightening; (2) frightened.
    even] quits with each other. (Peregrine thinks Sir Pol was responsible for Lady Pol's attack on him.)
    77. *'Twere . . . motion*] it would be an excellent puppet show.
    78. *i' the term*] when the law-courts are in session, and hence many clients visit the Inns of Court near Fleet Street.

1 Merchant.   Or Smithfield, in the fair.
3 Merchant. Methinks 'tis but a melancholic sight.
Peregrine. Farewell, most politic tortoise.

              [*Exeunt* PEREGRINE *and* Merchants.]

          [*Enter* Woman.]

Sir Politic.   Where's my lady?   80
   Knows she of this?
Woman.   I know not, sir.
Sir Politic.   Inquire.

              [*Exit* Woman.]

   Oh, I shall be the fable of all feasts,
   The freight of the *gazetti*, ship-boys' tale,
   And, which is worst, even talk for ordinaries.

         [*Re-enter* Woman.]

Woman. My lady's come most melancholic home,   85
   And says, sir, she will straight to sea, for physic.
Sir Politic. And I, to shun this place and clime for ever,
   Creeping with house on back, and think it well
   To shrink my poor head in my politic shell.   [*Exeunt.*]

ACT 5   SCENE 5

    [*Enter*] VOLPONE [*and*] MOSCA: *the first in the habit of a*
       commandatore, *the other, of a* clarissimo.

Volpone. Am I then like him?
Mosca.   Oh, sir, you are he;

---

78. *Smithfield*] locale of Bartholomew Fair, held in August.
80. *politic*] sagacious, diplomatic, politically savvy (said ironically, of course).
SD. Enter *Woman*] The Woman may have returned before this, during the hubbub.
82–3.] Oh, I shall be the talk of the town, the topic of the news reports and of mere boys serving on board ship.
84. *ordinaries*] taverns.
86. *for physic*] for the good of her health.

5.5. Location: probably outside Volpone's house.
1. *him*] i.e. the *commandatore*; cf. 5.3.114.

     No man can sever you.
Volpone.   Good.
Mosca.   But what am I?
Volpone. 'Fore heav'n, a brave *clarissimo*; thou becom'st it!
    Pity thou wert not born one.
Mosca.   If I hold
    My made one, 'twill be well.
Volpone.   I'll go and see   5
    What news first at the court.
Mosca.   Do so.   [*Exit* VOLPONE.]
                  My Fox
    Is out on his hole, and, ere he shall re-enter,
    I'll make him languish in his borrowed case,
    Except he come to composition with me.—
    Androgyno, Castrone, Nano!

       [*Enter* ANDROGYNO, CASTRONE, *and* NANO.]

All.   Here.   10
Mosca. Go, recreate yourselves abroad; go, sport.
       [*Exeunt* ANDROGYNO, CASTRONE, *and* NANO.]
    So, now I have the keys and am possessed.
    Since he will needs be dead afore his time,
    I'll bury him, or gain by him. I'm his heir,
    And so will keep me till he share, at least.   15
    To cozen him of all were but a cheat
    Well placed; no man would construe it a sin.
    Let his sport pay for 't. This is called the Fox Trap.
                        [*Exit.*]

---

   2. *sever you*] distinguish between the two of you.
   3. *brave*] splendidly dressed.
thou . . . it] it suits you.
   4. *hold*] retain, maintain.
   7. *on*] of.
   8. *case*] disguise.
   9.] unless he comes to an agreement with me.
   11. *recreate*] amuse.
abroad] outside the house.
   12. *possessed*] in possession of the house (with perhaps an unconscious
suggestion of being possessed by demons).
   15. *keep me*] remain.
   18. *for 't*] for itself.

Act 5   Scene 6

[*Enter*] CORBACCIO [*and*] CORVINO.

Corbaccio. They say the court is set.
Corvino.   We must maintain
   Our first tale good, for both our reputations.
Corbaccio. Why, mine's no tale; my son would there have
      killed me.
Corvino. That's true, I had forgot. Mine is, I am sure.
   But for your will, sir.
Corbaccio.   Ay, I'll come upon him   5
   For that hereafter, now his patron's dead.

[*Enter* VOLPONE *disguised.*]

Volpone. Signor Corvino! And Corbaccio! [*To Corvino*] Sir,
   Much joy unto you.
Corvino.   Of what?
Volpone.   The sudden good
   Dropped down upon you—
Corbaccio.   Where?
Volpone.   —And none knows how.
   [*To Corbaccio*] From old Volpone, sir.
Corbaccio.   Out, arrant knave!   10
Volpone. Let not your too much wealth, sir, make you furious.
Corbaccio. Away, thou varlet!
Volpone.   Why, sir?
Corbaccio.   Dost thou mock me?
Volpone. You mock the world, sir. Did you not change wills?
Corbaccio. Out, harlot!
Volpone.   Oh, belike you are the man,

5.6. The time must now be evening (see 4.6.61–2).

4. *Mine is*] i.e. my story is good too (though perhaps with unconscious
suggestion of the opposite: mine is a lie).

5. *come upon him*] make a demand or claim upon Mosca.

11.] i.e. Wealthy as you already are, don't let your covetous fear of being
disappointed in your hopes of more wealth drive you mad.

12. *varlet*] rascal; but also the title for a sergeant of the court.

13. *You . . . world*] i.e. As Volpone's secret heir, it is you who laughs at
everyone. (Said mockingly.)
   change] exchange.

14. *harlot*] rascal.
   you . . . man] you're the bigshot.

Signor Corvino? Faith, you carry it well;   15
You grow not mad withal. I love your spirit:
You are not overleavened with your fortune.
You should ha' some would swell now like a wine vat
With such an autumn.—Did he gi' you all, sir?
Corvino. Avoid, you rascal!
Volpone.   Troth, your wife has shown   20
Herself a very woman. But you are well;
You need not care; you have a good estate
To bear it out, sir, better by this chance—
Except Corbaccio have a share?
Corbaccio.   Hence, varlet!
Volpone. You will not be a'known, sir. Why, 'tis wise.   25
Thus do all gamesters, at all games, dissemble;
No man will seem to win.

> [*Exeunt* CORVINO *and* CORBACCIO.]

Here comes my vulture,
Heaving his beak up i' the air, and snuffing.

ACT 5   SCENE 7

> [*Enter*] VOLTORE.

Voltore. Outstripped thus by a parasite? A slave
Would run on errands and make legs for crumbs?
Well, what I'll do—

---

15. *carry it*] carry it off.
16. *withal*] as a consequence.
17. *overleavened*] puffed up, like bread with too much yeast.
18. *You . . . some*] some people.
19. *autumn*] harvest (of riches, as if money were grapes).
20. *Avoid*] Get out!
21. *very*] typical, thorough.
23. *bear it out*] carry it off.
better . . . chance] your fortune is indeed all the better as a result of your new inheritance. (The disguised Volpone is of course mocking.)
24. *Except . . . have*] unless Corbaccio is to have.
25. *You . . . a'known*] i.e. Ah, you prefer not to be publicly acknowledged as Volpone's heir.
27. *seem to win*] admit that he is winning.

5.7.2. *Would*] who would.
make legs] bow and scrape.

Volpone.   The court stays for your worship.
  I e'en rejoice, sir, at your worship's happiness,
  And that it fell into so learnèd hands,   5
  That understand the fingering—
Voltore.   What do you mean?
Volpone. I mean to be a suitor to your worship
  For the small tenement out of reparations—
  That at the end of your long row of houses
  By the Piscaria. It was in Volpone's time,   10
  Your predecessor, ere he grew diseased,
  A handsome, pretty, customed bawdy-house
  As any was in Venice—none dispraised—
  But fell with him. His body and that house
  Decayed together.
Voltore.   Come, sir, leave your prating.   15
Volpone. Why, if your worship give me but your hand
  That I may ha' the refusal, I have done.
  'Tis a mere toy to you, sir—candle rents.
  As your learned worship knows—
Voltore.   What do I know?
Volpone. Marry, no end of your wealth, sir, God decrease it!   20
Voltore. Mistaking knave! What, mock'st thou my misfortune?
Volpone. His blessing on your heart, sir; would 'twere more!

---

3. *stays*] waits.

6. *fingering*] (1) performing any work exquisitely with the fingers; (2) fingering of coins; cheating, pilfering.

8. *tenement . . . reparations*] house in need of repair.

9. *That*] the one.

10. *Piscaria*] fish-market.

12. *customed*] well patronized.

13. *none dispraised*] this being said without intent to criticize any other houses.

14. *fell*] fell into decay (not 'fell to the ground').

16. *hand*] agreement, by handshake or in writing.

17. *the refusal*] first refusal, option.

18. *toy*] trifle.

candle rents] rents from property which is deteriorating (like a lighted candle).

20. *decrease*] an intended and cutting malapropism for 'increase'.

21. *Mistaking*] committing a malapropism (with a suggestion of 'mistaking', wrong-doing, wrongfully appropriating).

22. *His*] God's.

would 'twere more] (1) I wish I could do more than just bless you; (2) I wish your misfortune was greater.

[*Exit* VOLTORE.]

Now to my first again, at the next corner.

ACT 5   SCENE 8

[*Enter*] CORBACCIO [*and*] CORVINO, MOSCA *passing* [*across
the stage, before them, handsomely dressed as a* clarissimo].

Corbaccio. See, in our habit! See the impudent varlet!
Corvino. That I could shoot mine eyes at him like gunstones!

[*Exit* MOSCA.]

Volpone. But is this true, sir, of the parasite?
Corbaccio. Again, t' afflict us? Monster!
Volpone.   In good faith, sir,
I'm heartily grieved a beard of your grave length   5
Should be so overreached. I never brooked
That parasite's hair; methought his nose should cozen.
There still was somewhat in his look did promise
The bane of a *clarissimo.*
Corbaccio.   Knave—
Volpone. [*To Corvino*]   Methinks
Yet you, that are so traded i' the world,   10
A witty merchant, the fine bird Corvino,

---

23. *my first*] i.e. Corvino and Corbaccio, whom I was taunting earlier (at
5.6.7–27).

5.8.1. *our habit*] i.e. the clothes bought with what we advanced to Mosca
and which should be our money. Mosca is wearing Volpone's '*clarissimo*'
clothes (5.3.105), of a kind restricted to use by rich merchants only (see
5.12.110–11).

2. *gunstones*] cannonballs.

3.] i.e. Is the rumour I hear a true one, that Mosca is the heir?

4. *Again . . . us?*] Have you come back to torment us again with your
jibes?

5. *a beard . . . length*] i.e. a man so old and wise as you.

6. *brooked*] could endure.

7. *That . . . hair*] with perhaps a pun on 'That the parasite should be heir'.
'Hair' and 'heir' are indistinguishable in the theatre.

methought . . . cozen] it seemed to me his very nose was that a of a cheater.

8. *still*] always.

8–9. *did . . . clarissimo*] i.e. that always threatened to be the ruin of a
Venetian grandee. (Ironic, since the grandee who will ultimately be ruined is
Volpone himself.)

10. *traded*] experienced; with a playful reference also to Corvino's occu-
pation as a merchant.

That have such moral emblems on your name,
Should not have sung your shame and dropped your
   cheese,
To let the Fox laugh at your emptiness.

Corvino. Sirrah, you think the privilege of the place   15
And your red, saucy cap, that seems to me
Nailed to your jolthead with those two *chequins*,
Can warrant your abuses. Come you hither.
You shall perceive, sir, I dare beat you. Approach.

Volpone. No haste, sir. I do know your valure well,   20
Since you durst publish what you are, sir.

Corvino.   Tarry,
   I'd speak with you.

Volpone.   Sir, sir, another time—

Corbaccio. Nay, now.

Volpone.   Oh, God, sir! I were a wise man
Would stand the fury of a distracted cuckold.

     MOSCA [*enters and*] *walks by 'em* [*again*].

Corbaccio. What, come again?

Volpone. [*Aside to Mosca*]   Upon 'em, Mosca; save me.   25

Corbaccio. The air's infected where he breathes.

Corvino.   Let's fly him.

     [*Exeunt* CORVINO *and* CORBACCIO.]

Volpone. Excellent basilisk! Turn upon the vulture.

12.] you that have such edifying moral representations of human behaviour associated with your name of 'crow' (as in the Aesopian fable of the crow
who, encouraged by the fox to sing, dropped the cheese held in its beak,
referred to in 13–14; see also 1.2.95 and note).

14. *emptiness*] (1) empty beak; see previous note; (2) vacuousness and
moral bankruptcy.

15. *privilege . . . place*] (1) prerogative as an officer of the court; (2) protection afforded by the precincts of the Scrutineo, in the ducal palace.

16–17. *cap . . .* chequins] A *commandatore* wore a red cap that had gold
medals of St Mark on each side of it.

17. *jolthead*] blockhead.

18. *warrant*] sanction.

20. *valure*] (1) worth; (2) valour. Cf. 1.5.100.

21. *publish*] proclaim.

23–4. *I were . . . Would stand*] ironic: 'What a wise man I would be to
withstand . . .'.

27. *basilisk*] a fabulous reptile that could kill with its glance; also known as
the 'cockatrice'. Mosca, by his very appearance, has frightened off the gulls.

ACT 5　SCENE 9

[*Enter*] VOLTORE.

Voltore. Well, flesh-fly, it is summer with you now;
　　Your winter will come on.
Mosca.　　　　　　　　　Good advocate,
　　Pray thee not rail, nor threaten out of place thus;
　　Thou'lt make a solecism, as Madam says.
　　Get you a biggin more; your brain breaks loose. [*Exit.*]　　5
Voltore. Well, sir.
Volpone.　　　　　Would you ha' me beat the insolent slave?
　　Throw dirt upon his first good clothes?
Voltore.　　　　　　　　　　　　　This same
　　Is doubtless some familiar!
Volpone.　　　　　　　　　Sir, the court,
　　In troth, stays for you. I am mad a mule
　　That never read Justinian should get up　　　　　　　10
　　And ride an advocate. Had you no quirk
　　To avoid gullage, sir, by such a creature?
　　I hope you do but jest; he has not done 't.
　　This 's but confederacy to blind the rest.
　　You are the heir?
Voltore.　　　　　A strange, officious,　　　　　　　　15

5.9.1. *flesh-fly*] blow-fly, a fly which deposits its eggs in dead flesh—here equated with 'Mosca', fly.

1–2. *it is . . . come on*] now is a time for you to flourish, but it won't last.

4. *solecism*] something deviating from the normal order of things. Cf. 4.2.43 and note.

5. *a biggin more*] another lawyer's cap.

7. *his . . . clothes*] the only good clothes he has ever had—Volpone's *clarissimo* gown.

This same] the disguised Volpone.

8. *familiar*] (1) ally or dependant; (2) attendant evil spirit.

9–11. *I am . . . advocate*] i.e. Since lawyers customarily rode mules in ceremonial procession to the law courts, Volpone's insult is to suggest that for Voltore to allow an uneducated rogue such as Mosca to outwit him is like allowing his mule to ride him. Justinian was the compiler of the Roman code of law.

11. *quirk*] lawyer's trick.

12. *gullage*] being made a fool of.

13. *he . . . done 't*] and that he (Mosca) didn't really dupe you.

14. *confederacy*] i.e. a secret agreement between you (Voltore) and Mosca.

Troublesome knave! Thou dost torment me.
Volpone.   I know—
    It cannot be, sir, that you should be cozened;
    'Tis not within the wit of man to do it.
    You are so wise, so prudent, and 'tis fit
    That wealth and wisdom still should go together.   20
                                    [*Exeunt separately.*]

ACT 5   SCENE 10

    [*Enter*] *four* Avocatori, Notario, Commandatori, BONARIO,
            CELIA, CORBACCIO, CORVINO.

1 Avocatore. Are all the parties here?
Notario.   All but the advocate.
2 Avocatore. And here he comes.

            [*Enter* VOLTORE, VOLPONE *following him.*]

1 Avocatore.   Then bring 'em forth to sentence.
Voltore. O my most honoured fathers, let your mercy
    Once win upon your justice, to forgive—
    I am distracted—
Volpone. [*Aside*]   What will he do now?
Voltore.   Oh,   5
    I know not which t' address myself to first,
    Whether your fatherhoods or these innocents—
Corvino. [*Aside*] Will he betray himself?
Voltore.   Whom equally
    I have abused, out of most covetous ends—
Corvino. The man is mad!
Corbaccio.   What's that?
Corvino.   He is possessed.   10

---

    17. *cozened*] cheated, outwitted.

    5.10. Location: the court of law.
    2 SD.] It is possible that Voltore and Volpone remain onstage at the end
of the previous scene as the court enters, merely coming forward at this
point; QF record no exit or entrance.
    4. *win upon*] override.
    7. *these innocents*] Celia and Bonario.
    9. *ends*] motives.
    10.] Possibly Corvino speaks aside or to Corbaccio, but he may well speak
aloud.

Voltore. For which, now struck in conscience, here I prostrate
    Myself at your offended feet for pardon.   [*He kneels.*]
1, 2 Avocatori. Arise.
Celia.   O heav'n, how just thou art!
Volpone. [*Aside*]   I'm caught
    I' mine own noose—
Corvino. [*Aside to Corbaccio*] Be constant, sir; nought now
    Can help but impudence.
1 Avocatore. [*To Voltore*]   Speak forward.
Commandatore. [*To the courtroom*]   Silence!   15
Voltore. It is not passion in me, reverend fathers,
    But only conscience, conscience, my good sires,
    That makes me now tell truth. That parasite,
    That knave, hath been the instrument of all.
2 Avocatore. Where is that knave? Fetch him.
Volpone.   I go.   [*Exit.*]
Corvino.   Grave fathers,   20
    This man's distracted. He confessed it now;
    For, hoping to be old Volpone's heir,
    Who now is dead—
3 Avocatore.   How?
2 Avocatore.   Is Volpone dead?
Corvino. Dead since, grave fathers—
Bonario.   O sure vengeance!
1 Avocatore.   Stay!
    Then he was no deceiver?
Voltore.   Oh, no, none.   25
    The parasite, grave fathers.
Corvino.   He does speak
    Out of mere envy, 'cause the servant's made
    The thing he gaped for. Please your fatherhoods,

---

15. *Speak forward*] Continue speaking.

16. *passion*] madness.

21. *now*] i.e. at 5 above.

24. *since*] i.e. since his appearance at the earlier part of the trial.

O sure vengeance] Bonario sees the (supposed) death of Volpone as heaven's vengeance on a ravisher.

27. *Out . . . envy*] entirely out of envy.

27-8. *the servant's . . . for*] Mosca has been named heir, the thing that Voltore hungered for, like a young vulture chick in its nest.

This is the truth, though I'll not justify
The other but he may be somedeal faulty.   30
Voltore. Ay, to your hopes as well as mine, Corvino.
But I'll use modesty. Pleaseth your wisdoms
To view these certain notes, and but confer them;
As I hope favour, they shall speak clear truth.
                    [*He delivers his notes to the court.*]
Corvino. The devil has entered him!
Bonario. [*To Corvino*]   Or bides in you.   35
4 Avocatore. We have done ill, by a public officer
To send for him, if he be heir.
2 Avocatore.   For whom?
4 Avocatore. Him that they call the parasite.
3 Avocatore.   'Tis true;
He is a man of great estate now left.
4 Avocatore. [*To Notario*] Go you and learn his name,
    and say the court   40
Entreats his presence here, but to the clearing
Of some few doubts.   [*Exit* Notario.]
2 Avocatore.   This same's a labyrinth!
1 Avocatore. [*To Corvino*] Stand you unto your first
    report?
Corvino.   My state,
    My life, my fame—
Bonario.   Where is 't?

29–30. *not . . . faulty*] not exonerate Mosca, but concede that he may be somewhat at fault.

32. *modesty*] restraint, moderation.

Pleaseth] may it please.

33. *certain*] (1) particular; (2) reliable.

confer them] (1) compare them; (2) discuss them among yourselves.

34. *As. . . . favour*] as I hope to be pardoned (with a suggestion too of 'as I hope to be saved').

36. *public officer*] i.e. Volpone as *commandatore*.

40 SD. To Notario] See 5.12.13–14.

40. *learn his name*] Thus far, Mosca has been referred to in court only as Volpone's parasite.

41. *but to*] only for.

43. *unto*] by.

state] i.e. estate and status.

44. *fame*] reputation.

Where is 't?] (interpolated scornfully) What reputation can you be talking about?

Corvino.   Are at the stake.
1 Avocatore. [*To Corbaccio*] Is yours so too?
Corbaccio.   The advocate's a knave,   45
    And has a forkèd tongue—
2 Avocatore.   Speak to the point.
Corbaccio. So is the parasite too.
1 Avocatore.   This is confusion.
Voltore. [*Indicating the papers*] I do beseech your fatherhoods,
        read but those—
Corvino. And credit nothing the false spirit hath writ.
    It cannot be but he is possessed, grave fathers.   50
                            [*They examine the papers.*]

ACT 5   SCENE 11

            [*Enter elsewhere on stage*] VOLPONE.

Volpone. To make a snare for mine own neck! And run
    My head into it wilfully! With laughter!
    When I had newly scaped, was free and clear!
    Out of mere wantonness! Oh, the dull devil
    Was in this brain of mine when I devised it,   5
    And Mosca gave it second; he must now
    Help to sear up this vein, or we bleed dead.

        [*Enter* NANO, ANDROGYNO, *and* CASTRONE.]

───

    44. *Are . . . stake*] i.e. are guarantees for the truth of my first report.
    45. *Is . . . too?*] i.e. Are you willing to stake your reputation on the truth of
what you averred earlier?
    46. *Speak . . . point*] i.e. Answer the question. To say that Voltore is a
lying knave is not to state directly that you were telling the truth.
    47. *So . . . too*] The parasite is lying, too.
    49.] i.e. But do not believe anything that the demon possessing Voltore
has written there.

    5.11. This scene may be an interpolation, since it interrupts the courtroom
sequence and since scene 12 in Q is still labelled scene 10. Perhaps it is to be
acted downstage or to one side while the *avocatori*, in tableau, consult
Voltore's papers.
    4. *wantonness*] arrogance, insolence; caprice, whim.
    the dull devil] probably, an excess of wine.
    6. *gave it second*] supported, seconded it.
    7. *sear up*] cauterize.
    bleed dead] will bleed to death.

How now! Who let you loose? Whither go you now?
What? To buy gingerbread? Or to drown kitlings?
Nano. Sir, Master Mosca called us out of doors,   10
    And bid us all go play, and took the keys.
Androgyno.   Yes.
Volpone. Did Master Mosca take the keys? Why, so!
    I am farther in. These are my fine conceits!
    I must be merry, with a mischief to me!
    What a vile wretch was I, that could not bear   15
    My fortune soberly? I must ha' my crotchets!
    And my conundrums! Well, go you and seek him.
    His meaning may be truer than my fear.
    Bid him he straight come to me to the court;
    Thither will I, and if 't be possible,   20
    Unscrew my advocate upon new hopes.
    When I provoked him, then I lost myself.
                    [*Exeunt* VOLPONE *and his retinue.*]

ACT 5   SCENE 12

    [*Four*] Avocatori, *etc.* [Notario, Commandatori,
    BONARIO, CELIA, VOLTORE, CORBACCIO, CORVINO].

1 Avocatore. [*With Voltore's notes*] These things can ne'er be
        reconciled. He here
    Professeth that the gentleman was wronged,
    And that the gentlewoman was brought thither,

---

9. *kitlings*] kittens.

13. *farther in*] deeper in trouble (since, with no keys, he is locked out of his own house and has nowhere to hide, and since Mosca appears to be taking over.)

conceits] ingenious plans.

14. *with . . . me!*] (1) i.e. curses on me! (2) with mischievous results for me.

16. *crotchets*] whimsical fancies, perverse conceits.

17. *conundrums*] whims, fancies.

18. *truer . . . fear*] more honest than I fear it is.

21. *Unscrew*] dissuade; redirect the behaviour of.

upon] (1) by means of; (2) in the direction of.

5.12. The *avocatori* may have continued to consult Voltore's notes during 5.11; see headnote to that scene.

2. *the gentleman*] Bonario.

Forced by her husband, and there left.
Voltore.   Most true.
Celia. How ready is heav'n to those that pray!
1 Avocatore.   But that   5
    Volpone would have ravished her, he holds
    Utterly false, knowing his impotence.
Corvino. Grave fathers, he is possessed; again, I say,
    Possessed. Nay, if there be possession
    And obsession, he has both.
3 Avocatore.   Here comes our officer.   10

               [Enter VOLPONE *disguised.]*

Volpone. The parasite will straight be here, grave fathers.
4 Avocatore. You might invent some other name, sir varlet.
3 Avocatore. Did not the notary meet him?
Volpone.   Not that I know.
4 Avocatore. His coming will clear all.
2 Avocatore.   Yet it is misty.
Voltore. May 't please your fatherhoods—
               Volpone whispers the Advocate.
Volpone. [Aside to Voltore]   Sir, the parasite   15
    Willed me to tell you that his master lives,
    That you are still the man, your hopes the same,
    And this was only a jest—
Voltore.   How?
Volpone.   Sir, to try
    If you were firm, and how you stood affected.
Voltore. Art sure he lives?
Volpone.   Do I live, sir?
Voltore.   Oh, me!   20
    I was too violent.
Volpone.   Sir, you may redeem it.
    They said you were possessed: fall down, and seem so.

---

5. *ready*] responsive, ready to help.
9–10. *possession . . . obsession*] entry into the body by evil spirits and attack by the devil without.
12. *invent*] find.
14. *Yet*] as yet.
19. *how . . . affected*] how loyal you were to Volpone's interests.
20. *Do . . . sir?*] i.e. He's as alive as I am.
21. *violent*] aggressive.

I'll help to make it good. *Voltore falls.*
                    God bless the man!
[*Aside to Voltore*] Stop your wind hard, and swell.
    [*Aloud*] See, see, see, see!
He vomits crooked pins! His eyes are set   25
Like a dead hare's hung in a poulter's shop!
His mouth's running away! [*To Corvino*] Do you see,
    Signor?
Now 'tis in his belly—
Corvino.   Ay, the devil!
Volpone. Now in his throat—
Corvino.   Ay, I perceive it plain.
Volpone. 'Twill out, 'twill out! Stand clear. See where it
    flies   30
In shape of a blue toad with a bat's wings!
    [*To Corbaccio*] Do not you see it, sir?
Corbaccio.   What? I think I do.
Corvino. 'Tis too manifest.
Volpone.   Look! He comes t' himself!
Voltore. Where am I?
Volpone.   Take good heart; the worst is past, sir.
    You are dispossessed.
1 Avocatore.   What accident is this?   35
2 Avocatore. Sudden, and full of wonder!
3 Avocatore.   If he were
    Possessed, as it appears, all this is nothing.
                    [*He indicates Voltore's statement.*]
Corvino. He has been often subject to these fits.
1 Avocatore. Show him that writing. [*To Voltore*] Do you know
    it, sir?
Volpone. [*Aside to Voltore*] Deny it, sir, forswear it, know it
    not.   40
Voltore. Yes, I do know it well, it is my hand;
    But all that it contains is false.
Bonario.   Oh, practice!
2 Avocatore. What maze is this?

---

24. *Stop . . . swell*] Hold your breath and puff yourself up.
25. *set*] set in a rigid stare.
26. *poulter's*] poultry seller's (also selling game).
35. *accident*] unforeseen event.
41. *hand*] handwriting.
42. *practice*] false practice, trickery.

1 Avocatore.   Is he not guilty then,
    Whom you there name the parasite?
Voltore.   Grave fathers,
    No more than his good patron, old Volpone.   45
4 Avocatore. Why, he is dead!
Voltore.   Oh no, my honoured fathers,
    He lives—
1 Avocatore.   How! Lives?
Voltore.   Lives.
2 Avocatore.   This is subtler yet!
3 Avocatore. You said he was dead?
Voltore.   Never.
3 Avocatore. [*To Corvino*]   You said so?
Corvino.   I heard so.
4 Avocatore. Here comes the gentleman. Make him way.

[*Enter* MOSCA.]

3 Avocatore.   A stool!
4 Avocatore. A proper man! [*Aside*] And, were Volpone
    dead,   50
    A fit match for my daughter.
3 Avocatore.   Give him way.
Volpone. [*Aside to Mosca*] Mosca, I was almost lost; the
    advocate
    Had betrayed all; but now it is recovered.
    All's o' the hinge again. Say I am living.
Mosca. [*Aloud*] What busy knave is that?—Most reverend
    fathers,   55
    I sooner had attended your grave pleasures,
    But that my order for the funeral
    Of my dear patron did require me—
Volpone. [*Aside*]   Mosca!
Mosca. Whom I intend to bury like a gentleman.
Volpone. [*Aside*] Ay, quick, and cozen me of all.
2 Avocatore.   Still stranger!   60
    More intricate!

---

49. *Make him way*] Make room for him.
50. *proper*] handsome.
54. *o' the hinge*] running smoothly, in order again.
55. *busy*] officious.
60. *quick*] (1) alive: (2) quickly.
cozen] cheat.

1 Avocatore.   And come about again!
4 Avocatore. [*Aside*] It is a match; my daughter is bestowed.
Mosca. [*Aside to Volpone*] Will you gi' me half?
Volpone. [*Half aloud*]   First I'll be hanged.
Mosca. [*Aside*]   I know
    Your voice is good. Cry not so loud.
1 Avocatore.   Demand
    The advocate.—Sir, did you not affirm   65
    Volpone was alive?
Volpone. [*Interrupting*] Yes, and he is.
    This gent'man [*Indicating Mosca*] told me so. [*Aside to*
        Mosca] Thou shalt have half.
Mosca. [*Aloud*] Whose drunkard is this same? Speak, some
        that know him;
    I never saw his face. [*Aside to Volpone*] I cannot now
    Afford it you so cheap.
Volpone. [*Aside*]   No?
1 Avocatore. [*To Voltore*]   What say you?   70
Voltore. The officer told me.
Volpone.   I did, grave fathers,
    And will maintain he lives with mine own life,
    And that this creature told me. [*Aside*] I was born
    With all good stars my enemies!
Mosca.   Most grave fathers,
    If such an insolence as this must pass   75
    Upon me, I am silent; 'twas not this
    For which you sent, I hope.
2 Avocatore. [*Indicating Volpone*] Take him away.
Volpone. [*Aside*] Mosca!
3 Avocatore.   Let him be whipped.
Volpone. [*Aside*]   Wilt thou betray me?
    Cozen me?

---

61. *come about again*] having reversed direction yet again.
63-4. *I know . . . loud*] You don't have to shout. Keep your voice down.
64. *Demand*] 'question', or 'let us question'.
    65. *Sir*] addressing Voltore, though Volpone then interrupts with his own answer.
    70. *What say you?*] The First *Avocatore* repeats his question in 65-6 to Voltore.
73. *this creature*] Mosca.
75. *pass*] be allowed.

3 Avocatore.   And taught to bear himself
   Toward a person of his rank.
4 Avocatore.   Away!   [*Volpone is seized.*]   80
Mosca. I humbly thank your fatherhoods.
Volpone.   Soft, soft. [*Aside*] Whipped?
   And lose all that I have? If I confess,
   It cannot be much more.
4 Avocatore. [*To Mosca*]   Sir, are you married?
Volpone. [*Aside*] They'll be allied anon; I must be resolute.
   The fox shall here uncase.   *He puts off his disguise.*
Mosca. [*Aside to Volpone*]   Patron!
Volpone.   Nay, now   85
   My ruins shall not come alone. Your match
   I'll hinder sure; my substance shall not glue you,
   Nor screw you, into a family.
Mosca. [*Aside to Volpone*]   Why, patron!
Volpone. I am Volpone, and this [*Indicating Mosca*] is my
      knave;
   This [*Indicating Voltore*], his own knave; this [*Indicating
      Corbaccio*], avarice's fool;   90
   This [*Indicating Corvino*], a chimera of wittol, fool, and
      knave.
   And, reverend fathers, since we all can hope
   Nought but a sentence, let's not now despair it.
   You hear me brief.

---

79. *And . . . himself*] and let the (supposed) *commandatore* be taught to
behave more courteously.
80. *his*] Mosca's.
81. *Soft, soft*] Hold on, wait a minute.
84. *They . . . anon*] Mosca and the Fourth *Avocatore* will be related by
marriage any moment, and thus in cahoots.
85. *uncase*] remove disguise.
86. *ruins*] ruin.
87–8. *my . . . family*] my riches shall not be used to insinuate you into a
good family by either sympathy or extortion.
89. *knave*] (1) menial servant; (2) rogue.
91. *chimera*] a mythical three-natured beast (traditionally part lion, part
goat, part serpent).
   wittol] willing cuckold.
93. *let's . . . it*] i.e. let's hear it, don't keep us in suspense, or disappoint us
(said ironically).
94. *You . . . brief*] i.e. That's all I have to say to you.

Corvino.   May it please your fatherhoods—
Commandatore.   Silence!
1 Avocatore. The knot is now undone by miracle!   95
2 Avocatore. Nothing can be more clear.
3 Avocatore.   Or can more prove
     These innocent.
1 Avocatore.   Give 'em their liberty.
Bonario. Heaven could not long let such gross crimes be hid.
2 Avocatore. If this be held the highway to get riches,
     May I be poor!
3 Avocatore.   This 's not the gain, but torment.   100
1 Avocatore. These possess wealth as sick men possess fevers,
     Which trulier may be said to possess them.
2 Avocatore. Disrobe that parasite.
                    [*Mosca is stripped of his fine costume.*]
Corvino, Mosca.   Most honoured fathers—
1 Avocatore. Can you plead aught to stay the course of justice?
     If you can, speak.
Corvino, Voltore.   We beg favour.
Celia.   And mercy.   105
1 Avocatore. [*To Celia*] You hurt your innocence, suing for the
     guilty.—
     Stand forth; and first the parasite. You appear
     T' have been the chiefest minister, if not plotter,
     In all these lewd impostures, and now, lastly,
     Have with your impudence abused the court   110
     And habit of a gentleman of Venice,
     Being a fellow of no birth or blood:
     For which our sentence is, first thou be whipped,
     Then live perpetual prisoner in our galleys.
Volpone. I thank you for him.
Mosca.   Bane to thy wolfish nature!   115

---

97. *These*] Bonario and Celia.
     100. *This 's . . . torment*] i.e. What one 'gains' eventually by such crimes is
not wealth but punishment and eternal torment.
     108. *minister*] agent, instrument.
     109. *lewd*] wicked, base.
     110. *abused*] deceived, imposed on.
     115. *I thank . . . him*] a mocking reminder of Mosca's thanks for the
command to whip Volpone earlier, at 81.
     Bane to] death to. (Wolfsbane is a poison of the aconite family.)
     thy] Mosca's first use of the second person familiar in addressing Volpone.

1 Avocatore. Deliver him to the *Saffi.*   [MOSCA *is led off.*]
    Thou, Volpone,
  By blood and rank a gentleman, canst not fall
  Under like censure, but our judgement on thee
  Is that thy substance all be straight confiscate
  To the hospital of the *Incurabili*;   120
  And since the most was gotten by imposture,
  By feigning lame, gout, palsy, and such diseases,
  Thou art to lie in prison, cramped with irons,
  Till thou be'st sick and lame indeed.—Remove him.
Volpone. This is called mortifying of a Fox. [*He is led aside.*]   125
1 Avocatore. Thou, Voltore, to take away the scandal
  Thou hast giv'n all worthy men of thy profession,
  Art banished from their fellowship and our state.—
  Corbaccio!—Bring him near.—We here possess
  Thy son of all thy state, and confine thee   130
  To the monastery of San' Spirito,
  Where, since thou knew'st not how to live well here,
  Thou shalt be learned to die well.
Corbaccio.   Ha! What said he?
Commandatore. You shall know anon, sir.
1 Avocatore.   Thou, Corvino, shalt
  Be straight embarked from thine own house, and
    rowed   135
  Round about Venice, through the Grand Canal,
  Wearing a cap with fair long ass's ears
  Instead of horns, and so to mount, a paper
  Pinned on thy breast, to the Berlino—
Corvino.   Yes,
  And have mine eyes beat out with stinking fish,   140

---

116. Saffi] bailiffs, as at 3.8.16 and note.
120. Incurabili] incurables.
125. *mortifying*] (1) sentencing to death; (2) humiliating; (3) subjecting of
the appetites to spiritual discipline; (4) rendering game (such as fox) tender
by hanging it up and beating it.
SD] Volpone may remain onstage, so that he can then come forward to
speak the epilogue, or he may be led offstage to re-enter for the epilogue. See
Introduction, pp. 18, 23.
128. *our state*] Venice.
130. *state*] estate.
138. *and . . . paper*] and are sentenced then to mount, with a paper.
139. *Berlino*] pillory.

Bruised fruit, and rotten eggs—'tis well. I'm glad
I shall not see my shame yet.
1 Avocatore.   And to expiate
Thy wrongs done to thy wife, thou art to send her
Home to her father with her dowry trebled.
And these are all your judgements—
All.   Honoured fathers!   145
1 Avocatore. Which may not be revoked. Now you begin,
When crimes are done and past and to be punished,
To think what your crimes are. Away with them!
Let all that see these vices thus rewarded
Take heart, and love to study 'em. Mischiefs feed   150
Like beasts till they be fat, and then they bleed.
                                        [*Exeunt.*]

VOLPONE [*comes forward to speak the Epilogue*].

Volpone. The seasoning of a play is the applause.
Now, though the Fox be punished by the laws,
He yet doth hope there is no suff'ring due
For any fact which he hath done 'gainst you.
If there be, censure him; here he doubtful stands;   5
If not, fare jovially, and clap your hands.

THE END.

---

142. *yet*] anyway (because his eyes will be 'beat out', 140).

145. *Honoured fathers*] presumably spoken as a joint plea, to which the *Avocatore*'s next phrase is in reply.

150. *Take heart*] take the matter to heart (not 'take courage').

150–1. *Mischiefs . . . bleed*] Evils are allowed to ripen like fatted beasts and then are cut down.

4. *fact*] crime.
you] i.e. the audience.

5. *doubtful*] uncertain of the audience's reception.

6. *jovially*] (1) as final judges (like Jove); (2) in a merry, rather than condemnatory, mood.

This Comedy was first
acted in the year
1605.
By the KING'S MAJESTY'S
SERVANTS.   5

The principal comedians were:

RICHARD BURBAGE.   JOHN HEMINGES.

HENRY CONDELL.   JOHN LOWIN.

WILLIAM SLY.   ALEXANDER COOKE.

With the allowance of the Master of REVELS.   10

---

3. *1605*] old legal calendar; probably February or March 1606.
4–5. *KING'S . . . SERVANTS*] The company at the Globe Theatre in which
Shakespeare was a principal shareholder.
6. *comedians*] actors.
10. *Master of REVELS*] a court official who licensed plays for both performance and publication.